GOD SPEAKS OUT

on

"The New Morality"

GOD SPEAKS OUT

on

"The New Morality"

A Production of
THE GRADUATE SCHOOL OF THEOLOGY
AMBASSADOR COLLEGE

By a collaboration of Faculty Members:
CHARLES V. DOROTHY, Ph.D., HERMAN L. HOEH, Ph.D.,
ERNEST L. MARTIN, M.A., RODERICK C. MEREDITH, M.A.,
BENJAMIN L. REA, Ph.D.,
with
HERBERT W. ARMSTRONG, *Chancellor,*
RALPH E. MERRILL, M.D.

Ambassador College Press
Pasadena, California
1 9 6 4

First Edition, October 1964, 250,000 Copies

Second Printing, April 1965, 50,000 Copies

Third Printing, July 1966, 25,000 Copies

Fourth Printing, March 1967, 25,000 Copies

Fifth Printing, May 1968, 25,000 Copies

Sixth Printing, January 1969, 20,000 Copies

Printed in The United States of America

NOT TO BE SOLD

This book is given FREE, as a Ministry of Love, by *The* PLAIN TRUTH magazine in conjunction with the Graduate School of Theology, Ambassador College.

The publishers must, regrettably, refuse to send this book to unmarried minors.

Although it is hoped that parents will recognize the urgency of placing this volume in the hands of their own adolescent children, that must remain solely the responsibility of the parents.

Contents

Preface

You live in a mixed-up world that has lost its way. *Especially* in the matter of sex and marriage.

What is *right*? What is *wrong*? In the modern rebellion against puritanical moral taboos, a bewildered world throws up its hands. It seeks a *new morality!* But where is the AUTHORITY for a *right* moral code? The world doesn't know!

Certainly there is no longer any dearth of printed instruction in the delicate field of sex and marriage. An avalanche of books has descended upon this confused world—authored, almost wholly, by medical doctors, psychiatrists, professional marriage counselors, and self-professed "sexologists."

Yet these books, somehow, have failed to supply the right answers. The morality problem has not been solved. What's *wrong?*

Does the problem of sex, after all, belong properly within the scope of medicine, or of psychiatry? Incredible though it may seem, the answer is *NO!*—except partially.

HOW did sex originate? *WHEN*, and *WHY* was the marriage institution founded? The world doesn't know! The world has lost the true GOD!

It was the Almighty Creator who *made* humans male and female. GOD was the Architect who designed sex. The ETERNAL set in dynamic motion sex stimuli.

But *WHY?* Strange as it may seem, *the world does not know!* The medical doctors *do not know!* The psychiatrists *do not know!*

HOW did marriage originate? The CREATOR Himself ordained the marriage union. But WHY? Why *marriage?*

The world, its doctors and psychologists, *do not know why!* Yet the gentlemen of these materialistic professions write the books purporting to give a confused world the *tragically* needed knowledge about sex and marriage.

The world has overlooked, ignored, and rejected the one sole AUTHORITY for morals. That *AUTHORITY* is the Great GOD, who created and who rules the vast universe!

GOD ALMIGHTY IS THE SOLE AUTHORITY FOR MORALS!

It is GOD who joins a man and woman as husband and wife.

Winston Churchill spoke, before the American Congress, of a great PURPOSE being worked out here below. The Eternal GOD is author of that supreme PURPOSE, and also of His PLAN for its accomplishment. Sex and marriage are indelibly connected with that PURPOSE—and directly associated with that PLAN.

The true GOSPEL of Jesus Christ is concerned with the SIN question, and the WAYS of RIGHTEOUSNESS. Two of the Ten Commandments safeguard the marriage institution. Two of the CAPITAL sins, carrying sentence of CAPITAL punishment, relate directly to wrong uses of sex.

The question of sex and marriage is intrinsically bound together with the SIN question, and the spiritual ministry of salvation.

The subjects of sex and marriage fall into the spiritual and moral categories, and therefore within the proper realm of the true Ministry of Jesus Christ.

The two Commandments relating to right or wrong uses of sex, like others of the Ten Commandments, involve physical actions, *but they are spiritual principles.*

Therefore this book, properly, has been a collaboration between those of Christ's Ministry, and those of the medical profession.

The Eternal Creator *made* sex to be a pure, clean, and wonderful blessing. The Biblical revelation gives adequate instruction, which, obeyed and followed, bestows upon the happily married pure and joyous delights beyond description.

But man has polluted, befouled, perverted, and misused every good thing God ever put within his reach. By wrong and perverted attitudes—by Satan-inspired interpretations of sex—by false moral codes—by flagrant misuses, and self-righteous repression of right uses—man has profaned God's freely proffered blessings into one of his greatest curses.

Sinning man has dirtied that which God made to be kept clean. Pseudo-pious religionists have, in their "chaste severity," forbidden, and condemned into *non*use that which a Holy God designed for clean and righteous USE!

In today's revolution of morals, God-rejecting professional men are leading the procession from prudish nonuse into promiscuous and sinful *wrong* use! Mankind, it seems, can go in every direction, and to every extreme, as long as it is *away from* the God-ordained *right* direction!

For many centuries past, the world has sorely *needed* the TRUTH, and the RIGHT KNOWLEDGE and instruction contained in this book.

At this late date, with humanity held in the satanic clutch of false interpretations, wrong teachings, harmful attitudes, following evil customs and injurious practices, it is impossible for the reader to reap the blissful joys intended by a loving Creator merely by instruction in physical details alone.

The earlier and middle chapters of this book are by far the most important. Every chapter is vital. Succeeding chapters can be *rightly* understood only in the light of what has gone before. It is important that you read it entirely through *from the beginning*. The astonishing knowledge and facts revealed in the early and middle portions of this book are as important as they are shocking.

No matter who you are, or how much instruction you may have received on the subjects of sex and marriage, you are going to find much surprising knowledge, new to you, as you proceed, chapter by chapter, through this book.

The impetus which started research and gathering of material for this book, in 1949, was the need to produce our own textbook for the *Principles of Living* course in Ambassador College. However, the accelerating demand from the constantly enlarging readership of *The* PLAIN TRUTH, now possibly exceeding two million people in all parts of the world, necessitated preparation of a work for the instruction of this vast number of people, in all walks of life, and in all levels of education.

Purposely, therefore, we have avoided the staid, dry, pedantic, professorial style of writing which seems to be typical of the average textbook written for colleges and universities. It has always seemed to us that such writing serves rather to appease the intellectual vanity of the author than to convey knowledge to the reader. One can acquire a good-sized headache trying to decipher such monotonously dignified verbiage. We have never approved of it. The purpose of words is to convey meaning. We have tried to make this text as plain and understandable as it is frank. We have endeavored to make it easy to read.

This work has been produced out of genuine concern, and deep compassion for a humanity *robbed* by false teachings, as well as by ignorance, of the joys, the delights, and the rich blessings a loving God made possible. But these may be OURS today, if only we will open our minds to receive what God reveals.

Read and reread it, from beginning to end, allowing your Creator to renew in you a clean heart, a right spirit, and an understanding mind!

And when you allow it to bring you the happiness the Holy God made possible, its producers will feel richly rewarded.

CHAPTER 1

WORLD IN REVOLT

Why This Book Had To Be Written

*T*ODAY THE WORLD is emerging from the age of hush. A moral revolution is sweeping the world.

The professional "authorities"—the psychoanalysts, the scientists, the doctors, the biologists and the marriage counselors—have decided that moral standards are in need of revision. And they *are being* revised radically—*downward*—under the catch phrase, *"The New Morality"!*

Few, indeed, realize the shocking *facts* of this accelerating downward plunge. It is rapidly becoming a greater threat to humanity than the hydrogen bomb! The plain TRUTH of the current moral collapse is staggering, almost beyond belief!

The "Old Morality"

"Christianity," entering the dark ages, absorbed the pagan dualism of Greece, and pasted the label "SINFUL" on sex.

Even as the United States entered the first World War, in 1917, it was still unlawful to publish, sell, or distribute any book disseminating knowledge of sex, or instruction on its uses. Sex was viewed puritanically as indecent, degrading, shameful. It was not only considered "not nice," it was positively "sinful."

People sorely *needed* proper instruction. But all teaching was forcibly withheld.

Parents taught their children nothing. They themselves knew nothing. Their parents had never taught *them!* And besides, it would have been too embarrassing! The commonly accepted attitude was: "keep our children innocent and pure through ignorance until marriage—then instinct will tell them what to do."

But instinct did not teach them. Humans, unlike animals, do not come equipped with instinct. Blindly, with a smattering of "gutter-acquired" *mis*knowledge, the newly married blundered their way into disillusionments, shattered dreams, bitter resentments, frustrations—and, too often, the divorce courts and broken homes.

A New "Morality"?

But today western civilization is throwing off the restraints. The revolt is on, against prudery, repression and ignorance. Knowledge, of a certain and wrong kind, has been flooding bookstore shelves and magazine stands. The new, wholly physical and sensual sex knowledge has been gulped in by curiosity-hungry minds. Yet this newly released knowledge has been misleading and damaging, far in excess of the former repressive ignorance. And this present tobogganslide in morals has become one of the world's most fateful DANGERS!

WHY has not this release of knowledge proved beneficial? Look at the facts as they have happened. Look at the actual results!

In 1917 it was illegal to disseminate technical knowledge of sex in the United States. Down through the centuries sex had been polluted. From ancient Egypt, through Greece, Rome, and organized "Christianity," sex had been regarded as evil—dirty—nasty. Not only was it sinful outside of marriage—but any use *in marriage*, except for the definite purpose of reproduction, was sternly labeled "SIN." Prudishness filled the atmosphere.

True, a very large percentage of girls and wives were kept "pure." Yet *some 90 per cent of marriages were rendered unhappy* because of false attitudes and sex ignorance. Divorces, through those centuries, may have been kept at a comparative minimum — due to religious convictions and economic barriers. But most divorces then, even as now, were caused primarily by this ignorance.

Then came World War I. It brought tremendous changes in thinking, in behavior patterns, in social customs, and in the "double standard."

In its wake, the legal barriers against sex instruction were knocked down—and the moral barriers began toppling simultaneously. Many medical doctors, psychoanalysts, "sexologists," and marriage counselors began grinding out volume after volume imparting sex knowledge. Bookstore shelves became well supplied with sex information.

But *something was criminally wrong* with this avalanche of sex literature. It revealed only *half* of the vitally needed knowledge—*the physical, biological half*—and even that from the purely materialistic, carnal, sensual approach.

Ignorant of the Creator's real PURPOSES of having made humans both male and female, and of the divinely intended functions of sex, these professional "authorities" actually started the western world on the fatal road of immorality and spiritual degradation that is leading, more rapidly than realized, to the utter destruction of humanity!

Yes, the professional "experts" decided that moral standards are in need of revision. And so, indeed, *they assuredly are!* But they are being revised in the *wrong direction!* They are being revised *in a downward spiral!*

Soon after World War I, Judge Ben Lindsey of Denver, Colorado, shocked the world with his public advocacy of "companionate marriage"— that is, the legalizing of temporary trial marriages. Once people recovered from the shock, too many stopped even bothering with trial *marriages*. More or less promiscuous premarital sampling became the campus fad.

Perhaps "credit" for starting this *IM*moral "New Morality" should go to Sigmund Freud, founder of psychoanalysis, who died in 1939. Freud attributed neuroses and many nervous and mental disorders to sexual repression and ignorance. Since the Roman Catholic definition of sex as degradingly sinful caused these disorders, "the way that seemeth right unto a MAN" was to reverse the definition to the opposite extreme of calling sex GOOD—*any* use of sex, in or out of marriage. If repression and self-denial caused neurotic disquiet, Freud and his followers reasoned, let's emancipate the people from restraints — revise the interpretation of "morality."

In a one-generation plunge, civilization in our world has swung to the opposite extreme of the moral pendulum. Premarital sexual experience is no longer being discouraged in many educational high places. Many a modern teen-age girl is being "emancipated" from the old taboos. Teen-agers are literally *leaping* to embrace the "new freedoms."

The western world is fast adopting a *new* interpretation of morals. Increasingly, modern wives no longer resign themselves to being only the last love affair of their husbands.

NOTHING IS MORE NEEDED, NOW, than a voice in the wilderness to cry out against this sudden moral collapse, and to supply THE MISSING HALF of sex knowledge, leading at least those who will, into the GOD-ordained TRUE MORALITY!

For both the old repression-in-ignorance morality, and the soul-damning so-called "NEW Morality" are as false as a subtle devil could devise them!

There *is* a GOD-given TRUE morality that is right, and will bring humanity happiness, joys, and blessings! Everybody in this world seriously *needs* the knowledge that no author, until now, has made available. They *need*, not only the physical details, but a knowledge of the Creator's PUR-

POSES in sex—its true MEANING—the related SPIRITUAL enlightenment—and the right God-intended ATTITUDE toward sex and marriage.

What KIND of Knowledge?

There is abroad today a teaching that KNOWLEDGE is the key to happiness—the solution to all problems. Given sufficient knowledge, say these intellectuals, and the world will banish all unhappiness and solve all problems.

So today we have a tremendous increase in knowledge. In *all* fields! Scientific knowledge. Technical knowledge. Medical knowledge. Mechanical knowledge. Knowledge from historical research.

The prophet Daniel foretold this amazing increase of knowledge. It is one of several sure signs of the end of this world—and the imminency of the *happy* WORLD TOMORROW!

Today bookstore shelves contain many books disseminating sex knowledge. But not only that. A veritable avalanche of sex literature floods the newsstands. Almost every issue of every magazine of popular circulation contains an eye-catching article on sex. Sex appeal is dominant in advertisements and radio and TV commercials. Sex is the major appeal in the motion pictures, in television, and in popular songs.

From every source and direction, it seems, sex consciousness and sex knowledge are being hurled at the public. Courses are being taught in many colleges and high schools.

But *what kind of knowledge?*

And from what SOURCES?

This torrent of sex information, plunging a new generation headlong down the cataract of promiscuity, *is wholly physical knowledge!* Its source is modern "science," medicine, and psychoanalysis. These are sources which have rejected the revelation of God.

All *knowledge* is not TRUTH. Half-knowledge, then, becomes a poisonous mixture of truth and error.

So today we have all this "knowledge" — *but NO HAPPINESS!*

The centuries of ignorance and prudery bore the fruit of unhappy marriages. But this new "enlightenment" is producing increasing unhappiness, destroying the meaning and sacredness of marriage, multiplying divorces, producing a bumper crop of juvenile delinquents, and reaping a harvest of venereal disease.

Modern civilization has leaped from the frying pan into the fire.

And WHY?

The FOUNDATION of Knowledge

Because these modern "authorities" producing this new flood of sex literature, are themselves ignorant of the true meaning and PURPOSES of sex. They have built a super-structure of "knowledge" without a FOUNDATION.

The FOUNDATION of knowledge is the Word of God!

The Holy Bible is the BASIS—the *starting* point—which supplies us with the only right *approach* to the acquisition of further knowledge. This will be explained later. Biologists, psychoanalysts, medicine men and marriage counselors have neither the true FOUNDATION of sex knowledge, nor the right approach toward it. They have approached it solely from the vantage point of human reason and carnal experience.

This new approach to sex knowledge is illustrated by a recent incident. An 18-year-old girl had been engaging for a year in premarital sex relations with her "steady" boy friend. She felt guilty and condemned. Finally she worked up courage to go to her pastor, confess her unchastity, and ask for guidance.

She braced herself for a stinging rebuke. Instead, the minister merely asked whether these experiences had been expressions of "deep feeling," or of temporary sensual gratification. The girl admitted they had talked casually of the possibility of being married some day, and said they really were "crazy about each other."

"Well then," counseled this minister, "you need feel no guilt at all about what you have done. As a matter of fact, to repress your desires of sex might even be a denial of your human instinct, and I would consider such denial of the natural sex urge to be unwholesome."

Perhaps you noticed that I did not say that this clergyman was a minister *of Jesus Christ.* If you care to turn to II Corinthians 11:14-15 you will find his connection identified!

This minister said, *"I would consider* such denial of the natural sex urge unwholesome." That is how *he* would consider it!

Today human "authorities" speak of how *they* consider such problems—or how *they* view various subjects. A doctor says, "This is my view." A biologist says, "It seems to me, thus and so." A psychiatrist says, "We are coming to believe . . . ." A minister says, "I would consider . . . ."

Yes, *men say:* —"I think . . ."—"I feel . . ."—"It might well be . . ."—"It would seem logical to suppose . . ."—etc., etc., etc.

God Almighty says, "There is a way that seemeth right to a man; but the end thereof are the ways of DEATH."

Would God Know?

Isn't it about time we ask: "What does GOD say about sex?" Is it just possible that the Eternal CREATOR could know anything about SEX? Well, *He ought to!* He *designed* and *created* sex, its stimuli, and its functions in the marvelous human body.

Why should a minister *of Jesus Christ* teach the TRUTH about sex? Jesus said: ". . . He which made them at the beginning made them male and female, and said, 'For this cause shall a man leave father and mother, and shall cleave to his wife: and they twain shall be one flesh.' Wherefore they are no more twain, but one flesh. What therefore God hath joined together, let not man put asunder" (Matthew 19:4-6).

God Almighty is our CREATOR! He designed the human body and mind. He made the human body to become the "temple of the Holy Spirit." And He designed some human bodies to be male, and some to be female. GOD thought out, planned and designed sex anatomy, both male and female. GOD made the human body so that it would function sexually.

Is what GOD purposed, planned, designed, and made, something that is EVIL? Here is what He Himself says about that:

"And God saw everything that He had made"—including the human body, male and female—"and, behold, IT WAS VERY *GOOD*"! (Genesis 1:31.)

WHO will say, then, that it was very BAD?—very EVIL? —very nasty? WHO will dare accuse GOD? What GOD made is not evil or sinful. *But man has power to put what God made to a wrong and sinful USE!* Sin is not the *thing*—sin is the *wrong use* of the thing—sin is the transgression of GOD'S LAW! Sin is *thinking* and *acting* contrary to God's purposes and COMMANDS!

I am a minister of Jesus Christ. I am commanded by Jesus Christ to lift up my voice—to cry aloud and spare not—and to show God's people THEIR SINS! I preach the repentance of SIN. I preach salvation *from* SIN!

The SIN question is a definite integral part of THE GOSPEL.

Does SEX have anything to do with SIN? Does SIN have any connection with sex? Two of the Ten Commandments have to do with SEX. The violation of the marriage covenant —whether before or after marriage—is a SIN. "Thou shalt not commit adultery," says the seventh of God's Commandments.

Marriage is a physical union, but a DIVINE institution, ordained by GOD. It is GOD who joins together a husband and wife as one FLESH. Marriage is of GOD—it is GOD'S

DOING—and His laws protect it. I am a minister of the living GOD, commissioned to TEACH people about holy matrimony, and God's laws protecting this sacred institution of His!

The tenth Commandment says: "Thou shalt not COVET." Of course a man could covet his neighbor's money, his goods, or his house. But he also can, and too frequently does, LUST after his neighbor's WIFE. He also may covet, or lust, sexually. This Commandment, too, enters the area of SEX.

The Eternal GOD instructed our first parents in the right uses of sex. Sex instruction is an integral part of MORAL and SPIRITUAL teaching. It belongs definitely within the field of CHRIST'S MINISTRY!

WHY is all this prolific dissemination of sex information of the past 40 years producing such EVIL fruit? A prime reason is simply that it has originated, *not* from God's Word, *not* from the pens of God's faithful and true ministers, but from the medical doctors, the psychiatrists, the "sexologists," and professional men in the purely secular and materialistic fields.

The "experts" and the "authorities" do not know it, but *there is a spiritual law!* That law is as real, as inexorable, as the law of gravity. When a man falls from a seven-story building, or a 70-foot-high precipice, the law of gravity is in action. It draws him rapidly downward. Then when he hits bottom, he is quite suddenly affected by another law. Inertia wallops him, probably fatally. For every sexual action, this spiritual law imposes a definite reaction. That law was set in living motion to *regulate* sexual behavior as the ETERNAL Himself intended.

Also there are PURPOSES in sex of which these authors are largely unaware. The real secret of happiness — both marital and premarital—has never been opened to their understanding.

Yes, there is this invisible LAW. And just to mention *one* of its reactions, premarital sex experience diminishes, in greater or lesser degree, capacity for REAL LOVE and happiness in a later marriage! If marriages were previously rendered unhappy by repressive guilt-stricken attitudes and ignorance, they become far *less* happy under this false "New Morality." The wrong kind of knowledge is more harmful than ignorance.

Today DIVORCES ARE ON THE RAPID INCREASE! About every fourth home, over the United States, becomes a divorce victim today. In Los Angeles it is one in three or less.

Premarital experience, becoming far more nearly universal than is generally known, is literally shattering young lives by the millions!

The New Campus "Morality"

Of all places where one would expect the TRUE knowledge to be disseminated, the very first should be the colleges and the universities. And yet the campuses housing these future leaders of the world are the very places where this swing to IMMORALITY seems to be most prevalent.

A newspaper headline said: "STUDENTS IN SEARCH OF A NEW MORALITY." Their "search" is leading directly to promiscuous IMMORALITY. University students are saying bluntly that with the waning of church and parental influence, "we decide for ourselves on codes of morality." A later chapter will bring these codes into sharper focus.

I am not only Christ's minister, charged with the moral responsibility of showing God's people their sins, and answerable for the commission to proclaim the RIGHT WAYS of GOD —I am also the chancellor of three colleges, two in the United States, and one in Britain. I am, therefore, quite concerned with the conditions developing on the campuses of the western world. And therein lies the impetus which has finally resulted in the publishing of the present volume— as will be presently explained.

Accompanying this trend into moral erosion on representative campuses, is the drift into intellectual materialism.

An article in a magazine of 14½ million copies circulation was captioned: *"Is God Leaving the Campus?"* The subcaption asked WHY so many students "end up without any genuine belief in God or the moral values." These thousands of students—future world leaders among them—are being fed on the prevailing diet of crass materialism, with true moral convictions largely discarded.

The result? Unbelievable thousands of premarital pregnancies; frustrations and broken lives; a shocking rise in mental breakdowns; and an astonishing number of campus suicides.

Those are the FRUITS!

Accompanying this moral revolution, too, has come a constant weakening of religious conviction, and a watering down of devotion. And, paradoxically, as this magazine article stated, "a new interest in religious values and ideas is sweeping the campuses." But this religious interest is, primarily, curiosity, and interest in *ideas*, but not in hearing or obeying the TRUTH!

Of course life on college campuses—especially co-ed—inevitably leads to romances and marriages. That is normal, and, under right conditions, as it should be.

But, on typical campuses, all is *not* as it should be! An appalling percentage of these marriages results in divorce. And divorce puts the participants through the wringer of emotional anguish, lonesomeness, and frustration. It results too often in broken lives, and the juvenile delinquency of child victims.

Where, and WHY Results Are Different

On our three Ambassador College campuses *things are radically different!*

Students come to these colleges to learn the TRUE VALUES! In their very first year they receive the *other half* of this needed knowledge—the half these sex-book authors *do not, themselves, understand.* These students learn the Creator's PURPOSES; they receive the knowledge of God-designed right uses.

And—yes, romances do, of course, occur on these campuses. But results are altogether different—and *most happily so!* There have been *NO* DIVORCES!

The factors leading to the establishment of this course of instruction in the original Ambassador College explain WHY this book had to be written.

Personally, I had learned much about the tragic *need* of this instruction during the previous years of my ministry. Christians are commanded literally to *live by* every Word of God—the entirety of the BIBLE! But often they need experienced help in applying Biblical teachings and principles to specific problems. My years of ministry have involved a great deal of counseling about personal problems. And marital and sex problems ranked high among those brought to me.

For many years I had known, passively, that the *real,* though unmentioned, cause of some 90% of divorces was sexual incompatibility resulting from ignorance and wrong attitudes. Of course its legal terminology in divorce actions usually is "mental cruelty." Then in 1949 a certain case induced special research of marital conditions in general. This brought acute awareness, with emphasis, *of the appalling TRAGEDY existent in a majority of all marriages!*

People generally were entering into the marriage relationship with no knowledge of the *right attitude* toward marriage in general and sex in particular. They were unaware of the divinely appointed PURPOSES of sex, and ignorant of vital physical details.

Ambassador College was founded to teach, not merely how to earn a living, but *how to LIVE!* Its motto has always been *"Recapture TRUE VALUES."* People entering the married state ignorant of God's truth about sex *do not know how to live!* Such unhappy marriages assuredly have not recaptured TRUE values!

Thus it was brought forcibly to the attention of the faculty the necessity of a course that would correct this tragic situation in the lives of Ambassador students.

On first thought it was assumed that such a course

should be taught by our college physician, Dr. Ralph E. Merrill. Dr. Merrill was a physician of wide experience and high standing in the medical profession.

In collaboration with Dr. Merrill a careful survey was made of the situation. We were reminded that Ambassador policy recognizes the Biblical revelation as the FOUNDATION of *ALL* knowledge — and as the approach to humanly acquired knowledge. In no area, we immediately realized, is this more true than in this field of sex and marriage.

GOD designed sex anatomy, and set in motion sex stimuli. GOD was the original Great Educator—and it was GOD who personally instructed our first parents about sex. Two of the Ten Commandments safeguard the *right uses* of sex in marriage. The Ten Commandments constitute an invisible SPIRITUAL law. Yet they involve *physical* actions.

Sex and marriage fall within the SPIRITUAL and MORAL category—even though they involve physical usage.

Dr. Merrill and the faculty decided that the teaching of this subject is the prerogative of the ministers of Jesus Christ. Only the true minister of God has the proper spiritual *approach* to this delicate yet vitally important subject.

There was, of course, close collaboration with Dr. Merrill, especially in the area of physical and biological details.

For this important course there was no textbook available which we felt we could endorse and place in the hands of our students. Of the vast accumulation of books on the subject of sex and marriage, there was, of course, a wealth of factual physical knowledge. Yet even these authors and "authorities" disagreed on many points. But none seemed to recognize a Creator—none approached the subject from the Biblical foundation—none realized fully God's PURPOSES —none viewed the subject from the viewpoint of God's revealed right attitude. None seemed to understand the TRUE morality of the Creator.

There was only one answer.

It was necessary to produce an adequate textbook of our own!

This was to be done as a combined effort between Dr. Merrill, certain of the faculty, and the Graduate School of Theology.

Our beloved Dr. Merrill died in 1958 before this work could be completed, though he had contributed the factual physical material needed for the book. Collaboration was continued, however, with his successors as college physicians.

Meanwhile, the course was taught as a collaboration between college physician and myself.

Since the establishment of this *Principles of Living* course, beginning the 1949-50 school year, including classes in general family relations and child rearing, hundreds of students have married who previously had taken this course. There has not been one instance, in all that number, of unhappiness due to sex incompatibility. There has not been a single divorce.

Jesus said, "By their fruits ye shall know them."

The fruits—the actual results—through the centuries, have shown that ignorance of what is contained in this book has led to widespread unhappiness, anguish and tragedy. And knowledge of what you are about to read, contrariwise, has paved the way to ideal happiness and joy in the lives of those who possess and follow it.

CHAPTER 2

Where Is the *Authority*
for Moral Codes?

*T*ODAY we see a world in revolt. The rebellion against medieval moral repression is sweeping the occidental world.

But WHERE are the rebels *going?* They don't exactly know. They know they will never return to former prudery. But they are confused. They are groping for some AUTHORITY for morals. Blindly they seek a "New Morality" which will approve IMMORALITY.

They no longer accept Roman Catholic authority. The Protestants never exercised authority.

College students, teen-agers, mixed-up married people —all look helplessly and hopingly toward the supposed modern professional leaders of moral and social standards— the psychiatrists, the doctors, scientists, and educators.

These professional men have been leading them in the moral rebellion—but in no definite and certain direction they conscientiously can approve. And when the blind lead the blind, they all fall into the ditch.

These "authorities" put a proud look on their faces and say: "I think," "I feel," "I guess," "We may well suppose," "It seems to me," "We are coming to believe," or "Here's the way I look at it." In their blind indecision they reject the one Supreme AUTHORITY on morals. They deny the God who made them, and refuse to acknowledge the authority of

His INSTRUCTION BOOK He sent along with His product!

Yes, just what *IS* the Holy BIBLE? Few seem to know!

It is the Maker's *Instruction Book!* But these professional leaders have never sought the PROOFS. If they were truly scientific, they would PROVE whether God exists—whether the Bible is His inspired Word!

Do you know WHY these "authorities" do not look at the PROOFS, but blandly throw God's revelation out the window? They regard it as a RIVAL! God's BOOK is the true Book of AUTHORITY! God Almighty is Himself the one and only supreme AUTHORITY! But these little men in their silly vanity have coveted that prerogative for themselves. They like to be accepted by a deceived people as "AUTHORITIES."

But be honest! Ask yourself: Does a real AUTHORITY speak their language? Does a true AUTHORITY say: "Of course we know little, as yet, but we may well SUPPOSE thus and so"? That is the language of the doctor, the scientist, the psychologist. The doctor *practices* medicine. Yes, that's right, he *practices*—on YOU! The scientist *experiments*. He doesn't KNOW — he *postulates* — he has a THEORY — he dreams up a HYPOTHESIS!

Jesus Christ was the SON OF GOD! Jesus Christ spoke with AUTHORITY! He didn't guess—He KNEW!

A young lawyer came to Jesus and asked, "What must I do to inherit eternal life?" Can you imagine Jesus answering in the terms of the *modern* minister, the scientist, psychiatrist, or doctor? Can you imagine Jesus answering, "Well, of course we don't know much about that, as yet, BUT, we may well SUPPOSE thus and so, and I FEEL this or that way about it, and IN MY VIEW, it may safely be assumed, etc., etc."?

You can PROVE the existence of GOD. You can prove it by the discoveries and laws of science. *Not* by postulates, but by proven *facts* of science. You can prove it by fulfilled prophecy. You can prove it by logic and rational reason. You can prove it by the laws of NATURE, and the very existence of LAW and ORDER in the created universe.

You can PROVE that the BIBLE is the very inspired WORD of the Supreme, Almighty, All-intelligent, Personal GOD, the CREATOR. So could these gentlemen who pose as "authorities" if they could deflate their egos and open their closed minds long enough to look at the proofs.

You can prove inspiration by fulfilled PROPHECY—by the facts of archaeology—by answered prayer—by other infallible proofs. It is SO PROVABLE that only the FOOL has said in his heart, "There is no God" (Ps. 14:1). (Write for our free booklets—"Does God Exist?" and "Proof of the Bible.")

The BIBLE *is* AUTHORITY!

Yet, it seems almost no one knows what the Bible really *IS*.

Original Manual of Sex

The Bible is our Maker's Instruction Book. When you purchase an automobile or electrical appliance, the maker sends with it an instruction book. This instruction book explains the purpose of the mechanism, what it is expected to do, and how to operate it.

The human individual—mind and body—is the most wonderful mechanism ever produced. With this human mechanism, the divine Maker sent along *His* Instruction Book. It reveals the PURPOSE for which we were placed on this earth. It instructs in the proper operation of this human mechanism so that it will accomplish its divinely intended PURPOSE.

This is *basic* KNOWLEDGE. It is knowledge *not otherwise accessible to or discoverable by man*. It is the FOUNDATION of *all* knowledge. It provides the right *approach* to the acquisition of *discoverable* knowledge.

For example. Educators do not know, scientists have never discovered, philosophers have never reasoned out, the real WHY of human existence. Is there, after all, real MEANING

to life? What is *THE WAY* to accomplishment of the divine
PURPOSE?

What is *THE WAY* to PEACE? The world's statesmen
and rulers do not know. The scientists do not know; they
can only invent and produce more terrifying weapons of
mass destruction. What is *THE WAY* to happiness? Money?
Those who have acquired it were seldom happy.

WHY do we get sick? What is *THE WAY* to perfect
health? The doctors don't know.

God's Instruction Book is the only source of this BASIC
KNOWLEDGE. It reveals PURPOSES and invisible but inexorable LAWS that govern peace, health, prosperity, content-
ment, happiness, joy, and eternal life. It reveals the PURPOSES
of *sex*, and the uses that lead to true happiness!

And this knowledge, in turn, provides the only right
approach to acquiring discoverable knowledge.

God did not equip humans with instinct. But He did
supply us with MINDS. He gave us eyes, so we can see. We
can hear, taste, smell, and feel. Additional knowledge is
accessible through these five sensory channels. We can retain in memory what we see, hear, or learn. We can reason,
think, plan, imagine, design. We can explore, investigate,
examine, measure.

God gave us hands. The human hand is a marvelous
mechanism. If an animal could be given a MIND with which
to design and plan, it still could not make and build, with
hoofs, paws or claws, what MAN is able to construct and
produce with human hands. So man can invent and produce
instruments, test tubes, laboratories, microscopes, telescopes,
with which to pursue further knowledge.

Evolution False Approach to Sex

But, unless he possesses the *right* FOUNDATION on which
to build, and the *right approach* to this discoverable knowledge, he fails rightly to UNDERSTAND or EXPLAIN or USE what
he discovers or produces. Man *has* pursued after SEX knowl-

edge. But *not from* the true FOUNDATION, or with the right *approach*.

The accepted *concept*, used as the *approach* to knowledge today, is the theory of evolution. Evolution is the skeptics' false explanation of the presence of a CREATION—including sex—*without* a CREATOR.

There is NO PROOF for evolution. There are assumed contributing or supporting factors, but they do not constitute PROOF. At best they could add what could *appear* logical support to something otherwise proved. I have *dis*proved the evolutionary hypothesis—by FACTUAL, rational and positive proofs. I have PROVED the existence of GOD, the AUTHORITY of the Bible, and therefore the FACT of CREATION.

But no scientist has ever *dis*proved the existence of God, or the inspiration and authority of the Bible; nor has any scientist PROVED the evolutionary theory to be true in actual fact.

I have before me, as I write, a recent book on the physiology and technique of marriage. It has enjoyed a wide circulation. The author is a well-known physician in Europe. He is learned in the knowledge possessed by the doctors, the biologists, the psychiatrists, the marriage counsellors and the sexologists. All his knowledge, however, is physical. This author has no FOUNDATION under his half-knowledge. He lacks the true approach.

In his Chapter 2, he approaches the PURPOSE and FUNCTIONING of sex from the false assumption that evolution is a fact. He notes the differences between animals and humans, and reasons that *ideal marriage* has developed through aeons of time from the animal state to the human potential.

He is ignorant of the true PURPOSES of sex in humans. Therefore he is rendered incompetent to teach his readers the right attitude toward, or the proper use and functioning of sex in the human family.

In all this avalanche of sex literature being hurled at

the public today, we have yet to find a single book or an article based on this true FOUNDATION, and *approached* with this vital knowledge.

Indeed, while the Bible is the FOUNDATION of *all* knowledge—whether history, science, anthropology, religion, sex, or whatever—there is possibly no field in which this basic revelation and concept is more vital than in this area of sex and marriage.

CHAPTER 3

But Was This Moral Code Christian?

*W*HAT A PARADOX! Solomon spoke prophetically of our time: "Of making many books there is no end." Altogether *too many* books have been written, in the last thirty-five years, on this subject of sex and marriage. Yet it is true, as the Creator says through the prophet Hosea, "My people are destroyed *for lack of knowledge.*"

An Ocean of Water—But Not a Drop to Drink

There is *tragic need* for this present volume!

The prophet Daniel said of our day: ". . . *knowledge shall be increased.*" So here is the paradox: Utterly beyond our realization, knowledge *has been increasing* since the turn of the century. Knowledge in the fields of science, technology, engineering, medicine—to name a few. And at the very same time, there is a FAMINE of *understanding* right and true knowledge.

I repeat: All this KNOWLEDGE—but no happiness! It's like the shipwrecked victim on a raft in the ocean—water everywhere, but not a drop to drink. What's WRONG?

The true facts will sound incredible. But in the following chapters the amazing truth will be made PLAIN.

When my wife and I were married, in 1917, we sought in vain for an authoritative book on the physical problems of marriage. Our parents had taught us nothing. Like *their* parents and grandparents before them, they knew too little about the embarrassing subject.

I did find six books which I purchased. One was a series of three volumes for males written by a pious minister: *What a Young Boy Ought to Know; What a Young Man Ought to Know;* and *What a Young Husband Ought to Know.* The companion series, written by a "Christian" woman physician: *What a Young Girl Ought to Know; What a Young Woman Ought to Know;* and *What a Young Wife Ought to Know.*

Just one thing was wrong with these six books. They did not *tell* us what we needed to know! It would have been unlawful. And, besides, judging from the sanctimonious flavor of the writing, I surmised that these authors would have been embarrassed—if, indeed, they themselves knew what a young married couple needed to know!

I have before me a book titled *Sane Sex Life and Sane Sex Living,* by H. W. Long, M.D. This book *does* tell what the newly married need to know—though, in certain technical knowledge it is about 40 years out of date. You see, it was written more than 40 years ago, and first published in 1919. But it was not then sold in any bookstore! That would have been illegal.

This book was made available only to members of the medical profession. Originally it had been used only in typed manuscript form, loaned by Dr. Long to married patients who had come to him tearfully pleading for help in their marital difficulties. This doctor had exhausted himself giving personal instruction verbally. To save time, he had typed the vital instruction to loan for private and confidential reading. In 1919 it was published in a book for other physicians to loan, also in strictest privacy, to *their* troubled patients.

The Dam Bursts

A few years later the legal floodgates opened. The tidal wave of sex books surged through, to be swallowed up by a public avidly hungry for the forbidden fruit of hitherto secret knowledge about sex.

This flood of newly released knowledge followed in the wake of the first World War. It came on the market contemporaneously with a postwar moral sag and an upsurge of psychoanalysis. This new "science" was attributing mental disquiet and neuroses largely—and some of its practitioners wholly—to sex repression, sexual maladjustments and frustrations, due to ignorance. This fast-growing profession, predominately sex-minded, exerted powerful influence toward the revision of moral standards.

The old taboos were being relegated to the limbo of superstition and dark-age ignorance. The new "enlightenment" was knocking down the moral bars. Sex, gradually, lost its *"Sinful"* label, and the sense of shame began to disappear.

Women were being "emancipated." They wanted the same rights as men—that is to say, they desired to descend into the same gutter. At least enough of them to start a trend. Of course, all men were not *in* that gutter—but the idea of the double standard assumed they were.

Three New Movements

Coincident also with the rise of the psychiatrists, and the relaxing of ethics and morals resulting naturally from the stresses and strains of a world war, three other movements were gaining tremendous momentum. These all combined to add impetus to the morals' "new look." These three were:

1) The "women's rights" crusade which was termed woman suffrage. Women wanted the same "rights" as men. It was more than a fight for the vote. Especially in America, women began to rebel against the Biblical edict that makes the husband the head of the wife. Marriage became a "fifty-fifty" proposition—temporarily. Of course *some* one has to rule, so the fifty-fifty *deal* merely bridged the transition into

the World War II *NEW* deal when the *wife* put on the trousers.

Women not only began to vote and make their voices heard in government, they began to rule the home, and run for public political office—(as I write, one is running for President of the United States!). They went into business. Women bobbed their hair and began to *feel* and act like men. They abolished the double standard. The old-time saloons became cocktail lounges and pubs. The legalized red light districts were abolished, and gradually premarital promiscuity began to give amateur competition to the *professionals.* Women—too many of them—had descended to man's level!

2) German rationalism and intellectual materialism permeated curricula in our institutions of higher learning. Education, as will be shown more vividly later, had always been basically pagan. But it also had had a certain "Christian" flavor. "Christianity" had clung to many basically pagan doctrines and customs, attempting to "interpret" them *INTO* the Bible. But it held to the name of Christ, dispensed "grace" even though turned into license—and it *had* retained certain standards of morals. And, it had acknowledged the Bible, though with its own interpretations. But it seems the Scopes trial not only ended in the death of William Jennings Bryan, it sounded also the death knell of the Word of God in education. The Bible was thrown out the window altogether, in favor of intellectualism's new Messiah—Science, and the theory of evolution.

3) The Modernist religious movement simultaneously leavened the Protestant ranks. The ministers "of the Gospel" were inoculated with the evolutionary serum in their pre-seminary college years. The seminary professors were themselves the victims of anti-God German rationalism absorbed in *their* student days. More and more, theological institutions were sending into pulpits young ministers addicted to Modernism. And they were becoming increasingly "broad-minded" in their attitude toward sex and marriage.

A fourth trend might be mentioned also. In America,

teen-agers began a new custom—"going steady." And the age of beginning to "go steady" has gradually lowered, until today even twelve- and thirteen-year-olds are starting it. This close familiarity has contributed its portion to the moral trend.

So THERE IS THE PROBLEM!

THERE is the state of affairs today.

Knowledge—But No Solutions!

KNOWLEDGE has rapidly increased. But it has been wholly *materialistic* knowledge. And this flood of sex knowledge has been only half complete. It has failed to reveal the Creator's PURPOSES. It has implanted a totally false interpretation of sex. It has produced wrong attitudes, led to wrong and sinful uses, and robbed humanity of the glorious blessings of GOD-INTENDED uses. A structure of sex knowledge was being built. But it was a superstructure *without a foundation*. The FOUNDATION OF ALL KNOWLEDGE—the revelation from God to mankind—was lacking.

And WHERE does this leave us, today?

It leaves us with a vast accumulation of KNOWLEDGE while at the same time *this civilization is being destroyed for LACK of RIGHT KNOWLEDGE!*

Permissiveness and promiscuity have replaced prudery and the sense of shame. The former evil has been replaced by one far more deadly! The unhappiness caused by dualism has been multiplied by the modern swing.

One of the most desperate needs of our time is a book disseminating the true, and heretofore unpublished, knowledge about SEX and MARRIAGE.

Moral standards, emphatically, are indeed in need of revision. But they cannot be *rightly* revised until wrong attitudes have been dispelled, and a right view established. God Almighty created sex to bring blessings, happiness. Wrong attitudes and uses have brought curses.

Before the full truth about sex and marriage can be

received, we need to know how present and former false concepts were acquired.

The "sex-is-evil" attitude came to us of today through the medium of the Roman Catholic Church. But where did *they* acquire it? The true facts are stranger than fiction!

NOT Christian!

Through the centuries the moral standards in the western world were regulated by the Roman Catholic Church.

Does that mean, then, that Jesus Christ started this teaching that sex is evil? Or, did the original apostles inject this dualism into Christianity? Is this concept to be found in the Bible?

The answer to these questions is an emphatic *NO!*

Yet this interpretation of sex was embraced by organized Christianity through the centuries. It is still the teaching of the Catholic Church. Many Protestants still cling to it. Many—and in rapidly increasing numbers—are breaking away from it.

The true facts about the appearance of this attitude in Roman Catholicism are astounding. They have been cloaked in mystery. The time has come for the shocking truth to be revealed.

We need, first of all, to understand some facts about creation, education, and early church history.

Man Is NOT An Animal!

Actually, education started in the Garden of Eden. The original Great Educator was the Creator Himself. He created the first man and the first woman. The first instruction came direct from God, in Person.

But *how* had He created these humans? And for what PURPOSE?

First, the Eternal created the fish in the oceans, lakes and streams, after the *fish* kinds. Then the birds of the air after the *bird* kinds, and winged land fowls after the *fowl* kinds. Then the land animals—cattle reproducing after the *cattle* kind; lions after the lion kind; dogs after the dog kind.

Then finally, God said: "Let us make man in *our* image, after *our* likeness." God now proposed to make man, *not* as an animal—*not* after the *animal* kind, *but after the GOD kind!*

MAN IS NOT AN ANIMAL!

The word "image" means, Biblically, the stamping with CHARACTER. It can also mean form or shape—does in some passages. But in Genesis 1:26, the word *likeness* refers to form and shape—appearance. And "image" here refers to God's *character*. Man was not *then* stamped with God's divine *character*-image.

God is composed of SPIRIT (John 4:24) but He formed man of the dust of the ground—material substance (Genesis 2:7). What was formed of this material substance became a living SOUL. The soul, says your Bible, is composed of MATTER, not spirit. And the soul that sins shall die (Ezekiel 18:4, 20). The soul is mortal. Man does not *have* a soul—he *is* a soul (Genesis 2:7).

This material man was *formed*—shaped—out of material substance. Thus, in form and shape, he bore God's likeness. God reveals Himself as having a face, hair, eyes, ears, nose, mouth, arms, feet. But man was made for the very purpose of *acquiring*—during his mortal lifetime—the CHARACTER of God.

Notice I Corinthians 15:45-54. The first man, Adam, was made a living *soul*. But Christ, the "last Adam," was made an immortal *spirit*. The first Adam—a living *soul*—was not immortal, not spirit, but was *of the earth—earthy* (verse 47). Then, verse 49, *we*—speaking to converted Christians—have borne the *image* of the earthy, in this life. That is, the *character* of sinful humanity. But through Christ the Christian *shall*—through the resurrection to immortality (verses 50-54)—bear the image of the heavenly. That is, the *divine character*.

Notice the first few verses of the first chapter of Hebrews. It speaks of the resurrected Christ, "who, being the brightness of His (the Father's) glory, and *the express image of His person. . . .*" The Moffatt translation renders this, more correctly, "He, reflecting God's bright glory and *stamped with God's own character. . . .*" "Image" means *character*.

The creation described in Genesis 1, brought into being the MATERIAL, from the earth, out of which God, the Master Potter, with our right decision, shall fashion, mold, and shape SPIRITUALLY, into His very own perfect *spiritual character*.

CREATION IS STILL GOING ON—God's *spiritual* creation.

God's PURPOSE is *to create us into the* GOD *kind*—to beget us as His children, so we may be BORN AGAIN—this time born of GOD into HIS divine family! Few readers, I know, will be able to grasp this tremendous truth. It is repeatedly revealed in your Bible—from Genesis to Revelation. Yet it has remained hidden from this world—just as God's wonderful truth about sex has remained hidden.

Animal vs. Human Sex Behaviour

I repeat, MAN IS NOT AN ANIMAL!

One may ask, do not all animals come equipped with sex? Do they not, like humans, reproduce after their kind? All mammals reproduce in the same manner as humans—yes! Are not animals made of material flesh and blood—the same as humans? Yes, *but not the same kind of flesh*. Have you not read, I Corinthians 15:39, that "All flesh is not the same flesh: but there is one kind of flesh of men, another flesh of beasts . . . ," etc.

God made cattle to reproduce after the cattle kind. But He *is*, by a spiritual creation still going on, reproducing MAN after HIS kind—after the GOD kind. Man is being made in the GOD image!

God possesses MIND. *Man* possesses MIND. Animals have mere brain.

Both animals and humans reproduce through sex. Yet there are some astounding *differences* between animal and human sex functions, to be explained later. There is a vast difference between humans and animals in relation to the Creator's PURPOSES of sex. These differences need to be understood.

But man *alone,* of all creatures that reproduce through sex, devises his own codes of morality. He has always rejected GOD's code.

Only MAN, by use of mind, exercises self-determined control over sex urges. Animals establish no moral codes. Animals are actuated by instinct. The animal brain is *set* by the Creator to act in certain ways under certain circumstances—much as you might set an alarm clock to ring at a certain hour.

Humans, like God, have MIND-power. Humans acquire knowledge which no animal brain can receive. What can any animal know about astronomy, chemistry, mathematics, literature, art, music? The human MIND has actual creative powers. From a vast labyrinth of acquired knowledge, the human mind can reason, plan, imagine, design, make decisions, and *will* to act according to personal choice. HUMANS WERE CREATED WITH THE POTENTIAL OF DEVELOPING RIGHTEOUS CHARACTER!

Human Mind vs. Animal Brain

Humans are endowed with the faculty to learn to know right from wrong. Human minds have ability to weigh facts, to judge, make decisions, and to exercise self-restraint and self-discipline.

My son had a dog. When the fact was flashed to that dog's brain, through the sense of scent, or hearing, that a member of the family was coming down the walk outside, the dog automatically wagged its tail happily. But when a stranger was coming down the walk, the dog just as automatically began to bark. Now can you imagine a dog reasoning thus: "A stranger is coming down the walk. Now let me think! Shall I set up a bark, or shall I restrain myself and keep quiet? O.K. I guess I'll practice self-restraint and resist the instinct to bark, this once."

A thinking, reasoning, *talking* horse may be interesting entertainment on a television show—the very impossibility of it attracts millions of viewers. But if it were a natural occurrence, that particular show-format would be a flop.

Pure instinct, in animal brain, sets off action automatically. Humans do not have this kind of instinct.

Humans have HUMAN NATURE. Human nature is a PULL —in the direction of vanity, self-gratification, self-interest. Like the pull of gravity, it is a *downward* pull. But the human mind can recognize this pull, decide whether to yield or resist, and then *will* to follow its decision.

Nowhere are the differences between animal *brain* and human *mind* more pronounced than in the area of sex.

Rejecting the Great Educator's Instruction

In creating man for this SUPREME purpose of the Great God, He created them *male and female*. It was the Almighty Eternal GOD who designed, formed, shaped male and female bodies. And the *"instruction book"* which the Maker sent along with His product—this human mechanism—is the BASIS for knowledge of HOW sex was intended to be used— and for what purposes!

The Great Creator was also the GREAT EDUCATOR—the very first educator to instruct humans. He instructed our first parents in SEX. He instructed them also in the right WAY of life—the way of true LOVE. For His Law *is* LOVE!

The Genesis account portrays the Great Educator instructing the first man and woman regarding the two basic philosophies of life. These were pictured by the two symbolic trees.

The one, the tree of LIFE, was freely offered. It represented THE WAY of *LOVE*—of outgoing concern for others, of giving, helping, serving, sharing. This was THE WAY of God's inexorable spiritual LAW, summed up in the Ten Commandments. God revealed THIS WAY as the way to peace, happiness, security, abundance. This law is fulfilled by LOVE (Romans 13:10). Two of the Ten Commandments concern SEX, and protect marital love against pollution.

The other philosophy of life—that of Satan—was symbolized by the forbidden tree of the knowledge of good and evil. That philosophy is THE WAY of vanity—of SELF—of taking, gratifying fleshly desire, coveting—lust. That false WAY is, simply, rebellion against God's Law.

God ordained and intended LOVE *in* a happy marriage. He forbade lust prior to, or outside of, marriage! Much, much more on this, in detail, later.

But WHAT HAPPENED?

Our first parents rejected the direct revelation of knowledge from God. They listened to the false teaching of Satan. From that day, humanity was embarked on the course of false education. Mankind had chosen, and succeeding generations have followed, the life-philosophy of vanity, self-desire, greed, competition, strife—taking, getting the most while giving the least—the way of hate and of WAR.

Incidentally, every book about sex so far published, save the present volume, so far as I know, has been based on the attitude of this world's false life-philosophy!

The most ancient records reveal that educational institutions, from dimmest antiquity, were organized and maintained by religions. But the religions of this world have always been pagan! Their religions are based on the satanic philosophy. As early as the tenth century B.C. we find the record of schools for the training of pagan priesthoods.

The academic form of curricular education—the form in vogue today—was originated by the pagan Greek philosopher Plato, 427-347 B.C. He was the founder of education of regular curriculum in a fixed place. He called it the *Academy*.

At the time of Christ pagan schools on the Plato model dotted the Roman Empire. As the Church of God grew and multiplied during the first thirty-eight years after Christ's ascension, and later, during the rise of what came to be called "Christianity," *no Christian schools existed.* All children—*if* they were educated—were educated in the *pagan* philosophies—and in the pagan concept of sex. You see, printing had not yet been invented. Textbooks had to be prepared, laboriously, entirely by hand, one at a time. And truly Christian textbooks were never produced.

The Incredible "Lost Century"

At this point an amazing, diabolical Great Conspiracy of Satan occurred. The unbelievable TRUTH of this masterpiece of deception has been successfully hidden from public notice for eighteen long centuries!

In the Book of Acts and other New Testament passages we have the well-preserved authentic history of the founding and the first 38 years' history of the original Church of God. But by the time of the Roman siege against Jerusalem, 70 A.D., the curtain is suddenly rung down on the stage of church history.

In 69 A.D., the Christians from Jerusalem, heeding Jesus' warning of Luke 21:20-21, fled north from Judaea to the east side of the Jordan. From that date their organized proclaiming of Christ's true Gospel ceased.

For the next hundred years, church history is virtually a blank. The historian Edward Gibbon terms this virtually non-existent history "scanty and suspicious."

IT WAS THE MYSTERIOUS "LOST CENTURY" OF CHURCH HISTORY!

When the curtain rises, about 170 A.D., we behold a "Christian" church hardly recognizable! In most vital points of doctrine and custom it is the very antithesis of the Church of the original Apostles founded by Jesus Christ. Yet it professes Christ. It proclaims His shed blood. It freely offers grace. It calls itself "Christianity."

WHAT HAPPENED during that lost century?

For 1800 years it has been cloaked in mystery. But suddenly God has seen fit to reveal in unmistakable clarity the facts surrounding this Master Conspiracy of Satan. For by it he has deceived the whole world!

The sure prophecies in your Bible say plainly that *the whole world* was to be DECEIVED! Satan was to deceive *all nations!* (Rev. 12:9; 17:2; 18:3.)

But HOW? He would have to use human instruments to bring about his Great Deception. He did!

Jesus Christ foretold the entrance into His Church of spurious ministers—false prophets. He called them wolves "in sheep's clothing" (Mat. 7:15). This was not an apostasy, or going astray, of Christians within the Church. His disciples were designated as "sheep." Jesus was not speaking of "stray sheep," but of "WOLVES." They were DECEIVERS— they pretended to be—they masqueraded as—sheep. They came in from the outside *for the very purpose* of destroying the sheep.

Jesus said they would come in His name—that is, pretending to be HIS MINISTERS. He said they would actually proclaim that Jesus was the Christ (Mat. 24:4-5), yet they would DECEIVE the MANY—not the few, the *MANY!* The Apostle Paul warned of the same thing (Acts 20:29-30). Actually what these deceiving false apostles *brought in* was the pagan BABYLONIAN MYSTERY religion *with its pagan interpretations of sex.* It was a religion of LAWLESSNESS, called "Mystery of Iniquity," and was already active, posing as "Christianity," by 50-51 A.D. (II Thes. 2:7). In this Scripture Paul tells us WHAT religion was brought in to deceive.

Paul branded them as, in true *fact*, the ministers of Satan (II Cor. 11:14-15). Yet they palmed themselves off as the apostles of Christ—but they were FALSE apostles (verse 13).

When Jude wrote, about 67 A.D., they had already crept in by stealth and false pretense, turning GRACE into *license* to disobey God's Law (Jude 4). In their letters James and Peter spoke of this opposition against God's Law. The

Apostle John combatted it in his letters, written in the 90's A.D. By that time these impostors had come and GONE— claiming that *they*, and their followers, NOT the true Church, constituted the original "Christianity," and the ONLY original true Church (I John 2:19). But they never were any part of the TRUE Church which Jesus founded (same verse).

The whole story of this Great Deception can be told only in a full-length book, yet to be written.

This much of summary may be revealed at this time:

The Great Conspiracy

These deceivers, actually the ministers of Satan, who is this world's *god* (II Cor. 4:4), were priests of the Babylonian Mysteries.

All the world's religions, until Christ, had been state religions, controlled by kings, emperors, or heads of government. All, but that of Israel, were superstitions maintained for the very purpose of exercising sway over the people through fear of one's fate after death.

These religions determined the sexual morals of the people.

Normally, when a country was overthrown, and a new government came to power, a new religion was introduced. But when Nebuchadnezzar's Chaldean Empire (Babylon) was overthrown, their Assyrian-Babylonian Mystery religion *did not die*. By the time of Christ, the prevailing religion throughout the Roman Empire was ROMAN paganism—a religion of Emperor-worship. Yet there was a colony of Babylonian-Mystery followers in Samaria. Samaria had been the capital of the northern Kingdom of Israel, until their captivity and removal from their land to Assyria. It is north of Jerusalem in Palestine. In 33 A.D. Babylonians were there. Their forefathers had been moved there by Shalmanezar, after the captivity of the Kingdom of Israel, 721-718 B.C. (II Kings 17:1-3, 6, 18, 22-24).

They were, by 33 A.D., a small remnant, but headed by a very ambitious priest—a sorcerer, named Simon (Acts

8:9). When Philip came to Samaria, performing real miracles, many of these people accepted Christ and were baptized (Acts 8:5-24). Their leader, Simon, saw his following disintegrating. He tried to purchase a Christian apostleship with money. The Apostle Peter rebuked him, saying he was "in the bond of iniquity." He was. He was chief leader of the "Mystery of Iniquity" spoken of in II Thessalonians 2:7. Iniquity is lawlessness—opposed to God's Law. This "Mystery" religion was the same old Babylonian Mysteries. It is called, in Revelation 17:5, by its true name, which is NOT "Christian," but "MYSTERY, BABYLON THE GREAT." That is, the *"Babylonian Mysteries"* having become GREAT at a later time.

This Simon the magician, called Simon Magus in history, marvelled at the phenomenal growth of this new INDEPENDENT Christian religion. Never had anything contained its virility, life, and power. He saw TWO main factors, which, in his carnal thinking, "made it tick."

First, this religion had a CHAMPION—a HERO for people to worship. That Hero — Christ — had been persecuted, finally martyred. Simon knew mass psychology. He knew people sympathize with the "underdog." And here was a man who had come back, by a resurrection, as a Champion to triumph over His enemies!

People would FOLLOW such a Champion! They would worship such a Hero! He determined to simply "take over" the NAME of Christ to gain followers for himself!

And thus Satan used this Great Conspiracy to DECEIVE THE WHOLE WORLD (Rev. 12:9; 17:2; 18:3).

These deceivers claimed the NAME of Christ. They proclaimed the shed BLOOD of Christ for the remission of sins— they offered GRACE—because this was POPULAR, as long as they did away with OBEDIENCE to God and His Law. They substituted penance for repentance. Satan, *their god*, was represented as being the Creator. They then invented a fictitious devil, appearing as a diabolical being with horns, a tail, and a pitchfork. All the while the *real* Satan palmed himself off as "an angel of *light*" (II Cor. 11:14), this world's god.

This Simon the magician, leader of these priests of the BABYLONIAN MYSTERY religion, had gone along and been baptized with the others, when Philip preached at Samaria (See Acts 8:12-13). Even though the Apostle Peter strongly rebuked him for trying to buy an apostleship with money— and condemned him as being "in the bond of iniquity"—that is, bound to the Babylonian MYSTERY religion of INIQUITY or LAWLESSNESS *opposing* the Law of God (compare Acts 8:18-23 with II Thessalonians 2:7 and Revelation 17:5)—nevertheless this Simon went on *pretending* he was a Christian. He had been baptized.

Now notice, in the 8th chapter of Acts, verses 9-11: This Simon used sorcery. He bewitched the people of this district of Samaria. He claimed to be a GREAT religious leader. And *all* of the population of Samaria—followers of the BABYLONIAN MYSTERY religion—gave heed to Simon— accepted him as LEADER—from the least to the greatest. Even the most important leaders of the people accepted him. The people said of him: "This man is that POWER OF GOD which is called GREAT" (*Revised Standard Version*, verse 10). He had been so accepted for a long time.

Now here comes an astounding, surprising FACT. For many centuries before this, the chief religious head of the pagan religions had been given the title "Pater," meaning "Father." But sometimes it was spelled "Patre"—even as, today, in Spain and South America priests are called "Padre." And, USUALLY, it came to be spelled "PETER!"

Also the chief headquarters, or chief place of worship, was called by the title "PETER." This was not a NAME, but a TITLE. Even heads of ancient families came to be called "arch-Peters" or "Arch-Pater," which came to be "PATRI-ARCH." Strange? Surprising? Yes, but TRUE.

This Simon the magician, who had deceived the people with his tricks of magic, was the LEADER and HEAD of the remnant of the BABYLONIAN MYSTERY religion. His followers attached the word "GREAT" to his name—the actual *originator* of the CHURCH labeled "MYSTERY, BABYLON THE GREAT" in Revelation 17:5. Yes, *he* was the "SIMON PETER" who was the FIRST "PAPA" or "FATHER" or PATER—PETER—of *that church.*

What Sex Teaching?

This Simon was inspired—by *his* god—to desire to found a UNIVERSAL religion. But what interpretation of SEX did he bring with him, from the religion of ASSYRIA and BABYLON?

Various other names had been attached to this religion. When this Simon had wormed his way in, pretending to be a member and apostle in GOD's CHURCH, even during the very first century, Christ speaks of him and his followers as "Nicolaitanes" (Rev. 2:6). The true apostolic CHURCH is represented as *hating* the deeds of these Nicolaitanes.

What were these deeds—and the teachings on which they were based? They are clouded in some mystery. Every effort was made, during the following two centuries, to destroy every secular record of them. They *couldn't* destroy what GOD inspired in the BIBLE!

The resurrected Jesus (inspiring John from heaven) mentions a direct connection that occurred a few generations later between these Nicolaitanes and "the doctrine of Balaam." What was this doctrine of the Nicolaitanes that came from Balaam's doctrine?

The *Encyclopedia of Religion and Ethics* (Hastings) says Clement of Alexandria refers to this sect as IMMORAL. Tertullian made similar charges of self-indulgence and lustfulness. The article speaks of "the explicit comparison with the teaching of Balaam (Rev. 2:14) in the two particulars of sanctioning, and even recommending, fornication, and compromise with idolatry." Balaam was a recognized prophet (pagan) and soothsayer. He counselled Balak to seduce Israel from its allegiance to The ETERNAL by alluring the people into the immoralities associated with the Moabite nature-worship—sexual immorality.

Even the *Catholic Encyclopedia* says these Nicolaitanes "led lives of unrestrained indulgence." The sect "claimed to have derived from Nicholas the doctrine of promiscuity."

Now Nicholas of Antioch (not the Nicolas of Acts 6:5) is identified with a Bishop Nicholas *of* SAMARIA, said to have become a heretic in company with Simon the magician! (This last according to the *Dictionary of the Bible* by Hastings.)

Actually, it is probable that these names have simply been confused, and that the Nicholas of Samaria is indeed Simon himself, and one and the same as Nicholas of Antioch. This would mean that Simon himself was, after all, the original bishop "Saint Nick," or Santa Claus!

Now HOW do we reconcile this religion of lustfulness and sexual promiscuity and unbridled fornication with the teaching that sex is SINFUL?

An account I well remember reading in a Bible Encyclopedia some 37 years ago stated the doctrine of the Nicolaitanes thus: They took the principle of the Scripture: "But where sin abounded, grace did much more abound" (Rom. 5:20). The argument was that bestowing GRACE glorifies God and His great POWER. If SIN abounds, then GRACE abounds much more. Therefore, the more we sin, the more GOD'S GRACE abounds—and the more GOD is glorified by forgiving so much *more!*

That sort of satanic reasoning was the basis of the ancient "temple prostitutes."

The more sinful they paint fornication—or ANY use of sex—the GREATER was God's glory in forgiving it and bestowing grace. This was their diabolical argument. This was their doctrine!

In this ancient pagan religion they even had an order of women who wore black garb, did certain physical duties and tasks, were kept in seclusion, like a convent. You will find them described in the *Encyclopedia of Religion and Ethics*, Volume VI, article "Hierodouloi" (Graeco-Roman). This term, it explains, designated certain temple ministrants, who were below the rank of priests, and usually, if not invariably, of servile status. Actually, these were the "temple prostitutes." "At Eryx and Corinth, then, we see that the *hierodouloi* were nothing but female prostitutes," continues the article, "who gave all, or a share of, their gains to the temple. . . . There is, therefore, no doubt that the term *hierodouloi*, in all the instances so far discussed, means serfs, whose bodies were absolutely at the god's service and the priests' discretion, to be used either for purposes of labor or prostitution."

Now, of course, the fornication committed by the priests with these women was kept *completely secret*. These were "dedicated" women! Their priests took the place of their god. The fornication was represented as a holy act—a sort of being married to their god!

Nevertheless, this entire rotten and foul pagan doctrine represented sex as EVIL, then claimed to glorify God by carrying it to excessive indulgence, thus allowing God to bestow the *greater* grace in forgiving it.

No wonder the resurrected Jesus, who inspired Revelation 2 and 3 as a direct quotation from Him, says to the apostolic Church: "Thou hatest the deeds of the Nicolaitanes, *which I also hate*"—and, to the later Church in Pergamos, "So hast thou also them that hold the doctrine of the Nicolaitanes, *which thing I hate*" (Rev. 2:6, 15).

Babylonian Mystery Deceptions

The message to the Church in Smyrna says: "I know the blasphemy of them which say they are Jews, and are not, but are the synagogue of Satan." The Apostle Paul explained that a Christian is a Jew *spiritually* (Romans 2:28-29). So Jesus referred to those following Satan's WAY, and Satan's ministers, who professed to be the true Church.

Again, these Babylonian Mystery followers at Samaria professed to be JEWS when it suited their purpose—and, again, Gentiles when *that* suited their purpose. Example: the woman Jesus encountered at Jacob's well, in Samaria. This woman—like the other Samaritans—was in the Babylonian religion. She had been living successively with six men, in fornication (John 4:5-7, 16-18). When it suited her purpose, she claimed to be Jewish—a descendant of Jacob (verse 12), but then when it suited her purpose to call herself a Gentile, she did (verse 9). There is reason to believe that Simon the magician was the man she was currently living with. This event in Jesus' life is not without significance!

One other significant fact.

There were those in Pergamos who held the doctrine of Balaam (Rev. 2:14). This seems to be directly connected with the doctrine of the Nicolaitanes (verse 15). Balaam was the PETER—chief priest of the pagan mystery religion—of his day. Balaam's headquarters, or chief place of worship, was *Pethor*. In the Hebrew language the "h" was commonly not pronounced. In today's English, therefore, the chief headquarters place of worship would be "PETOR"—or PETER!

How MUCH there is that has been kept a MYSTERY—covered up—kept from the knowledge of the world! Today God is revealing much that Satan has tried to cover!

So TWO POWERFUL FACTORS operated to inject pagan attitudes and teachings into a deceived professing Christianity.

1) All children attended schools where the textbooks were PAGAN. They grew up accepting *pagan* teachings, customs, and attitudes. They were reared in pagan concepts of SEX. Even the "Christian" leaders were reared from childhood under this paganized influence.

2) The "Christian" religion which spread, late in the first century and on through the second, third, and fourth centuries, through the Empire, was this counterfeit "Christianity," spawned by paganism. The true Church had fled, become scattered. Its members were branded "heretics."

It is not so strange, then, after all, that pagan interpretations of sex should have flowed at full tide into this fast-growing counterfeit "Christianity." It was not, after all, a *"new"* concept, but the SAME inherited conception that had been accepted for generations in this pagan religion.

CHAPTER 4

Origin of Pagan Dualism

*W*E NEED to understand, now, precisely *what was* this pagan interpretation of sex. We need, also, to know the facts of its origin.

What was the real *source* of this attitude of "shame" which flowed on the tide of the Babylonian Mystery religion into the Roman world, now wearing the label "Christianity"? How, in a word, did this concept come to be accepted as "Christian"?

Emphatically it was not the teaching of Hebraism, nor of Jesus. Never was it embraced or taught by the original apostles. It is not to be found in the Scriptures.

The Soul Is Composed of Matter

This teaching reached Roman "Christianity" by way of Greece. But it flowed, at an earlier date, into Greece from Egypt. Yet it stems from a still much earlier source, actually in the Garden of Eden. There we find its real author!

God had told the first man, Adam, that he, as a man, was wholly physical. Here was the newly created man. Grasp the significance if you can! Suddenly, a full-grown adult MAN received consciousness.

He looked around. Everywhere he saw BEAUTY! There were colorful flowers, stately trees, green lawns, entrancing shrubs, shimmering pools, the audible laughter of a rippling stream. He was surrounded by breath-taking magnificence.

Then the man looked at himself. He must have wondered: "WHAT AM I?" Once, I remember, I fainted. Then, when consciousness again came *suddenly*, the question was gasped, involuntarily: "Where *am I?*" But Adam must have wondered, not only *where*, but *WHAT!*

And God told him. "You are DUST." After the man had sinned, God said: ". . . out of [the ground] wast thou taken: for DUST *THOU* ART, and unto dust shalt THOU return."

God did *not* say "dust your BODY is." He said the conscious MAN was dust—composed of matter. The revelation of God is plain: "God formed MAN of the dust of the ground" (Genesis 2:7). This man, composed of physical matter from the ground, *became* a soul (same verse). This Scripture does not say God put an immortal soul *into* a material body. It says God breathed BREATH into his nostrils—into the MAN's lungs. God breathed this breath—this air—into the man's nostrils, just as all men breathe air in and out of their nostrils—just as dumb animals do!

This man, composed of matter out of the ground, *became* a breathing, living soul. The soul, then, came out of the ground. The *soul* is composed of *matter*, not spirit. The word "soul" is translated from the Hebrew *nephesh*. It means "life of animals."

The Spirit Is Not the Man

Elsewhere the Bible speaks of a spirit *IN* man. But this spirit is *not the man*—it is something that is *IN* the man. Connected with the physical brain (matter) of the man, it forms human MIND. It merely imparts the power of intellect and personality. But Satan counterfeited this.

Satan does not represent this spirit as merely something that is *IN* the MAN. Satan palmed it off as an immortal soul. Satan led people to believe this spirit *IS* the man, not something *IN* the man. Satan then led men to believe the BODY is merely the HOUSE in which the MAN (falsely represented as an immortal soul) dwells.

The spirit that is *IN* a man has no consciousness *of itself*. It cannot *know*, apart from the physical brain. It cannot *see*, of itself. Coupled with the brain, it can see only through the physical eye. It cannot hear without the human ear. PROOF: A blind man has this human spirit *in* him—but it sees NOTHING. This spirit is *in* a deaf man. But he cannot hear, though he has full powers of MIND otherwise.

If this spirit cannot see without a functioning physical eye, nor hear without a properly functioning physical ear, in a *living* man, it most certainly cannot see or hear apart from a *dead* man.

Neither can it *know* or *think* apart from the physical brain. By a physical drug the physical brain may be rendered unconscious. This drug cannot affect the spirit in the man—yet he *knows nothing* while the brain is rendered unconscious, even though his spirit is still in him.

Thus, as the Bible plainly says, dead men "know not anything." This spirit is not the man. It is merely something IN him which imparts intellect or MIND power to the brain. It is *not* a ghost. It is spirit *essence*. It is merely an ingredient added to the brain which produces human MIND. It is a HUMAN spirit. The MAN with this spirit can know only PHYSICAL things. It requires the addition of *another* Spirit — God's HOLY Spirit — to open the human mind to comprehension of spiritual things (1 Cor. 2:9).

GOD says that what came from the dust was the MAN. Satan deceives men into believing that what came from the ground was *not* the MAN, but the HOUSE in which the man dwells — the GARMENT the *man* wears — the PRISON which holds the "immortal soul" captive!

Jesus Christ said, "That which is born of the flesh [matter from the ground] *IS FLESH* [matter from dust]." Nowhere does the Bible say man *IS* a spirit. It says man is mortal. It says the soul that sins shall DIE.

Jesus Christ said man may be BORN AGAIN—next time,

born of GOD, who is a SPIRIT. *Then*, He said, we shall *be*
SPIRIT. But now we are FLESH! Christ came to reveal the
HOPE of humanity—to be BORN of GOD, by a resurrection
from the dead. Born into the very GOD FAMILY. That is
what salvation is! Satan has blinded a deceived world from
this GREAT *HOPE!* He seeks to destroy all this, deceiving
men into believing man is already immortal—an "immortal
soul" that *can't* die—could *not* be resurrected from the
DEAD!

Thus Satan seeks to destroy the Gospel!

But what has all this to do with the origin of this teaching that sex is evil?

IT HAS *EVERYTHING* TO DO WITH IT!

Satan uttered the first recorded lie in the history of
mankind. He told mother Eve she would *not* surely die —
or, in other words, that she was an "immortal soul." But
GOD says souls that sin *SHALL DIE* (Ezek. 18:4, and Ezek.
18:20).

History's First Recorded Lie

Notice how SATAN HIMSELF put in human minds the
sense of shame and guilt toward sex.

In the "Creation chapter," Genesis 1, it is written that
in creating man, God created the physical sex organs—". . .
male and female created He them" (verse 27). "And God
saw everything that He had made, and, behold, it was VERY
GOOD" (verse 31). The physical organs of sex, then, God
pronounced "VERY GOOD."

God gave the first man and his wife full instruction in
regard to His intended purposes and uses of sex, as we shall
cover in detail later. God *ended* His instruction—His teaching—of necessary basic spiritual *and* physical knowledge,
as recorded in Genesis 2:24:

"Therefore shall a man leave his father and his mother, and shall cleave unto his wife: and they shall be one
flesh."

Then follows verse 25: "And they were both naked, the man and his wife, and were not ashamed."

NOTICE CAREFULLY! God had been personally *with* Adam and Eve. The three had been talking together. Adam and Eve were naked. *Nothing* in God's instruction regarding husband-and-wife relationship had caused them to experience any sense of shame in regard to sex. In the privacy of this one married couple, bound in marriage by the Holy God who was speaking with them, there was absolutely no sense of shame in regard to sex.

Now continue right on—next verse! See what now happened!

Remember, as originally inspired and written, the Bible was not divided into chapters and verses. These were added by uninspired men much later, as a matter of convenience in Biblical study. The very next verse, continuing immediately, is verse 1 of chapter 3:

"Now the serpent was more subtil than any beast of the field which the ETERNAL God had made. And he said unto the woman, Yea, hath God said, Ye shall not eat of every tree of the garden?"

Immediately Satan begins to discredit God's teaching. He subtilely and craftily implies, "Look! God knows better than that! God was misrepresenting! Now listen to ME, and I will lead you into truth!"

God had told Adam and Eve that the wages of sin is DEATH—for eternity—ETERNAL punishment! God told them they were MORTAL, and could DIE! Satan uttered the first recorded lie of history:

"Ye shall not SURELY die!"

In other words, "Why, God was deceiving you. He knew you are IMMORTAL SOULS!"

Satan Implants Sense of Shame

The Genesis account is exceedingly brief and condensed. It merely *summarizes*, in fewest words, these conversations and events. We learn much from later passages, and from history.

Filling in the omitted gaps and details, it becomes clear that what Satan said, in more detail, was approximately this:

"You won't *surely* die—why, *you* are an immortal soul that *can't* die. Did God tell you that you were made from the dust of the ground? That's only a half-truth! It is only your BODY that was made out of matter. The real YOU is a spirit. YOU are an immortal, immaterial SPIRIT. Since you are immortal, and shall live into eternity, *you* have lived *from* eternity. God didn't create YOU. *You* have always *been!* All that God created was that BODY you can see and feel. And that BODY is evil! It is nasty, especially those sex organs you are leaving uncovered! Why, SHAME on you! Don't you know that physical sex is degrading, filthy, shameful? WHY didn't God tell you that? You see, God was deceiving you. All that GOD made is filthy, shameful, evil. Go cover up your nakedness! Hide it! The real *you* is a holy, righteous, pure immortal SPIRIT—but your BODY is the PRISON that an evil God has entombed you in—a degrading, sinful, filthy BODY. Yes, you ought to be *ashamed!*"

As soon as Satan got in his lying, deceptive talk, and the woman had obeyed him, eating the forbidden fruit, and her husband deliberately had eaten it with her, the next verses tell us this:

"And the eyes of them both were opened, and *they knew that they were naked;* and they sewed fig leaves together, and made themselves aprons" (verse 7).

Now continue, next verse:

"And they heard the voice of the ETERNAL God walking in the garden in the cool of the day: and Adam and his wife hid themselves from the presence of the ETERNAL God among the trees of the garden. And the ETERNAL God called unto Adam, and said unto him, WHERE ART THOU? And he said, I heard thy voice in the garden, and I WAS

AFRAID, BECAUSE I WAS NAKED; and I hid myself" (verses 8-10).

Notice God's answer!

"WHO TOLD THEE THAT THOU WAST NAKED?" (Verse 11.)

Yes, *WHO* put the sense of shame about sex in the minds of Adam and Eve?

It was SATAN who had been telling them things!

GOD DIDN'T!

All the time GOD had been talking to them, instructing them in true and right knowledge, they were naked. But NOTHING in all God taught them gave them any sense of shame toward sex. This idea that sex is evil CAME FROM SATAN. It was an accusation against GOD—an attempt to make what GOD designed appear to be contaminated and degrading. It was inextricably tied up with the false "immortal soul" lie!

WHY God Covered Them

But absolutely *nothing* in what you have just read justifies nudism, or nudist colonies. That is not the teaching of God at all! Rather, God Himself *clothed* Adam and Eve. Let's now learn how—under what circumstances, and WHY!

When God had talked with Adam and Eve, immediately following their very creation, He was instructing them in a situation of husband-and-wife privacy. As long as they were *the only* humans, alone by themselves (so far as any other humans are concerned), God gave them no instruction to cover their bodies.

God is *everywhere* present at all times—*omnipresent!* When a husband and wife, today, are *alone*, in the privacy of their own bedroom, GOD is invisibly present!

But, when their children, and other people—the PUBLIC —ALL LIVING—are introduced, *then*, we read that GOD HIMSELF *clothed* Adam and Eve. Notice it! It appears later, in the same chapter:

"And Adam called his wife's name Eve: because she

was the mother of ALL LIVING [her children—their family —the public]. Unto Adam also and to his wife did the ETERNAL God make coats of skins, and clothed them" (Gen. 3:20-21).

Notice the expression: "The ETERNAL God ... clothed them." The Hebrew word God inspired Moses to write here, for *"clothed,"* is *labash*. It does *not* mean to cover nakedness —to hide nakedness—or any such meaning.

The Hebrew word meaning to *conceal* nakedness is *kasah*. But the word Moses was inspired to write, *labash*, means, rather, the donning of apparel, raiment. It refers rather to *outer* garments than underclothing. It implies the idea of adorning, or decorating, or displaying, rather than concealing or covering over, or hiding.

So notice, God did NOT *kasah* them—did *not* cover nakedness, conceal nakedness, but rather He *labashed* them —adorned, clothed them.

Of course this clothing *did* cover nakedness. The difference between the two Hebrew words, *labash*, and *kasah*, is one of purpose and intent, rather than the *fact* of being covered. Both do cover nudity. But the Hebrew *kasah*, carries the connotation of *concealing*, or *hiding* something, while *labash* includes no such meaning, and implies *adding* attractiveness rather than *hiding* shamefulness. In other words, although God's clothing did cover their bodies, it DID NOT imply any sense of shame!

This *does not* mean, under any circumstances, that God would approve nudity. NOT AT ALL. God CLOTHED man! God intended man to KEEP CLOTHED! God intended that we NEVER expose or exhibit the pubic region of our bodies—but THE REASON is *not* because the pubic region which GOD designed and made is degrading or evil, *but rather*, as a matter of proper modesty and decorum!

It is a matter of propriety—of courtesy to others— that we take care of certain eliminative functions *privately*. This does not imply there is sin or evil in going to the toilet. It is a matter of etiquette—consideration for others—rather than to cover up something WRONG. In the same manner, God wills that we wear clothes—that we *do not expose* the sex region of the body—as a matter of decorum and propriety—but NOT because the sex organs which God designed are themselves evil.

Clothing Necessary

There are two additional reasons.

God designed sex for use *only* between a husband and wife whom GOD has joined in holy wedlock. He designed sex for righteous uses—and one of them is to bind husband and wife together in a *loving* relationship unshared with any other. The very *privacy* of this marriage relationship makes it sacred, makes husband and wife *dear* to each other in a *special* way never shared with any other. This entire loving, sacred, precious relationship is greatly impaired, *or destroyed*, when shared with any other. That is why fornication and adultery are so harmful to their participants, and therefore CAPITAL SINS.

The second additional reason for avoiding indecent or lewd exposure is that undue exposure of the female body is automatically lust-arousing to the carnal male mind. Burlesque and girlie shows, strip-tease acts, and all such exhibitions, are deliberately intended to attract male admissions for profit, through lust.

God did not intend a man to expose himself even before his own sons. The example of Shem and Japheth, sons of Noah, *backing up* with a garment on their shoulders, *to cover* the nakedness of their father, ought to be sufficient. And here the Hebrew word for *"covered* the nakedness" (Gen. 9:23) is *kasah*, and not *labash*.

Nevertheless, these passages in Genesis show positively that the origin of the concept that sex is evil and shameful originated with SATAN—and not from God!

The pagan world accepted this lie. As a teaching, or doctrine, it became a universally accepted dogma. This fable was popularized by the Greek philosopher Plato, founder of the curricular system of education. Plato wrote it in his book *The Phaedo*.

"Shame" Tied to "Immortal Soul" Lie

It was from this "immortal soul" doctrine that the concept of sex as evil itself stemmed.

Notice how it developed!

This "immortal soul" doctrine teaches that man is DUAL. While it claims falsely that the "immortal soul" is the real man, and the body is merely the prison in which he is entombed, yet it teaches inconsistently that man is DUAL—both soul and body.

Thus, the real MAN is represented as being *spiritual*, pure, good, righteous, already having immortality. It represents the body—the FLESH—as being essentially evil, filthy, nasty. Sex organs and sex functioning are physical—of the BODY, and therefore fleshly, sensual, and evil.

This satanic doctrine is the very antithesis of GOD'S revelation of the true FACTS. It is a diabolical LIE!

God formed MAN of the dust of the ground. MAN *is* FLESH. And God beheld everything that He had made, and, behold, IT WAS *VERY GOOD!* It is what man thinks and *does* that is sinful. But Satan blasphemes the Holy GOD, by saying that what *God made* was very filthy, nasty, evil, and sinful.

Satan represents the "spirit in man" as being, itself, the conscious MAN. The true FACT is, the "spirit IN man" merely imparts certain characteristics to the physical BRAIN.

Animals have BRAINS, the same as humans. Yet animals *do not have* MINDS! Animals cannot reason from memorized facts and knowledge, draw conclusions, make decisions, will to act according to a thought-out plan. Animals cannot imagine, formulate plans, invent mechanisms. Animal BRAINS cannot devise codes of morals, and exercise self-discipline according to reasoned-out decisions. Animals, in a word, have BRAINS and instinct, but their brains are incapable of SCIENTIFIC KNOWLEDGE accumulated by the human MIND.

WHY is this?

What is the real difference between animal BRAIN, actuated only by instinct, and human MIND?

God's Word explains it, in I Corinthians 2: "For what man knoweth the things of a man, save the spirit of man which is *in* him?" (Verse 11.) It is this spirit that is *IN* man, which, added to material BRAIN, gives this human brain the functions of MIND. But this Scripture *plainly* says that this spirit is merely something that is *IN* the MAN. It is *not* the *man!*

What Man's Spirit Imparts

This spirit *in* man cannot, of itself, see anything. The human BRAIN *sees* through the human physical EYE. It hears through the physical ear. The spirit *in* man cannot know, or think, or remember, *of itself*. Of itself, it has no consciousness. It merely *imparts* human mind-powers and personality to the human brain.

A man dies, and in that very day his thinking stops, his thoughts cease (Psalm 146:4). Notice it! A man dies, and HE—the *man*—returns to the earth. "In that very day his thoughts perish." Dead people are totally unconscious—they know nothing (Eccl. 9:5). When this spirit leaves man at death, it has no consciousness—IT SLEEPS (I Cor. 11:30; 15:51; I Thes. 4:14).

But this spirit is *not* the "soul"—that which God formed out of material dust became the SOUL! *The soul is* MATERIAL *—not spiritual.*

This HUMAN spirit imparts to the human brain the power of MIND. Without it, no man could comprehend HUMAN knowledge—*which is wholly physical and material knowledge.* This knowledge is confined to that which enters the mind through the five sensory channels. But such a mind *still* cannot comprehend spiritual knowledge.

Spiritual things cannot be seen with the eye, heard with the ear, felt with the hands. The greatest minds—scientific, philosophical minds—cannot really come to know and understand SPIRITUAL truths.

Just as no animal BRAIN, without this human SPIRIT that is IN MAN, can have MIND and comprehension of PHYSICAL knowledge on the HUMAN plane; even so, no HUMAN MIND can have comprehension of spiritual things on the *divine* plane, unless or until the HOLY SPIRIT of GOD has been imparted to this human mind.

Notice it—the same verse: "For what man knoweth the things of a man, save the spirit of man which is in him? *even so* the things of GOD knoweth no man, but the Spirit of God" (I Cor. 2:11). Read the verses before and after. Get the whole meaning in its context. It becomes PLAIN!

Satan has deceived the whole world into counterfeiting this human spirit, and representing it as an immortal soul. *That is Satan's* LIE!

NOW SEE WHERE ALL THIS LEADS!

This satanic, dualistic teaching flowed from Egypt into Greece. It was first introduced by Socrates, a SEX pervert. Then his pupil Plato popularized it in his book *The Phaedo.* Plato founded the system of pagan schools, on the curricular form.

By the time of Christ, these pagan schools, as stated before, dotted the Roman Empire. They were the *only* schools. They inoculated into the unsuspecting minds of children this dualistic concept. Automatically children in the western world, becoming "Christian," absorbed the concept that sex, being of the flesh, was filthy, evil, and sinful.

This "hush-hush" attitude of "shame" toward sex was bound up in the pagan myth of the "immortality of the soul"! This was the heart and core of both Hellenistic philosophy, and the pagan religions.

There were, of course, various pagan religions. Yet they all stemmed from the same Semiramis origin. This original paragon of licentiousness—this white harlot married to the black despot Nimrod—was the real Isis of Egypt, the Isi of India, the Fortuna of pagan Rome, the Ceres of Greece. Also she was the goddess Ishtar of Assyria and Babylon—the Astarte of Phoenicia (in both cases pronounced EASTER)—to this day celebrated in the spring of the year as a supposed Christian festival! Yes, Semiramis also was the original Venus!

The World Into Which Jesus Came

This dualistic teaching was the basic hypothesis of all Grecian thought, writing, and religion. It was, as Cole styles it, "the soil in which the pale flowers of asceticism grew. Sex was regarded as low and degrading, an act in which man descended to the level of the beast."

Into such a world Jesus Christ came.

IN such a world Simon Magus launched his spurious "Christianity." During that first 446 years, the children of "Christians" were, of necessity, taught in these pagan schools. They grew to adulthood accepting the ASSUMPTION of this dualistic interpretation of sex as a matter of course. It was never questioned. They supposed it was the "Christian" view.

By the beginning of the 6th century this concept was firmly rooted in western "Christianity."

The invasion of the barbarians from the north, and fall of the Roman Empire in 476, ended this system of pagan schools. But the concepts and beliefs were by then firmly established. From the 6th to the 12th centuries the Roman Church conducted the monastic schools and the cathedral schools. These were operated for the teaching of the monks and the priests. However, during all this time there were no *printed* books. Textbooks had to be produced by hand, one at a time. And the heritage of the old pagan texts continued on.

CHAPTER 5

Fixing Catholic Dogma
of Sex

*T*HE ROMAN WORLD of the first four centuries, A.D., had inherited this dualistic view of sex from the Greeks.

But even though this concept was generally assumed, we must not suppose that the expanding Roman Catholic Church neglected to refine, and in specific terms define the interpretation as a dogma.

It was Augustine, who lived 354-430, who first translated this general Hellenistic attitude into definite terms of theological doctrine. He was the real father of the Catholic teaching on sex. And since the Protestant world has passively assumed the Catholic view without any specific definitions of its own, Augustine was the pioneer interpreter of the sex-is-evil idea generally held until the present generation.

To *understand* this sense of "shame" toward sex, therefore, we need to know certain essential facts about Augustine.

Augustine's Early Life

The *Encyclopaedia Britannica* describes him as one of the four great fathers of the Latin church. He was actually not a Roman, or Italian, but a North African—a dark-white Canaanite. He was born at Tagaste in North Africa of a pagan father and a Christian-professing mother.

Vainly his mother tried to instruct him in the Scriptures. But his early studies in the Latin philosophers, Seneca,

Cicero, Vergil, and Lucretius prejudiced the young man and convinced him—without examining it—that the Bible was full of contradictions. He had, also, some acquaintance with the writings of the Greek philosophers.

His father set his heart on making young Augustine a rhetorician, and sent him to the University of Carthage to study rhetoric.

Prior to this, he was once taken very ill. Afraid he might die, he called for baptism. But when the danger passed soon, he deferred, and then neglected the baptism entirely.

From his father young Augustine inherited a sensually passionate nature. This, remember, is the real FATHER of the sex attitude that prevailed in all Christendom until the present generation! He entered into an illicit premarital sex relationship with a girl, while still in his teens. This fornication continued for fifteen years. A pregnancy and a son resulted.

At Carthage he decided to devote himself to literary pursuits. Here he soon abandoned what little Biblical teaching he had imbibed from his mother.

A turning point in his life came in 373, at age 18. He read Cicero's *Hortensius*, which aroused within him a passionate desire to study philosophy. And we should be reminded that *philosophy* means the thoughts, reasonings, theories, speculations and explanations of life, purposes, values, ethics and ways, written by men cut off from God— men ignorant of God's authoritative revealed knowledge. Only the Creator Himself can tell us WHY we are here, the true meaning of life, the true values and the right ways. The world's philosophy, therefore, is pure fable. It is, of course, carnal and pagan. It is man's attempt to know that which is to him UNKNOWN and utterly inaccessible to the carnal mind. Yet this was the intellectual and spiritual food digested in Augustine's formative years.

Augustine sought vainly to find some *meaning* to life. He leaped from one phase of speculative thought to another.

Nothing satisfied him. He wanted a *world*-view that was all-embracing.

He Absorbs Pagan Dualism

This search led him into Manichaeism, a pagan mixture of Persian Zoroastrian dualism and Gnosticism. This doctrine teaches that man's "soul" sprang from the "Kingdom of Light," but is imprisoned in "the Kingdom of Darkness" which is the BODY, from which it seeks to escape. This weird teaching enthralled him. He became a fervent member of the sect. It seemed to him to solve the mysteries of the world. He accepted it as the explanation of his own personal problem with sex. It led him into a fanciful and mystic religious world, embellished with a wealth of Oriental myth.

He remained wedded to this strange religion for nine years. It gave him, for the time being, great peace of mind. Its ideal was chastity and self-restraint. Sex, being of the physical body, was evil and degrading. His conscience had troubled him greatly, because he was bound in the fetters of sensuality. But now, even though he lacked the moral will power to break these fetters that enchained him, he seized on the HOPE that death ultimately would free his "pure soul" from the prison of his body.

As the years passed, he occupied himself increasingly with the exact material sciences. Gradually these studies convinced him of the incompatibility of Manichaean astrology with the facts. Yet, from Manichaeism he had absorbed a belief in celibacy.

The Manichee ideal of chastity—the virtue of celibacy, self-restraint from the "degrading" use of sex—of the continent life utterly denying the temptations of sex in any form, and under any conditions, had been too deeply imbedded in Augustine's mind to be ever given up. So, even though he did give up this Persian religion as a whole, he clung tenaciously to its interpretation of sex.

In 383 the celebrated Manichaean Faustus sought vainly to hold Augustine within the ranks of that religion. But in the discussion, Faustus was unable to solve all the world problems that had puzzled and worried Augustine. The result: instead of holding Augustine as a Manichaeist, Faustus disillusioned him. All except Manichaeist teachings of the evils of sex, that is.

Swayed by Agnosticism

After this, Augustine went to Rome, where he opened a school of rhetoric. This he continued but a short time. He accepted a professorship at Milan and left Rome. Here he was swayed by new influences.

Augustine was subject to being swayed by various influences, unsound though they were. He was torn between two strengths within himself. On the one hand, he possessed an unusually intellectual mind. Being carnal, he was filled with intellectual vanity. He took deep pride in the conviction that he was a Thinker. He was always trying to understand the mystery of life. But he never knew where to find it—in GOD'S WORD! On the other hand he had been unable to control his sex appetite. As one writer states it, "he could not subdue his lust of the flesh. . . . He was still tormented by guilt over his 'habit of satisfying an insatiable lust.'"

At Milan his inner mental conflict in the search for truth continued. He soon associated himself with a group of professional intellectuals called "The Academics," or, "The New Academy." This was a school of thought followed by the philosophic successors of Plato. They had changed from the dogmatism of Plato to the extremes of agnosticism. Where Socrates, teacher of Plato, has said: "This alone I know, that I know nothing," Arcesilaus said: "I cannot know even whether I know or not."

This Neo-Platonist society, also known as the Skeptics, denied the existence of absolute truth. Augustine's thinking was greatly influenced by this group. Of course he failed to find truth here, but it influenced him to seek for truth outside the world of materialism.

Yet the factor that troubled Augustine was the existence of evil. His own inability to control his sex nature racked his conscience. If there was any PURPOSE in existence, why do we find pain, suffering, and evil present? If there be a God, *why* would He allow it?

In this Neo-Platonic association, Augustine found partial solution in the theory that evil does not actually exist—it is merely the absence of good. One ought to be astonished at the ridiculous nonsense the carnal "intellectual" mind of vain "thinkers" will embrace. Much in this Neo-Platonic system of thought became the FOUNDATION for Augustine's later theology—and thus of Roman Catholic teachings.

At Milan, Augustine also came under the influence of Ambrose, Bishop of Milan. The literary quality of Bishop Ambrose's sermons attracted Augustine. Also they overcame many of his objections to the Bible. Ambrose was a man of worldly culture, combined with the maturity of the "Christianity" of the period. Augustine sought vainly an opportunity to engage Ambrose in philosophic discussion—but found the Bishop inaccessible. Gradually, however, Ambrose's sermons drew Augustine toward embracing the Catholic faith.

Augustine Embraces Catholicism

The mental struggle now going on within him was becoming intolerable. The thought of divine purity condemned him for his equally strong love of the world and sensuality. All that held him back from now embracing Catholicism was his inability to control sex and live in continence.

It was in the summer of 386 that he received a visit from a Catholic compatriot named Pontitian. He was shaken deeply to learn from Pontitian that two young officials, both engaged to be married, had suddenly turned their backs on the world, and had entered on a monastic life.

Conscience-stricken, Augustine ran out into the garden, and flung himself under a fig tree. A passionate burst of weeping seized him. He seemed to hear a voice. It bade him: "*Take up and read.*"

He procured a Bible. As most religionists, churchmen, and the clergy of this world do, he took a single brief passage of Scripture by itself, without regard to context, imputing to it his own meaning. The ministers of this world's "Christianity" quote certain isolated verses from the Bible regularly. In many cases they impute to these a meaning entirely at variance to the real meaning of the passage in its context. And all the while they studiously *avoid* numerous *other* passages which clearly and plainly teach the very opposite of the meaning they are attempting to *read into* the passages they do quote and wrongly interpret.

The passage to which Augustine happened to turn was Romans 13:13-14: "Let us walk honestly, as in the day; not in rioting and drunkenness, not in chambering and wantonness, not in strife and envying. But put ye on the Lord Jesus Christ, and make not provision for the flesh, to fulfil the lusts thereof."

Augustine said later: "I had neither desire nor need to read further. As I finished the sentence, as though the light of peace had been poured into the heart, all the shadows of doubt dispersed. Thus hast Thou converted me to Thee, so as no longer to seek either for wife or other hope of the world."

There was absolutely nothing in this passage on which his eyes had lit which forbade a man to seek a wife—nor in any other teaching of the Bible. There was positively nothing in this passage which suggested celibacy or a life of retiring to the seclusion of the monastery. Neither this passage nor any in the Bible teaches that Christians must *leave* the world. There is nothing in the Bible to justify the monastery system. Rather, in Christ's own real "Lord's Prayer," in John 17, Jesus prayed thus for His followers: "I pray *not* that thou shouldest take them out of the world, but that thou shouldest keep them from the evil" (verse 15). Actually, He commanded His Church: "Go ye *INTO* ALL THE

WORLD, and preach the gospel to every creature" (Mk. 16:15).

But Augustine's mind was filled with ideas, convictions, and philosophies absorbed from Manichaeism, from the Skeptics, the Neo-Platonists, the pagan thinkers and philosophers, and his own stricken conscience. Therefore, to such a troubled mind, this Biblical passage was falsely interpreted to mean, "Withdraw from the world entirely. Do as these two men had done—flee from the world into the seclusion of hiding." This actually did much to firmly establish the monastic system in Roman Catholicism. I deem it well that the reader realize how some of these pagan ideas, teachings, and practices came to be accepted as "Christian," though they are in fact the very antithesis of REAL Christianity!

Entering Monasticism

Now it so happened that at this precise moment Augustine was engaged to be married. He had sent away his unmarried partner in fornication. However, unable to control his sex appetite, he had indulged in fornication with a third woman.

Now, upon what has been termed his "conversion," Augustine withdrew with a few male companions to the seclusion of a country estate near Milan. He announced himself as a candidate for baptism. His religious opinions and habits still were largely unformed. He did seek sternly to discipline himself, according to what he supposed to be right, awaiting baptism. He was baptized on Easter, 387, in his thirty-third year.

Then Augustine spent a year in Rome, in literary work. In the autumn of 388 he returned to Tagaste. There he formed a small religious community, which he headed. Their mode of life was semi-monastic, but this experience of seclusion is said to have formed the basis for the monastic system.

Augustine's fame began to spread. Many invitations for more active ecclesiastical life began to pour in. After two and a half years in retirement he went to Hippo, where the lay people ordained him a priest. Finally he became Bishop of the See there.

What Augustine termed his conversion—when he heard the voice, and read the two Biblical verses—changed his whole life. His lust of the flesh was now so far overshadowed by his thirst for the spiritual that it no longer was a problem.

But he did not banish reflections on the interpretations of sex from his *mind*. On the contrary, as he rose to prominence and greatness in Roman Catholicism, he virtually *fixed* the doctrine of the Church in regard to sex.

In this he was subject to powerful influence, both by the various teachings, philosophies, and pagan schools of thought to which he had been partisan, and also by his own former problem and struggle with his own conscience. He never shook off the influence of the Hellenistic dualism that sex, being of the flesh, was in itself intrinsically evil.

Augustine never did entirely rid himself, either, of his earlier aversion to the Scriptures—especially those of the Old Testament. Yet he was forced to recognize sex as a FACT of CREATION—an act of God. To that extent he was impelled to modify his dualistic views sufficiently to call the Creation good.

He could not escape the admission that God intended man to marry. Otherwise God would have provided some different method for the reproduction of the human *kind*. But he did reason in his mind that, before what he *assumed* to be the "fall," man had originally been created so that sex and reproduction should have been entirely different. He reasoned that, before the "fall," sex would have been wholly a matter of the *mind*, and solely for procreation. There would have been no passion, no sensual, physical attraction whatsoever.

Apparently it never did occur to him to see in sex any such thing as an expression of LOVE between a happily married husband and wife, bound together by GOD. To him it was wholly LUST. It had always been so in *his* personal

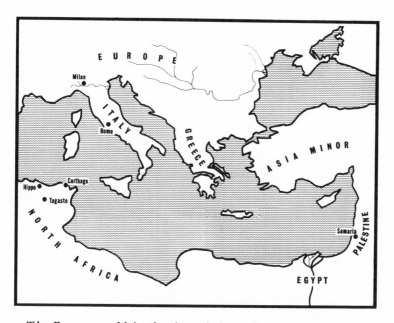

*The Roman world in the time of Augustine. Born in Tagaste,
North Africa, in 354, Augustine attended the University of
Carthage. Later, in Rome, he opened a school of rhetoric. At
Milan he met Bishop Ambrose, who persuaded him to embrace
the Roman Church. Augustine became Bishop of Hippo in 396.*

experience. It had been painted in this color, solely, by the
Manichees.

Augustine never did become sufficiently versed in the
Word of God—he never did drink in sufficiently of the
MIND of Christ as revealed in the sacred Scriptures, to com-
prehend God's purposes in sex.

Two things should be noted in this connection. It is
many times more difficult to UNlearn error than to learn
new truth. Augustine never succeeded in erasing from his
mind many of these pagan concepts and attitudes and philosophies he had absorbed from earlier pagan associations.
And secondly, he never came to regard the Bible as his
source of knowledge—as the infallible AUTHORITY for faith

and practice. He followed, instead, tradition and custom.

He it was, who in large measure established Roman Catholic doctrine and practice as it continued through the Middle Ages. And from the founding days of Simon Magus (Acts 8) on through Constantine, Augustine, Leo I, Thomas Aquinas, the Council of Trent, and on to the present, the Roman Church has never regarded the Bible as its basic AUTHORITY or source of belief and practice. The Catholic Church teaches that the Bible is *not* a sufficient guide "to heaven." For Catholics, authority resides in THE CHURCH, not in the Bible.

If this were not so, there would be no need for this book. The Catholic concept of sex was not derived from the Bible. It does not teach the *revealed* knowledge and purposes of GOD in regard to sex. It teaches the doctrines of THE CHURCH. And it was this Augustine who first began to define the CHURCH position on sex in definite terms. That is the reason, if we are to understand the real SOURCE of this view of SHAME in regard to sex, we need to examine and understand the real SOURCE of Augustine's interpretation.

So it was that Augustine the Bishop viewed sex through the eye-glasses of Augustine the Manichaeist, and Augustine the Platonist *"Thinker"*—out of his own conscience-stricken experience. The concepts absorbed from Hellenistic dualism, and other assumptions received from the Skeptics and Neo-Platonic philosophers, influenced him heavily.

Among the errors he carelessly ASSUMED to be true was the idea of the "fall of man." He supposed, falsely, that God had created a perfect man—who was an immortal soul composed of spirit, fused with, and housed in a body of flesh. He assumed that this soul was endowed with a holy, pure, righteous nature, perfect in character. Then, when God wasn't looking, Satan came along and WRECKED God's perfect handiwork. Man "fell" to a *lower nature*—one of lust—concupiscence—evil desire for sensual gratification.

When God finally beheld, with horror, the wreckage perpetrated by Satan—when God came to realize how Satan had thwarted His PURPOSE—He had to think out some plan for "repairing the damage." In other words, redemption is God's effort to *restore* fallen man to a condition *as good as* Adam was, before the "fall."

God Contradicts Augustine

This concept is the very reverse of Biblical TRUTH. God's Word reveals that God formed MAN—not a prison-house in which man dwells—but the MAN, of the dust of the ground. This man *became*, or was, when breathing, a LIVING SOUL. The soul, says Genesis 2:7, is composed of MATTER out of the ground. The soul is mortal. The soul is *the breathing body*. It can SIN, and the soul that sins shall DIE (Ezek. 18:4, 20).

Man did not "fall" to a lower NATURE of concupiscence. Human nature in us all, today, is the *same* human nature that, in Adam, *caused* him to SIN! IF Adam had been created "free from inordinate inclinations to sin," as a Catholic catechism states it—IF he had been created with a higher spiritual nature *unable* to sin—he simply could not, and would not, have sinned. If God had created Adam so he would not, or could not, sin, then THAT would have defeated God's PURPOSE!

But God could never defeat His own Purpose. Nor was Satan allowed to thwart it. His PURPOSE is still, today, BEING CARRIED OUT! God's PURPOSE *STANDS!* (Isa. 14:27; 46:9-11.)

Man did not "fall"—in the sense that his nature was changed to a lower nature. It was SATAN who *FELL!* (See Luke 10:18.) And it is Satan who has deceived the whole world, using a great false church as his instrument!

But, Augustine reasoned, Adam "fell" into a nature of concupiscence; and this concupiscence is transmitted, as original sin, by the very act of sexual intercourse which brings about conception. Therefore, no sexual union ever takes place—even for the purpose of reproduction in holy wedlock—without the corrupting lust of the flesh. All babies, he reasoned, are born as a result of this odious concupiscence. And they, in turn, receive concupiscence by heredity.

This is simply false and unscriptural teaching. It was this *false teaching* which instilled a false sense of shame, and a feeling of GUILT, in the minds of married people.

Yet Augustine had his own explanation of this guilt complex. He reasoned that "the fall" produced it. The sense of shame toward sex, he reasoned, was transmitted to each generation by heredity. But he did not receive his ideas from the Bible. He reasoned from personal experience, supposing all men to be like him.

He, himself, possessed a *strong* sex drive combined with a *weak* will to control it. So Augustine excused his personal weakness—even though plagued by a guilt-stricken conscience—theorizing that all human wills, because of inherited "original sin" due to the "fall," are totally impotent in the area of sex.

No man, he argued, can master his own body. And because of the odiousness of the act by which conception occurs, this sense of shame was passed on by heredity.

His perverted reasoning bridged over the *fact* that it was *this false teaching* which instilled the unhealthy attitude toward sex, and induced the sense of guilt. He himself, was guilty of *causing* much of the suffering, unhappiness, and frustration that has come to succeeding generations.

HOW Was Christ Sinless?

But WHAT ABOUT CHRIST?

If concupiscence—original sin—the state of sin—is universal in all men—if it is passed on by heredity—if man has no power to resist concupiscence and master his own body—HOW EXPLAIN A SINLESS CHRIST?

Ah! This was a dilemma! But Augustine thought his way around it!

His explanation was the doctrine of the "Immaculate Conception."

Few non-Catholics properly understand this doctrine.

It refers, *not* to the conception of Jesus in the womb of His mother, Mary, but to that of Mary.

In brief, the doctrine, as now taught, is this:

Because of the "fall," this "original sin"—this *state of sin*—this concupiscence—is transmitted by the father at the instant of conception. Because Mary was to receive the great dignity of becoming the "Mother of God," she was preserved free from "original sin," in the very instant of *her* conception. Apparently Mary's parents are supposed to have lived so righteously that they were changed from a carnal or human nature, to a spiritual or divine nature.

Thus, according to this doctrine, Mary was born sinless. She was *preserved from* "original sin." The Catholic Church has always attributed to Mary the fullest possible measure of holiness *and freedom from sin.*

Anyway, as Augustine reasoned, there was none of this concupiscence or hereditary sin in Mary at all. It was not there to be passed on, by heredity, to Christ. And since Jesus had no *human* father, but was begotten by GOD, through the Holy Spirit, Jesus was preserved from the stain of sin. He was thus made sinless, *because* there was no contaminating sex act involved in his begettal in Mary's womb.

The world has little realized the tremendous scope and ramifications of Satan's many deceptions connected with this subject of sex!

When David cried out, "Behold, I was shapen in iniquity; and in sin did my mother conceive me" (Psalm 51:5), he was not accusing his mother of committing sin in the act of his conception. This Psalm is David's heart-rending prayer of REPENTANCE, and his broken-hearted and tearful plea for forgiveness. It followed his act of adultery with Bathsheba and the murder of her husband. David is not trying to excuse himself by blaming the guilt on his mother. He is confessing *his own sin!* He is speaking of the *human nature*, which was in David from the very instant of conception. He referred to the sinful nature *in him* from the instant of conception. *The act of conception*—in marriage—

IS NO SIN, but obedience to the COMMAND OF GOD (Gen. 1:28, and 9:1).

There is not ONE WORD of Scripture to imply that the *purpose* of the virgin birth was to free Christ from the taint of sin! There is NO TAINT OF SIN connected with *any* birth. Even the *birth* of the child of unwed parents IS NOT A SIN! The fornication that brought about conception *was a sin*— on the part of the *parents*. But there is no sin on the part of the *child*. Such children are under NO CONDEMNATION— should feel none.

Jesus Christ was HUMAN, born of a HUMAN mother— and He paid the debt of HUMAN sins for *all* humans who confess them *and repent and believe*. But His only Father was GOD, not a human man. Conception was produced by the Holy Spirit from GOD. Jesus' divine begettal, from God, made Him the Son of GOD. His birth of the virgin Mary, who was HUMAN, made Him the Son of MAN. As a man, he suffered death for the sins of MAN. As a divine Person, *by whom* the Father had created mankind, He gave a life of greater value than the sum total of all other human lives!

How GREAT are the ways of GOD!

But as a HUMAN, Jesus *was* TEMPTED in *all points*, just as we are (Hebrews 4:15). The temptation—the desire— was the same as with all men—but Jesus never harbored that desire. He put it instantly out of mind. He kept so close to God—His thoughts and affections so constantly on things above—as we are commanded to do (Col. 3:1-2), His mind so positively and vigilantly on the awareness of the *true* values as opposed to the false, that every wrong desire was banished before it could conceive.

The True Definition of Sin

Let James make clear what does constitute SIN. Of course the basic definition of sin is stated by John—"sin is the transgression of the Law" (I John 3:4), referring to the spiritual Law of God. And again, "All unrighteousness is sin" (I John 5:17)—and David defined God's Commandments as righteousness (Psalm 119:172). But James explains not only *what* is sin, but *how* it takes place. He says: "Every man is tempted, when he is drawn away of his own lust, and enticed. Then, *when lust hath conceived*, it bringeth forth sin: and sin, when it is finished, bringeth forth death" (James 1:14-15).

The Revised Standard translation renders it into more precise English: ". . . each person is tempted when he is lured and enticed by his own desire." It is plainly stated in Hebrews 4:15 that Jesus "was *in all points* tempted like as we are, YET WITHOUT SIN." James states that the temptation never comes from God. Paul explains there is a "law of sin" "in our members" (Rom. 7:23)—that is, in human flesh. This law is, simply, human nature. And human nature is merely a *"pull,"* like the downward pull of the force of gravity. You hold a book in your hand. Gravity exerts a *pull* downward—but you can resist, and hold up the book.

Jesus was *human*, and in human flesh—as well as divine. This human "law"—the automatic *pull* of the flesh and its natural desires—was in Jesus. He was *tempted*—IN ALL POINTS, including sex temptations—yet WITHOUT SIN. The *desire* was present *in His flesh*. That *desire* came to His mind to tempt Him. But the instant awareness of the *pull* of the flesh in the wrong direction entered His mind HE PUT IT OUT! Too often WE DON'T! That's the difference! It is when your mind *retains* this desire of the flesh—this temptation—and it "conceives" into yielding—DOING wrong—that it becomes SIN.

The *temptation is* NOT *sin*.

Jesus was required to withstand the ordeal of being TEMPTED by Satan himself, before He qualified to replace Satan as GOD and KING of the world (Mat. 4:1-11)—and that, after He had been physically weakened by forty days' fasting. But the very fast which depleted physical strength increased *spiritual* power.

In this supreme temptation at Satan's hands, Jesus was tempted with overwhelming physical desire. He was HUNGRY, to an extent few men have ever known. The *desire* to eat food was TREMENDOUS. He had the *power*, as the Son of GOD, to turn stones into bread which his stomach *craved*. But He did not yield to this desire. He rejected it instantly. He did not say: "Let me think it over." He did not harbor the temptation *in His mind*, and allow that desire to increase until it overwhelmed Him. But immediately, the instant the temptation was put to Him, He thrust it out of mind. Instead of obeying Satan and taking things into His own hands, He *trusted God* for His bodily need, rejecting what He knew to be *the wrong way* to supply His stomach's need.

Sin is wrong DOING! It is *transgression* of God's Law. Jesus never sinned. All other humans, including YOU and me, *have!* The difference is that we have harbored wrong desires in our minds—allowed the temptations to overwhelm us and so weaken our spiritual resistance that we yielded in physical action. Sin is a spiritual principle—but concerned with PHYSICAL actions! We have allowed these temptations to remain in our minds long enough to take root—to conceive—to take the action of wrong *doing*. Jesus never did. That's the difference.

Non-Biblical Teaching

Augustine taught, contrary to God's Word, that Jesus was kept free from sin by virtue of being born of an immaculately conceived mother—that He was above even being tempted. IF that had been true, Jesus could not have paid the penalty of HUMAN sin for you and for me! Neither could He have died.

The satanic immortal-soul doctrine presupposes that Jesus never died in reality. Satan's lie tries to make us believe that Jesus was an immortal Spirit being inside a body. But Jesus *died*. Jesus was DEAD! He was resurrected *from the dead* (I Cor. 15:3, 12-20).

Jesus simply kept closer to God—and to TRUTH—than Augustine. Augustine tried to excuse his own sexual sins by postulating that no man can resist concupiscence. So he had to invent a different Jesus (II Cor. 11:4) who was actually *not* a MAN but a divine being never tempted by sex. This is not true. Jesus had the same human fleshly desires as Augustine and all other men. He simply never yielded to those desires.

How DIFFERENT are the false reasonings of Augustine and Satan's deceiving church from the TRUTH taught by the true Church of God, as recorded in THE BIBLE!

Augustine's reasonings were based, not on the Word of God, but on his early pagan associations and personal failures. So he reasoned that all sexual *desire*, whether harbored and acted on or not, was concupiscence and therefore sin.

Of course, Jesus said: ". . . whosoever looketh on a woman to lust after her hath committed adultery with her already in his heart." But Jesus was talking, not about a temptation *resisted*, but the committing of an action, *in his thoughts*. In other words, whoever looks on a woman, and harbors sex desire, or lust, has committed adultery. Even though the inordinate desire is carried out *in his mind only*—not in actual physical contact—it still is AN ACTION—it is wrong DOING. He has done it in his mind. It was a mental action, not physical—yet the *intent* was there.

But Jesus was not talking about a case of a man happening to glance at a voluptuous female in a bathing suit, and in a flash recognizing that here is TEMPTATION—and in that same flash turning eyes the other way and walking off with *clean and pure thoughts* in his mind. Such a man under such circumstances recognizes temptation, refuses to harbor it, does *not* let his mind dwell on illicit desire, immediately puts a thought of God, or of Christ, in his mind. This man *did not* commit the ACT, either mentally or physically. HE DID NOT SIN. Sin is wrong DOING, either mentally or physically.

Augustine's corrupted thinking led him to rate celibacy as a *blessed state* compared to begetting children in marriage! Even the desire to be married—when the *purpose* desired was to rear children to be "saved" through Christ—was, in his warped reasoning, a low desire compared to being a celibate or a virgin.

Even though God's inspired instruction to mankind in I Corinthians 7 teaches otherwise, Augustine *interpreted* this chapter in accordance with his contrary ideas!

He termed marriage a "medicine for immorality." That is, marriage ideally ought to be engaged in *only* by those unable to contain themselves as virgins. It was merely the least of the evils—a lesser evil than fornication. And, further, sex, he reasoned, even within marriage, when not entered into for the express purpose of having children, *is a sin!* This is totally contrary to I Corinthians 7—yet it is the Catholic position still! Of course it is spoken of as only "venial sin"—yet it is termed SIN. Incidentally, the grading of sin and the term "venial" is a Catholic term—not Biblical!

To quote from Cole, in explaining how the Hellenistic interpretation of sex flowed from Greece into Roman Catholicism, Augustine "simply accepted the tradition as it was passed on to him from earlier hands, but he did systematize and solidify it, making it definitive for the medieval Church, and it is his mind which still dominates the Roman Catholic interpretation of sex." (*Sex in Christianity and Psychoanalysis*, by William Graham Cole.)

The Reasoning of Aquinas

During the Middle Ages, Catholicism, without altering basic tenets, did adapt to the ways of the barbaric Teutonic tribes who overran the Roman Empire. Its outstanding theologian of that era was Thomas Aquinas. This leader made a few minor alterations and adaptations in the Catholic teaching regarding sex.

Thomas Aquinas, unlike Augustine, was an avid follower of the philosophy of Aristotle. Accepting Augustine's pronouncements regarding sex in the main — continuing, of course, the general thesis that sex is itself essentially evil and shameful, he nevertheless made a few additions. In these he harmonized the philosophies of Aristotle and the barbarians. It is significant that he followed pagan philosophies—NOT THE WORD OF GOD!

In harmony with the pagan Aristotle, Aquinas was not quite so suspicious of physical pleasure as Augustine. He softened just slightly in this direction. He put major emphasis on devotion to thought, contemplation, using the *mind* in human REASON. The Word of God puts emphasis on the fact that human reason, unguided by God's Word, is unreliable and leads into false beliefs and ways. "There is a way that seemeth right unto a man," says God, through the wise Solomon, "but the end thereof are the ways of death" (Proverbs 14:12 and 16:25). The Bible warns repeatedly against vain reasonings.

Paul writes, to the Romans: ". . . when they knew God, they glorified Him not as God, neither were thankful; but became vain in their imaginations [REASONINGS], and their foolish heart was darkened. Professing themselves to be wise, they became fools . . . who changed the truth of God into a lie" (Romans 1:21-25).

But Thomas Aquinas glorified mental contemplation and human reason. The greatest good was to devote oneself to it. Whatever contributed to it was good—whatever hindered it was evil. A quiet life devoted to thought was much higher than a life of action and accomplishment. This, of course, was diametrically contrary to Biblical teaching.

In the vanity of his supposed "intellectuality," Thomas Aquinas arranged the "sins of sex" in order of their supposed sinfulness. When sex desire disturbed or interrupted mental thought and processes of reason, it was sin. It must never disorder one's occupation with reasoning.

He listed what he termed "unnatural vice" as the most sinful of sex sins. Among these, the worst was bestiality— the lowest depth of sin to which a man can sink. Next, in categorical order of "unnatural vices" he listed homosexuality, and lastly masturbation.

By this time marriage had become a sacrament. Aquinas

granted that marriage was not only acceptable by divine law, but also in harmony with his reason. He thought it was necessary for the world in general, though, like Augustine, virginity and celibacy were higher. Marriage was especially approved if a man's *reason* dictated it. Marriage, as a sacrament, was a sternly perpetual bond until death, and divorce and remarriage were forbidden.

The opinions and declarations of Augustine, and of Thomas Aquinas, had remained just that. They were not actually official Church dogma. Yet they were accepted and followed within Catholicism *as if* they had been official doctrines.

But Luther's "reformation" forced the Ecumenical Council of Trent. The Church now found it necessary to dogmatize doctrines and make them official, especially respecting sex and marriage. Luther had broken with the policy of celibacy.

The Council of Trent

This Council was not truly "ecumenical." It included no Protestants nor the Greek Orthodox Church. It was Roman Catholic only.

It made no change in the general concept that sex itself is an odious and shameful thing. It merely left that general concept in the public mind as it was before. It did officially make marriage a sacrament of the Church. It had to find some way to make sex in marriage for the purpose of reproduction appear at least *permissible*—in view of God's command in Scripture: "Be fruitful and multiply."

This difficulty was solved by declaring that "sacramental GRACE" of matrimony can remove the guilt of sin, but only *when* the motive is procreation. It must, of course, be understood that "sacramental grace" refers only to marriages performed officially by a Catholic priest, under Catholic terms and conditions. And "grace," remember, means "undeserved" or "unearned pardon, or gift."

They allowed one other condition of receiving this "free

pardon" from the Church. It was termed "rendering the debt." If a husband *demanded* sexual union when procreation was not the motive, and the wife was "forced to give in," her act was called "rendering the debt." The Church graciously "pardoned" her, bestowing its "grace." She, therefore, was not committing sin—but the husband who demanded this "debt" was guilty of sin—though it was termed "venial" sin.

The position of this Council—the position of the Roman Catholic Church always—is that the only AUTHORITY is the Roman Catholic Church. They do not recognize GOD, or CHRIST, or the BIBLE as supreme authority. The position is that the CHURCH has usurped that authority.

In the Work of God, which God through Christ carries on around the world, by the instrumentality of *The* WORLD TOMORROW broadcast, *The* PLAIN TRUTH magazine, the Ambassador Colleges, the only AUTHORITY is GOD ALMIGHTY, who speaks through CHRIST as the living Personal Word, and the BIBLE as the written Word of God—the *Instruction Book* of the Creator to the mankind of His creation!

And so we see:

1) that humans are not animals of instinct; that humans know nothing at birth—humans must learn and *be taught;* that humans were made free moral agents, allowed to make wrong choices, commit wrong acts; that the first Teacher of the first humans was the Creator—but the humans and their descendants rejected revelation; that pagan thought—the reasonings of human minds *cut off* from God and His TRUTH formed the pagan teachings and customs of this world, swayed by Satan's deceptions; and that the pagan concept of sex, adopted and perpetuated until our time by the Roman Catholic Church, has been false and harmful.

2) that the western world, somehow, has come to assume that these pagan teachings masquerading as Christianity actually are the teachings of the Bible!

This dualistic attitude that sex is evil in itself, and

shameful, has caused tragic unhappiness in countless millions of marriages.

This is emphatically *NOT* the teaching of God, or of the Bible. It has been a CURSE to humanity.

CHAPTER 6

The New Morality

*T*HE "sense of guilt" interpretation of sex had been weighed in the balance by a repressed world and found wanting.

But today we have emerged into a different world. Knowledge has suddenly increased with the acceleration of an explosion.

Yet today's world is not exchanging its traditional pagan concepts for the truth of God. In no sense is it returning to its own Creator and His ways and laws.

Rather humanity now is taking a rocket-speed plunge into a new "morality"—or more properly, *IM*morality—of its own. It is fleeing farther than ever, and with accelerating speed, away from its Maker and the happiness He made possible.

The dualistic interpretation destroyed happiness in a high percentage of marriages. The "new morality" will destroy civilization.

Before we examine the TRUE WAY, it is essential that we open our eyes to the facts as they now exist. I doubt seriously that my average reader realizes the true state of affairs. To call them shocking is an understatement!

"Morality," it seems, is the major interest in the western world. Look at the news! The hydrogen bomb—the possibility of erasing human life from this planet, snuffing out all our lives—the Cold War—the flight to the moon—all these have subsided in interest behind news of Elizabeth Taylor's latest "love" life; the Profumo scandal and the illicit sex lives of Christine Keeler and Mandy Rice-Davies; and other sensational sex news.

Every issue of every magazine of popular circulation, it seems, uses an article on sex to entice readers at the newsstands. For example, this chapter is being written in Düsseldorf, Germany, in May, 1964. As my wife and I passed through the lobby of our hotel, a few moments ago, returning to our room, she picked up at the newsstand a copy of *Reader's Digest*, United States edition. Pasted over the front cover was the usual newsstand sticker advertising in big type six articles to tempt the purchaser. First to hit the eye is: "Too Much Sex on Campuses," and, in small type underneath: "page 59." Turning to page 59, the subheading states that the obligation to teach students how to cope with their sex problems is being neglected by too many colleges.

The article, condensed from *Ladies' Home Journal*, quotes an Oregon State University professor: "The conclusion that we have done a thoroughly unsatisfactory job of sex-human-relations education, probably most of all in the colleges, is simply inescapable."

But *how can* the colleges teach what the educators themselves do not know? Education has gone materialistic. The TRUTH that would bring the people the true FREEDOM of happiness—freedom from frustrations in marriage; from the nightmare of premarital pregnancies; from broken homes and juvenile delinquents; from disillusionments, perverted minds, broken lives—this TRUTH can come only from GOD and from HIS WORD! But God is not very welcome on the average campus today, nor is His Word taken seriously.

On the three Ambassador campuses this obligation toward our students is *not* neglected! And *these* students enjoy this true FREEDOM from unhappiness and tragedy!

The Shocking FACTS!

Take a quick over-all view of conditions in the western world. In Sweden, the mother of a 19-year-old son was being interviewed by a British newspaper woman. The son came in, gave his mother a kiss on the cheek, and was off for the remainder of the day.

"My son is so thoughtful of me," said the Swedish woman. "I used to walk into my kitchen, on rising of a morning, and frequently find a strange teen-age girl in a kimono searching the refrigerator. When my son learned that I was not too happy over this, he was very considerate. Now he takes his girl-friends elsewhere for the night."

Shocking? It is common practice in Sweden today for teen-age boys to bring their girl friends to their own homes to sleep with them for the night. This sort of thing is not discouraged in Sweden. Rather, there are government agencies for disseminating information regarding contraceptives, and protection from venereal disease. If an unmarried girl becomes pregnant, there are public welfare agencies to help her. If she wishes to have her baby, provisions are made to give her aid, including the delivery of the baby. If not, she may be granted official permission to have an abortion. And legally!

Divorce may be obtained in Sweden with no difficulty at all. No "evidence" or "grounds" required. Marriage is not "until death do us part," but until the next divorce. This "new morality" in Sweden bears the fruit of tragedy, despondency, frustration.

The Profumo scandal in London merely happened to be one that "got found out." That is not to say that all top officials carry on such illicit "love affairs" with girls other than their wives. But, so far as successful men generally are concerned—according to the world's concept of "successful men"—such affairs are not at all uncommon. And the two "professionals" tried at court for perjury in the aftermath— Christine Keeler and Mandy Rice-Davies—showed no sense of shame or feeling of guilt. Rather, they thought their "profession" entirely honorable!

A French publication, not long ago, announced a "new religion" in France. Freedom from all restraint in sex urges—

complete freedom to do as one pleases—that was the new religion.

Listen to a Senior Editor for *Look* magazine: "We are witnessing the death of the old morality. . . . Conditions are changing so fast that the established moral guidelines have been yanked from our hands. *No single authority rules our conduct.* No church lays down the moral law for all. . . . We are heading into danger. We are in the midst of a moral crisis—because the great majority of Americans, who want to try to live moral lives, *no longer can be certain what is right and what is wrong.* . . . We are groping, painfully and often blindly, for new standards that will enable us to live morally and decently." (Emphasis added.)

What is meant, here, is that people now want to adopt a moral standard which calls fornication, adultery, homosexuality "moral." They want Society to approve and adopt a standard which enables them to be promiscuous, unfaithful, or perverted—and have it accepted as living morally and decently. But to continue, the *Look* Senior Editor said:

"*The experts feel* strongly that we cannot turn back to earlier, more rigid behavior patterns. . . . We must find a new moral code that will fit the need of the society we live in."

Misrepresenting the Bible

WHY would it never occur to "the experts" to learn the standards of the Creator? It is the "experts"—the professional leaders—the theologians, the educators, the doctors, the psychiatrists, the marriage counsellors—who set the patterns and establish the codes. They feel they cannot turn back to the rigid, prudish, straight-laced, repressive code of past centuries, resulting from the dualistic attitude of shame and sense of guilt in marriage.

What is really WRONG is the concept, generally assumed, that this sex-is-evil attitude is the harsh Law of God—the teaching of the Bible. So the Bible gets discredited. God is banished from their thought. And, in the thinking of misguided men, they must now do away with the sex-is-evil notion altogether. They must now adopt a sex-is-GOOD code.

Too many "religious" people have conceived of SIN as being wrong *things*, instead of the wrong doing—the wrong *USES* of things. Some of the "very religious" have taught that any alcoholic beverage is SIN! A deck of cards or a pair of dice is SIN! The theater is SIN! It is only their *wrong use* that is sin!

And the "wisest" of the psychiatrists, the physicians, the church leaders, and the educators cannot comprehend that SEX has GOD-ORDAINED purposes—that the right or wrong of sex is a matter of *HOW IT IS USED*—not a matter of whether SEX ITSELF is evil or good!

Sex knowledge has increased. But, I repeat, this avalanche of sex knowledge released these past forty years is only half true, because only half complete. It does not reveal God's PURPOSES and LAWS of sex. Therefore it is deceptive, soul-damaging, and is leading this world to the brink of total destruction!!

Illicit Sex Police-Protected?

But to continue:

Over our UPI teletype, at the News Bureau on the Ambassador College campus, Pasadena, came this dispatch from LONDON: "In London's parks the birds and the bees take lessons from the boys and girls—as many a blushing tourist can testify. Today the youth of Britain was assured that it can continue the free-for-all-wrestling that passes here for courtship without undue interference from the police."

Do people generally realize the extent of this sudden "social revolution"? Committing fornication openly on park benches, or park lawns!! It ought to be shocking—revolting!! But people have become calloused, indifferent, unconcerned! It's time people WAKE UP! Their "social revolution" has brought modern society to the precipice of total destruction.

But to continue the above UPI dispatch: "Scotland Yard, taking into account a recent court decision, has circulated a confidential memo warning its detectives and constables that couples cannot be arrested on suspicion of offending public decency: this goes not only for the parks, the famous squares, the main boulevards and all the other open places where the mating urge seems to seize upon the young Briton, *but in particular, parked cars. . . .*"

It is in parked cars that girls most often lose their virginity. Now fornication in parked cars is openly permitted in London. Police interference is barred.

"Many Americans," continues the dispatch, "have wondered how the British ever got their reputation for being staid and conservative. Any tourist who can take his eyes from the screen of some London cinemas is apt to see hotter love scenes in the back rows than Hollywood can produce."

A London Vicar of the Church of England has barred kissing by teen-agers in his church. "My church is not the place for courting," he said. "I was amazed to find that many teen-agers were only interested in sex. I'm no square. Young love is only natural and healthy—but there is a time and place for everything. Church is not a courting haunt."

Switch the scene back to Los Angeles.

Symptom: Fourteen girls missed graduation exercises at a Los Angeles high school. . . . *Reason:* advanced pregnancy.

The New Teen-Age Disease: "Automania"

From the *New York World Telegram & Sun:* " 'Automania,' a Nassau County judge says, is a new teen-age disease. It's an over-obsession for cars manifest in stolen autos, wild joyrides, backseat intimacies.

"All across the broad sweep of the United States, an infectious malady is spreading with the persistence and virulence of the plagues that pre-dated this age of antibiotics. The malady goes by the name of teen-age immorality. It is reflected not only in a cauldron of promiscuity, illegitimate births, abortions, venereal disease, homosexuality and 'shotgun' marriages, but in related behaviour patterns that offend against the accepted mores. These include delinquent behaviour, truancy, runaway-itis, thievery, heavy drinking, and addiction to narcotics and related habit-forming potions. . . .

"There was not a single sociologist, psychologist, or youth expert whom we interviewed while preparing this series who did not agree that waywardness among today's juveniles has soared to the point of defying all precedent. . . .

"Juvenile arrests have increased 116% in the last 10 years. The cost of youth crime is up to $4,000,000,000 a year. A million young people under 18 were jailed last year. *The U. S. Senate Juvenile Delinquency subcommittee has reported that 20% of all our young people between the ages of 10 and 17 have court records for misbehaviour.*"

THAT IS ONE IN EVERY FIVE!

PARENTS! Do you know what *your* teen-age children are doing? Don't be too sure! These are not fairy tales you are reading. These are FACTS! This is the *condition!* This is the world that is influencing *your* children *more than you realize!*

Now continue this report:

"The *most* eye-popping figures relate to the fruits of SEX DELINQUENCY. The vital statistics division of the U. S. Public Health Service says there are now approximately *a quarter of a million illegitimate births a year.* This is an increase of 60% over the past ten years, and the rate has tripled in the last 25. The rate of increase in legitimate births during this period is far less.

"The quarter of a million figure would be much higher except for special circumstances. There are 15 states which do not specifically report on illegitimate cases. No births to married women are ever reported as illegitimate, and many cases of illegitimacy are concealed through the falsification of records. Furthermore, it is estimated that *about two million illegal abortions are performed every year.* Then there are *the vast number* of cases where the product of illicit young 'love' becomes legitimatized through a hasty 'shotgun' wedding. . . . *The greatest percentage increase in the ranks of those who breed illegitimate progeny are products of so-called good families on the right side of the tracks. . . .*

"The Council of School Parents in high-income, status-happy Darien, Connecticut, issued an eye-opening report recently revealing 'an alarming number of pregnancies in high school' and 'an unbelievable amount of necking and petting going on . . . involving even youngsters from the sixth and seventh grades . . .' The Council's publication quoted a girl student as saying, 'Accepting a date to the drive-in movies is like accepting a date for sex relations.' "

"Going Steady"

A new evil, not generally recognized as an evil, is the American custom of "going steady." Teen-agers have their arguments. One impelling motive is the feeling of insecurity of these times. "Going steady" provides "security"—the boy or girl is assured of dates. Then too, as boys today become more and more girlish and feminine, and less and less masculine, many are becoming more bashful. Asking a girl for a date seems to be an ordeal. What if she turns the boy down? The thought strikes fear into the boy's heart.

From the *Los Angeles Times* comes this dispatch by Dorothy Ricker in the "Teen-age Mail": "Some time ago when I conducted a national poll on teens going steady, 72% of the girls and 74% of the boys answered 'Yes' to the following question: 'Do you think dating only one person leads to more physical intimacy [fornication] than dating more than one?' "

A few years ago, the going-steady custom was followed primarily by young people in the late teens—17 to 19. A little later the 15- and 16-year adolescents were going steady. And now the children of 13 and 14 are beginning the practice —and, in some cases, even 11- and 12-year-olds.

The "new psychology" of the "experts" accompanies hand-in-hand the "new morality." Under this particular satanic sway parents are sparing the rod and spoiling the children. Permissiveness is being accepted as the "intelligent" and modern formula for child rearing.

And where is this leading? Many directions—all of them WRONG! Few parents realize what is really happening to their children. Children are influenced far more by *other children* than by their parents—unless parental training is *far* more intelligent than that of this perverted "new psychology."

College Campus Morals

Take, for example, the daughter who has been carefully reared and kept morally clean up to age 17.

Here is the case history of one such girl. The reader may have read it in the May, 1964, *Reader's Digest*. She entered college early. It was a sophisticated atmosphere. Most of the girls were a little older, and the product of the "new psychology" in permissive child rearing. Other girls did not conceal their amusement at her ideals of chastity. She was terribly old-fashioned.

In her second year at college, she weakened under this pressure—not only from young men who had "a line" about the "rightness" of allowing "love" to be freely expressed, but pressure from the girls as well. Few college students can stand up against such pressures. The girl "fell for the line" of a certain boy, decided it was love, and yielded. She began to believe premarital sex was the right thing to do, after all.

Then the bombshell exploded—and her life with it! The boy friend married another girl. She discovered she was pregnant. She refused, on counsel, to take her problem to her parents. Instead she underwent an illegal abortion. Discouraged, frustrated, she was unable to maintain passing grades, and left college, her whole life wrecked.

I quote from the article: "Officials [of the college] supposedly dedicated to bringing her to mature womanhood, never knew why she had failed."

I do thank God that, at three colleges, I have been given the opportunity to see that students do receive proper and full instruction not only, but also reasonable regulations designed to forestall and prevent such tragedies!

Look further at this campus state of affairs. These are things few parents know. Few students, making application for admission to a college, realize the influences and the pressures that will be exerted.

From the *London Daily Mail* comes this bit of news:

"Oxford's top undergraduates—two of them girls—suggested a 'sex charter' to university authorities yesterday. Its main points were:

"1) Undergraduates' private sexual behaviour should be *their own responsibility*.

"2) Authorities should punish undergraduates *only if* they have seriously damaged the institution's moral reputation, or if their behaviour has 'clearly' amounted to an imposition on friends' freedom or welfare.

"A circular letter, signed by 27 undergraduates, most of them officers or ex-officers of university clubs, was sent to 200 dons inviting their approval of the charter. It claims the charter, which follows the expulsion of a girl undergraduate found with a man in a room at St. Hilda's College, would avoid further friction between undergraduates and the authorities."

To return once again to the article in *Reader's Digest*, the author, a Superior Court woman judge, says: "What distresses me is that many girls are overwhelmed by the pressures to conform" (on college campuses). "They believe that if a girl remains chaste she's likely to be stricken from available-for-dates lists. Nice girls, too timid to defy the crowd, make sexual commitments for the security of 'belonging.' For those girls missing the warmth and security of home, *the sexual answer to loneliness can lead to the loneliest of lives*—an almost total absence of feeling. . . . It is the parents' duty to talk frankly to a college-bound daughter. . . . But the odds are against even the best-advised girls if colleges are indifferent to student attitudes. . . . From the first day students arrive, colleges should spell out acceptable standards of social behaviour" (emphasis ours). But do they?

At the three Ambassador Colleges, the acceptable standards of social behaviour *are* spelled out in emphatic terms. Standards at these colleges are those of the Creator, designed for our happiness. Students are not left in ignorance of the TRUE VALUES. Students are taught the inexorable Laws of God which REGULATE happiness, well-being, enjoyable living—with no corroding aftertastes!

Shocking Rise in Illegitimate Births

Illegitimate births, reported above for America, are prolific all over the western world. The London *Daily Telegraph*, reporting for Great Britain, says: "Illegitimate births now stand at one in six. The figure for London was considerably higher. . . . *Roughly two out of every three babies born to girls of 20 and under are conceived outside marriage.*"

I have before me, as I write, a later edition of the London *Daily Telegraph* for May 20, 1964. A large two-column top-of-the-page headline says: "BIRTH CONTROL ADVICE TO SINGLE GIRLS."

The story says: "A decision on whether information and advice about contraceptive techniques should be given to single girls by the Family Planning Association will be made at the association's annual meeting in London next month.

"It is proposed that advice at the association's 413 clinics should be given at the doctor's discretion." The news story states that some of the members are arguing "that probably 'most' people have premarital sexual intercourse. In this case the association should give advice to all who seek it. They believe this would reduce the present high rate of illegitimacy. Abortion, pregnant brides and 'shotgun weddings' could also be reduced."

The argument, in other words, is this: Since most young people are indulging in premarital sexual intercourse anyway, let's *encourage* the practice by giving further instruction. The story says the proposal will have it opponents. The proposal is too recent to report here the decision of the annual meeting. But now to return to the earlier report from the *Daily Telegraph.*

"Another pointer was the increase of convictions for homosexual offenses. *'The greatest danger facing the health of the nation today* is the so-called new morality,' Dr. Ernest Claston, assistant Secretary of the British Medical Association said. 'The moral landslide now undermining our civilization was *receiving the sanction of religious leaders.* Certain doctors were advocating a new teaching on sex. . . .

" 'Today our nation, with all its prosperity and potentiality, its skills and science, its institutions and inventions, *is in greater danger than it has ever been in its long and proud history.* The reasons are that it is allowing its grip on moral standards to slacken and that it has no longer an adequate purpose. This is partly due to the failure of leaders who say they do not know what is going on—"I never realized it". Sex has become an obsession and promiscuity a national problem.

Theologians Employ Deceit

" *'But now comes a new and subtle stratagem. From religious bodies emerges a "new morality".* You can find this in the Cambridge school of theology, the Quaker report on sex, the Bishop of Woolwich's book "Honest to God", in the so-called South Bank religion, and in broadcasts, speeches and articles.

" 'The subtle and clever thing is that this new morality is induced so plausibly. While appearing to retain traditional virtues, it allows for *the exceptional case.* So anyone becomes an exception. *In the name of compassion, it condones adultery, fornication and sodomy.'* "

There are the conditions as they actually are today.

And *where is the responsibility?* It is with the theologians, the doctors, the psychiatrists—the leaders. But most of all, it is with the theologians.

These theologians masquerade as the ministers of Christ.

I will give you, plainly, their *true* affiliation later. But *IF* they were the ministers of Christ, it would be their responsibility to be LEADERS, not followers—to cry aloud—lift up their voices—show the people *their sins!*

See, now, where even theologians themselves and other officials place the blame—and then we shall see where GOD ALMIGHTY places the guilt!

I quote again from a report by a Senior Editor for *Look:*

Remember, he is quoted above as saying a great majority of Americans, who *want* to try to live moral lives, no longer can be certain what is right and what is wrong. God is out of the picture. What *authority* is left? To whom can they turn? The *leaders* are not telling them the TRUTH!

"Most Americans," says the *Look* report, "hate to admit we are in a crisis. But *its bitter fruits* are all around us: the beatnik, the racist, the wild kid, the price-rigging executive, the pregnant high-school girl, the dope addict, the vandal, the bribed athlete, the un-cared-for aged, the poor, the criminal. Television depicts shoot-'em-up violence as the American way, and the movies uphold stardom as a warrant for four husbands and a lover. . . .

"In Lansing, Michigan, Governor George Romney says, 'Our greatest danger is the decline in religious conviction and moral character. *This is more serious to our future than the external threats we face.'* . . .

"Since we live in a society without a supreme moral authority" . . . [and I break in to ask, "WHAT'S HAPPENED TO GOD?"] . . . "where can we get moral standards? Not from the church, says Dean Samuel Miller of the Harvard Divinity School. 'The church has become almost as monastic as the orders in the Middle Ages. *There seems to be no connection between what happens in the church and what happens in society,* except that people living in a desperate age use it to tranquilize their disturbing experiences—like some kind of lullaby.' "

Listeners to *The* WORLD TOMORROW world-wide radio program, and readers of *The* PLAIN TRUTH have heard and read, repeatedly, that the "Christianity" of this day seems to have *no connection* with adherents' social, business, professional or political lives—nothing to do with how we live. The sole mission of the church, as generally conceived, it seems, is—or used to be—merely "to get people 'saved'"— and this consists, ordinarily, of "confessing Christ," "accepting Christ," "making the decision for Christ," or "giving the Lord your heart and the preacher your hand." But most Protestant denominations have turned "modernist" and no longer believe even in "being saved." WHAT HAVE THEY LEFT! Religion has become, as aptly phrased in the above quote, a tranquilizer and a lullaby!

But to continue the *Look* report:

"The churches . . . have failed to supply moral leadership, and because *their responsibility is the greatest*, their failure is the worst. Harvard Divinity School's Dean Miller says, *'The church simply does not have a cutting edge'*"— it has thrown away the two-edged sword!!! "'It has taken the culture of our time *and absorbed it.'* . . .

"Yale's Chaplain Coffin agrees: *'We churchmen are gifted at changing wine into water—watering down religion. The problem of the church today is ineffectiveness. We've never had attendance so high and influence so low.'*"

Shocking 46-Nation Report

In mid-summer, 1964, the International Planned Parenthood Federation held a Conference at Church House, Westminster, London. It was attended by representatives from 46 nations.

To say that the report of that congress, published in newspapers throughout the world, was shocking is a gross understatement.

The London Sunday Times reported that there was general acceptance among most representatives present of premarital sexual intercourse—even involving boys and girls *in their early teens!*

The Planned Parenthood associations have been organized to promote the *planning* and intelligent spacing of children by *married people*. But unless they are grossly misrepresented by newspaper dispatches, they appear to be more active in disseminating contraceptive techniques to the unmarried than in enlightening *married* people concerning the intelligent planning of production of offspring.

There is arising grave concern and fear over the anticipated population explosion during the coming century. These associations, supposedly, are intensely concerned, and are formed for the purpose of regulating the birth rate in order to save civilization.

But the news that seems to make the headlines concerns their efforts to get contraceptive information to the unmarried adolescents.

An American delegate said, "We are in the midst of a changing of sex 'mores.' "

"You can't solve anything by turning the clock back," insisted Dr. Thorsten Sjovall of Sweden. What he means is, the sex-is-sinful repression has been tried for many centuries and found wanting. The world is turning to the "sex-is-virtuous" AMORALITY, regardless of how used—in or out of marriage—heterosexual or homosexual. To turn the clock back would be to go back to the sense of shame and guilt. The Creator's purposes and instruction seem utterly unknown. Therefore, the doctor knows of no solution except to approve immorality.

The conference brought out vastly different conditions in certain different nations. For example, a fourteen-year-old girl in Sweden is not a whit embarrassed, no matter who sees her, as she abstracts a contraceptive from a slot machine in a public place. But Jordan is a different world. Until recently a fourteen-year-old Arab girl might have been put to death by her parents for having premarital sex relations. However, even in Moslem Jordan, times are changing, moral attitudes are relaxing, although a girl would still risk social disgrace for engaging in premarital sex.

Iron Curtain country delegates said their sex problems

are much the same as elsewhere. "Lovemaking" is encouraged, as long as pregnancy is prevented. In Turkey, 12,000 girls and women a year die from illegal abortions.

A Danish youth, the Conference was told, recently urged on a television interview that girls of fourteen should be provided with contraceptive means by the school doctors.

Yet in Italy a young man could be fined for kissing his girl friend in public, and brought into court for being found making love. But in Italy, too, morals are fast beginning to relax. They have merely started in that direction a few years behind such nations as Sweden, the United States, France and Britain.

Violence Accompanies Immorality

Dr. Sjovall of Sweden was not at all disturbed by the general promiscuous sex immorality in Sweden. This is merely termed "emancipation." But he *was* quite concerned at the increase of violence and belligerence—teens "shoving their weight around"—and organized riots. Dr. Sjovall ought to observe the *facts!* The violence, the disrespect for authority, the riots, the rise in juvenile crime, has directly *accompanied* moral laxity and sex promiscuity! They go hand in hand!

Dr. A. Guttmacher is president of the Planned Parenthood World Population Federation. He mentioned that a fifth of United States brides are pregnant before marriage, and *for teen-agers the ratio is two out of every five.* In view of this, he foresees a decline in opposition from churches and parent groups.

"Parents, themselves," he said, "are becoming more sophisticated. They know, for example, that their son and daughter must go to college equipped with contraceptives. So long as they are taught responsibility to each other I think some better humans may come out of this 'new morality.' Hypocrisy is going under." In other words, teen-agers don't have to hide or pretend—they can commit fornication more openly.

Such quotations should give the reader a better idea of professional "thinking" along the lines of morality today!

In attendance was Frau Volker from Germany, mother of two boys. When she attended her first family planning conference ten years ago, she was shocked by the frank acceptance of premarital sex, especially by the Americans and Swedes.

"Through my clinic, I have ceased to be shocked," said Frau Volker. "I now accept that girls go to bed with boys, either because it is the fashion, or because they do not want to lose a friend. The *problem* we have to tackle is that *70% of our marriages are now due to pregnancy.*"

This German mother did not consider promiscuous teenage fornication a problem. The *problem* was lack of contraceptive protection against premarital pregnancies!

Many members of the Planned Parenthood Federation are going to read this book. I wish they could open their eyes to the *fact* that, in their *acceptance* of premarital sexual intercourse, they are influencing an *increase* in the birth rate among unmarried adolescents, rather than regulating and retarding the birth rate among the married.

Statistics seem to show that contraceptive education of juveniles *is not decreasing premarital pregnancies!*

Even in marriage, contraceptive knowledge does not prevent pregnancies *unless* there is vigilance. Even among married people, possessing contraceptive knowledge, and planning at the time to avoid pregnancy, carelessness is producing a bumper crop of "accidents." If carelessness in the use of contraceptives on the part of *the married* is resulting in so many pregnancies, *how much more* will be the exposure to pregnancy under the conditions to which the unmarried must resort!

Who Is to Blame?

This chapter could continue on and on, ad infinitum. There is no end of accounts, reports, and news of today's widespread and still spreading moral degeneracy.

But where is the blame?

I can state it in two ways: 1) Few realize that God Almighty foretold these very conditions 2,500 years ago and more, and that the Eternal Himself places the blame in plain and unmistakable terms! In the following chapter, I intend to show you precisely what the Creator says, and where He fixes the guilt. 2) This world-calamity has befallen mankind *because* of a lack of the TRUE AND WHOLE KNOWLEDGE REVEALED BY THE *CREATOR* OF SEX! The *guilt* is placed *by* the Creator on those who profess to represent HIM, but have turned their backs on HIS knowledge, and HIS Message to the people, and disseminated lies in the guise of truth!

Then, after that, I propose to proclaim to those who will read, and heed, the TRUTH OF GOD in respect to sex.

GOD created sex. GOD designed sex anatomy. GOD designed and created the nervous, emotional, and psychic systems, all of which combine to put POWER and intense *drives* into sex functions. What GOD designed, created, and set into living motion is *VERY GOOD!* God made this to be put to a right, a clean, a healthy, a *moral* and a spiritual USE! But He also endowed man with the power of free choice, and the ability to pervert, misdirect and misuse what He made for man's good!

What was designed to make possible the highest physical *blessings*, man has polluted and turned into his greatest physical CURSES!

MAN seeks FREEDOM in reverse! Instead of freedom from curses, he seeks freedom for the perversions, the dissipations, the illicit and evil acts that *produce* curses! There is a great difference between freedom *to* commit sin, and the FREEDOM *FROM* SIN, which Jesus Christ gave His life to make possible. *You* need to ask: Just what do you *mean*—FREEDOM?

CHAPTER 7

Pinning the Guilt Where
It Belongs

WHOSE IS THE GUILT? The pagan teachings about sex brought the curse of ruined marriages, resentments, bitterness, frustrations and neuroses. The New Morality is wrecking lives, breaking up homes, threatening the destruction of civilization.

The Creator designed sex to bring blessings and happiness—to bind together husband and wife in love—to protect and preserve the institution of the home and family.

But look at the mountain of woe and anguish piled up by a society that has rebelled against its true GOD, rejected the divine Maker's knowledge, lost its way and blundered on in the misleading paths of human devising.

Two Extremes From Happiness

The "sex-is-evil" doctrine resulted in unhappy marriages. As one physician wrote, back in the years B.N. (Before the New Morality): "Many a newly wedded couple have wrecked the possibility of happiness of a lifetime on their honeymoon trip; and it is a matter of common knowledge to the members of our profession that *the great majority of brides* are practically raped on their entrance into the marriage relation." This was the result of ignorance regarding the physical details of marriage. To disseminate such knowledge was a crime by law.

Because of this ignorance, the physician continued,

"The ordinary figure of a 'bull in a china shop' can but faintly describe the smashing and grinding to powder of the most delicate situation that can occur in all human experiences. Ideals that have touched heaven are rudely crushed to atoms; hopes beyond the power of words to express go out in despair; dreams become a hideous nightmare; and love, which was as pure as crystal waters, is muddied, befouled, and made into a cesspool. *And all this because of ignorance.*"

That was before World War I. Wives, disillusioned, said: "All men are BRUTES!" Husbands resented their frigid wives, became bitter and frustrated.

But men were not brutes. Brutes do not make these blunders. Brutes do not *need* the knowledge these men were denied. Brutes are equipped with instinct. But *men* must *learn*—or be taught. And teaching in this sorely needed area of knowledge was denied men and women, and prohibited by law in modern times, until a generation ago.

Then World War I started the revolt against Puritanism and repression. The legal bars finally came crashing down. But the avalanche of sex knowledge suddenly released was purely physical knowledge. Again I repeat, it was only *half* true, because only half complete. The most vital factor in the realm of sex is RIGHT ATTITUDE. The authors of the flood of books on sex were devoid of UNDERSTANDING of the Creator's purposes and living LAWS regulating sex.

Man, from the Garden in Eden, has rebelled against his Maker—has rejected and lost the necessary knowledge revealed by the Maker for man's happiness and well-being.

God says: "There is *a way* that *seemeth right* unto a man, but the end thereof are the ways of death." So man reasoned out *the way* that *seemed right!*

What had been WRONG? The concept that *sex is evil*—that *knowledge* about it must be prohibited—and the resulting *sense of shame*, and *feeling of guilt*.

They revolted against Puritanism and repression. The psychoanalysts lent an aura of professional respectability to the revolt. They theorized that neuroses resulted from inhibitions and repression of natural sex urges.

The way that seemed logical and right, therefore, was to reverse the teaching, and institute a "New Morality" accepting sex as GOOD—to cure neuroses by abolishing repression and changing to permissiveness and promiscuity. If repression and inhibitions caused psychic disturbance, the "cure" was to abolish repression and inhibitions—to call sex GOOD—to make it available whenever and wherever impulse or desire led.

Since ignorance produced "brute" husbands and "frigid" wives, the solution that *seemed right* was to release the full knowledge of biological details—to emancipate women from the sense of dread, shame, and guilt and to show them—as well as men—how to enjoy sex.

Yes, that way SEEMED RIGHT!

Just one thing was WRONG with it—it failed to take into account the Creator's PURPOSES, and invisible yet living and inexorable LAWS respecting sex. And that one thing WRONG resulted in taking humanity out of the proverbial frying pan and throwing it into the fire! If the fruits of dualistic interpretations were BAD, the new interpretation of the NEW MORALITY is bearing fruits that are FATAL!

Already it has been tried in the balance and found wanting. Its results ARE ALL *BAD!*

But WHO IS to BLAME?

Sex and Psychiatry

This "New Morality" wears the cloak of respectability, because it is advocated by professional leaders—the psychiatrists, the doctors, the theologians. And, now, even the politicians are beginning to endorse the new "freedoms" by the powers of governments!

First, the father of modern psychoanalysis, Sigmund Freud, theorized that neuroses and emotional disturbances were caused by sex repressions, inhibitions, and ignorance.

Next, the doctors swung into line in the direction leading gradually to this "New Morality." Then the educators, rejecting the knowledge from GOD, disseminating only materialistic knowledge, allowed the new permissive teachings to be injected into educational institutions.

The educated clergy are reared in the educational system. Gradually the younger ministers coming along absorbed the new "liberal" teachings. And today much of the clergy is coming to endorse the "New Morality."

Now observe, please, that even ministers themselves fix the BLAME.

I have quoted in Chapter 6 the sentence of Dean Samuel Miller of Harvard Divinity School, and of Yale's Chaplain Coffin—that there is no supreme moral authority—no connection between religion and *how we live*, but that religion has become a tranquilizer and a spiritual lullaby; that the Church does not have "a cutting edge"—that is, it *does not have the Word of God*, which is the "two-edged sword." Also that they are "changing wine into water—watering down religion."

The attitude of the churches, and the theologians, was well expressed by a London businessman with whom I have had dealings in the purchase of college property. "We must," he said, "adapt our religion to the changing conditions of a changing world."

The Voice of God—Where?

Instead of being THE VOICE OF GOD to *prevent* society from plunging off the precipice into the tragic cataclysm of moral degradation, the theologians "adapt" their religious codes and their preaching *to conform* to this changing, degenerating world! As quoted in the preceding chapter, instead of *leading* the world into the *right* ways of God, they allow the WORLD to *lead them* into degeneration and degradation; they have REJECTED God's WAYS—His LAWS—and have "taken the culture of our time *and absorbed it*."

Now hear further evidence, before I reveal what God Almighty foretold of these modern theologians.

An article by David Boroff, in the August, 1961, *Coronet*, summarizes the situation. Speaking of the Protestant clergy, he says in part: "A change-over in attitude has taken place, with powerful implications for the whole range of sexual activity—marital, premarital, even extramarital. . . . Fundamentalists in all parts of the country still regard sex as *sinful* and the body as something to be distrusted. And such attitudes are deeply rooted in the American mind. . . .

"However, much of Protestantism *no longer wishes to be identified with repression and Puritanism.* 'In fact,' says Professor Roger Shinn of New York's Union Theological Seminary, 'repression is a Christian heresy.' "

His reasoning: The "Old Morality" teaching that sex is sinful and that virtue demands the utter nonuse of sex brought only unhappiness, suffering, and curses—therefore it was a "Christian heresy." The "way that seemeth right," consequently, is to reverse everything—go to the opposite extreme—invent the "New Morality" and call sex GOOD, and say that the utter freedom-of-use under any and all circumstances now becomes virtue. This could hardly be classified as intelligent reasoning!

Continue a few quotes from the *Coronet* article:

"In recent years, Protestant theologians . . . have been influenced . . . by the findings of psychiatry—especially the revelation of the psychic damage that may be done by sexual repression. This new set of attitudes is shared by thousands of Protestant clergymen and is taught in such great centers of Protestant learning as the *Union Theological Seminary* and the *Harvard* and *Yale Divinity Schools.* According to Dr. Seward Hiltner, a Protestant theologian, since man is a 'whole or total being, sex is good if it serves the fulfillment of man as a total being.' "

This reasoning allows the application that ANY illicit use of sex may be good—under certain circumstances. God's teaching—to come in the next chapter—will show *what* uses

of sex God designed for WHAT GREAT AND BENEFICIAL PUR-
POSES—a wonderful knowledge designed to bring supreme
happiness and blessings—of which these human leaders know
nothing!

Continuing the *Coronet* quotes: "How can people practice a liberal ethic without falling into the trap of 'anything
goes'? Protestant theologians offer a few very hard and fast
rules . . . 'When I counsel,' a minister told me, '*I'm not in
the habit of telling people what to do*. I merely outline the
question so they can find the answers themselves. There
simply isn't any fixed answer for every question.' "

In other words, this theologian avoids committing himself, or making himself legally liable for wrong results. He
knows that in all too many cases the person counselled will
"decide for himself" the way of fornication, adultery or
sodomy.

"One minister was visited by a married man," continues the *Coronet* article, "who was having an affair and
was suffering from the pangs of guilt. . . . It turned out,
however, that this man was married to a bedridden invalid
with whom sexual relations were impossible. 'The only function I could serve was to relieve the man's feeling of guilt,'
the minister said."

Churchmen Themselves Blame Theologians

Many Protestant churchmen are placing the blame
squarely on the theologians. Methodist Bishop Hazen G.
Werner is quoted in the *Augusta Chronicle* (Georgia,
U. S. A.) of September 29, 1961: " 'We have been dried out
by the hot winds of secularism. We who are to overcome the
world *have been overcome by the world*.' "

This shift toward the false "New Morality" on the part
of upwards of 50% of the clergy is actually drawing some
ministers and priests into the vortex of committing immorality themselves. From Panama City, Florida, came this AP
news story: "Twenty men, including three church figures
and two school teachers, have been arrested on perversion

charges, officers said today. Sheriff Charley Abbott and Police Chief Tom McAuley said an investigation into *an extensive homosexual ring* is continuing. They said the men arrested are accused of molesting about 50 children. The officers said all were booked on charges of lewd, lascivious and unnatural sex behaviour."

Here is another report on how theologians are rapidly changing their views on chastity. It came over our UPI wire service at the Ambassador College News Bureau, Pasadena campus, on May 1. From Green Lake, Wisconsin: "A united quest for an effective approach to sex and family problems in the 1960s brought more than 600 scientists and clergymen together to clear cobwebs and open dead-end paths in basic Protestant church thinking. . . . Delegates (summoned by the National Council of Churches and the Canadian Council of Churches) have asked themselves, for example, whether fear of pregnancy is a deterrent today to premarital sex relations. *More effective contraception is forcing a review of the Christian case for chastity,* local ministers say. Where, then, does the pastor look for explanations opposing extramarital sex? *Are there any remaining arguments against the practice?*

"Sex relations out of wedlock is only one of many problems causing serious thought by theologians, medical men, sociologists and laymen at the weeklong conference. . . . Many persons feel American and Canadian Protestantism has not found the way to deal with them. 'There has been a major shift in our thinking about sex,' said Dr. Silvanus M. Duvall, co-chairman of the conference, *'from the attitude that it is a sin* to be repressed, to a feeling that *it is something good and should be enjoyed.'* Dr. Duvall, who has co-authored several books, said pastors are unable to meet today's problems with yesterday's preachments because their people are confronted by a social revolution."

I could weary the reader with reports and evidence piled upon evidence of the shocking facts showing it is THE PREACHERS who are primarily to blame for this moral debacle! *Not all* preachers! A large percentage—some place it as high as 50%—still follow the "Old Morality" that sex is evil. Of course *that* is a perverted PAGAN teaching. But the *trend* is rapidly toward the "New Morality." Every year the percentage of ministers embracing this licentious course becomes larger!

GOD Pins the Guilt

God has given a very serious responsibility and charge to His ministers! But of course *these are not HIS ministers!* God has charged us who are *His* ministers: "CRY ALOUD, *spare not, lift up thy voice like a trumpet, and show my people their transgression!"*

Through the Apostle Paul, Christ commands His ministers: "I charge thee therefore before God, and the Lord Jesus Christ, who shall JUDGE the quick and the dead at his appearing and his kingdom: PREACH THE WORD; be instant [keep at it] in season, out of season; REPROVE, REBUKE, EXHORT with all long suffering [patience] and doctrine. For the time will come when they will not endure sound doctrine; but after their own lusts shall they heap to themselves teachers, [the people] having itching ears; and they shall turn away their ears from the truth, and shall be turned unto fables" (II Tim. 4:1-4).

That time has come. People are filled with LUST. They heap to themselves, in the pulpits of churches, men whom GOD HAS NOT CALLED, who are willing to "tickle the people's ears" by approving *SIN*—adopting the "New Morality"— teaching that SIN is righteousness!

God has called HIS ministers to thunder forth HIS TRUTH without fear or favor—to show His people THEIR SINS in great POWER! *The* WORLD TOMORROW is GOD's broadcast —around the world. It THUNDERS FORTH God's TRUTH! *The* PLAIN TRUTH is GOD's magazine. It makes HIS TRUTH dynamically *PLAIN*. It never compromises with SIN. I am going to be persecuted for writing and publishing this book—

but HUNDREDS OF THOUSANDS WILL READ IT—and they shall have been WARNED, regardless of criticism, false accusation, character-assassination, falsely imputed ulterior motives!

GOD ALMIGHTY NEVER CALLED THESE "NEW MORALITY" MINISTERS! They come before their congregations in Christ's name, but THEY SPEAK *LIES* to deceive the people FOR FINANCIAL GAIN!

LISTEN to God's stinging indictment against them:

"WOE be unto *the pastors* that destroy and scatter the sheep of my pasture! saith the LORD" (Jer. 23:1).

Notice that carefully! God does not say *"My* pastors" —they are *not* HIS ministers. But He does say that the people of their congregations are HIS people! Not converted people—but His racial, national people, the descendants of ancient ISRAEL—who have LOST their identity and become the "LOST sheep of the House of Israel." (If you have not read the booklet, *The United States and the British Commonwealth in Prophecy*, remember it is FREE—write for your copy *now!*)

Continue: "Thus saith the LORD God of Israel against *the pastors* that feed MY people: . . . For the land is *full of adulterers*" (verse 10). Yes, the "social revolution" is approving adultery, fornication, homosexuality. The pastors are *absorbing* the world's degeneration and *approving it!* And this is actually bringing a CURSE on the very LAND! *Continue:* ". . . for because of THE CURSE [see marginal reference] the land mourneth"—or, more plainly from the RSV reading: "For the land is full of adulterers; because of the curse the land mourns, and the pastures of the wilderness are dried up."

Continue, verse 11: "For both prophet and priest are profane; yea, in my house [the churches] have I found their wickedness, saith the LORD. Wherefore *their way* [contrary to GOD'S WAY] shall be unto them as *slippery* ways in the darkness: they shall be driven on, and fall therein: for I will bring evil upon them . . . ."

The theologians will be PUNISHED—in God's own time.

What they sow, deceiving the people, they shall reap!

Shocking Homosexuality in the Ministry

These ministers of Satan (see II Cor. 11:13-15) commit adultery and walk in lies —"they strengthen also the hands of evildoers, that none doth return from his wickedness: *they are all of them unto me* AS SODOM ..."! (Jer. 23:14). The Sodomites were DESTROYED for homosexuality, the most repugnant and nauseating of sex SINS! Yet today's "New Morality" clergy are approving it! Many are participating in it!

Listen to reports PROVING IT!

Here is a London newspaper report: "The archbishop of Canterbury, Dr. Geoffrey Fisher, tonight spoke in the House of Lords in support of a change in British law *to make homosexual acts* between consenting adults in private *no longer a criminal offense.* The Archbishop said *the right to decide one's own moral code* and obey it, even to a man's hurt, was a 'fundamental *right of man* given to him by God, and to be strictly respected by society and by the criminal code.' "

THAT FROM THE HEAD MINISTER OF THE CHURCH OF ENGLAND!

You doubt that many preachers, themselves, are homosexuals and adulterers? You just read, above, from the 23rd chapter of Jeremiah, that GOD says they are! Now read additional evidence!

A Congregationalist minister, Pastor Robert W. Wood, wrote a book, *Christ and the Homosexual.* A newspaper review of his book in a Pasadena paper said: "Mr. Wood seems . . . interested in proving that 'homosexuality is the creation of God (since God is the Creator of everything); and as such it is just as good as any other creation of God.' He says further that homosexual love"—HE MEANS *LUST*— "can be truly sacramental, or holy, in the eyes of God. He seriously discussed the desirability of *performing marriages between two persons of the same sex.*

"A homosexual, he says, *'can be a successful clergyman.'* There is no hint that a spiritual leader ought to be more mature than that. Mr. Wood maintains that *the rate of homosexuality in the clergy is higher than in most other professions.* The author even suggests that this perversion may one day be useful in solving the problem of over-population." (It certainly did solve the "over-population" of Sodom and Gomorrah!!!) "He says that homosexuality is not a sin, and that under certain conditions in certain ways it may even be morally right."

I have much, *much* more evidence—*many* more such reports. Theological seminaries—several of them—are known to have, as students being trained to become pastors of churches, *a high percentage of homosexuals.* I have reports that homosexuals are ORGANIZED—and that there is a determined campaign to seek out, seduce, and "convert" to this loathsome perversion CHILD "converts."

One juvenile court chief counsellor testified 50 children came before him within six months, for involvement with adult homosexuals. A reliable magazine article reported that a high portion of the men in the State Department at Washington, D.C., are homosexuals!

Some men who profess to be the ministers of Jesus Christ argue that the Bible nowhere condemns fornication or homosexuality (sodomy). The Bible repeatedly, again and again, in strongest language CONDEMNS these things. The minister who says it doesn't is lying, and he *is* a *liar!* It would more than fill the remainder of this chapter to enumerate all such passages. But hear just one:

"BE NOT DECEIVED: *neither fornicators,* nor idolaters, nor adulterers, *nor effeminate,* nor *abusers of themselves with mankind* [homosexuals] . . . shall inherit the Kingdom of God" (I Cor. 6:9-10). However, if one REPENTS, turns *from* such perversion or unfaithfulness, and accepts the payment CHRIST made for his sin, he may be forgiven.

Verse 11 says: "And such were some of you: *but ye are washed,* but ye are sanctified, but ye are justified in the name of the Lord Jesus, and by the Spirit of our God."

God Holds Ministers Guilty

Now listen further to GOD's indictment in Jeremiah 23:

"Thus saith the LORD of hosts, Hearken not unto the words of *the* prophets [preachers] that prophesy [preach] unto you: *they make you vain:* they speak a vision of their own heart, and *not* out of the mouth of the ETERNAL. They say still unto them that despise me, The LORD hath said, Ye shall have peace; and they say unto every one that walketh after the imagination [reasoning] of his own heart, No evil shall come upon you" (verses 16-17).

This is a PROPHECY! It is for OUR DAY, *now!* It is speaking of the clergy of the United States and the British Commonwealth of Nations—the actual people descended from the ancient House of ISRAEL! This Message was not preached to them by Jeremiah—for they had been removed from their land of Samaria in captivity more than a hundred years before Jeremiah wrote! This writing was not taken to them or preserved by them—but was preserved by the House of JUDAH.

Do you realize that the CHURCH of God of the New Testament is actually *built* upon the very FOUNDATION of the PROPHETS of the Old Testament, as well as Christ and the Apostles of the New Testament? Notice, Ephesians 2:20, the Church is "built upon the foundation of the apostles *and prophets*, Jesus Christ himself being the chief corner stone."

Now notice—grasp clearly—what God says of today's clergy in Britain and America: The people, as a whole, have turned from God—He says they "despise me." Our lands are full of adulterers.

And does the clergy cry out against these sins?

No, God sees a HORRIBLE THING—the *pastors themselves commit adultery* and walk in lies (verse 14)—they "strengthen also the hands of evildoers, that none doth return from his wickedness"—that is, they tell the people that their sins are right—holy and good. They encourage the SINS, so that their people DO NOT REPENT and turn *from* sin. They preach a *false* Jesus (see II Cor. 11:4) whom they deceive people into believing saves people IN their sins, instead of *from* their sins!

They tell the people NO HARM—NO PUNISHMENT, but only "peace," will come from their adultery, fornication and sodomy (verse 17). In other words, as Paul wrote Timothy, quoted above, the time *has* come when the people will not endure God's TRUTH. They "heap to themselves teachers"— they employ pastors—that will tickle their ears with lies, vanity, and fables instead of God's TRUTH. The people are REBELLIOUS against God and His LAW. They are "a rebellious people, lying children, children that *will not hear the law of the LORD*: which say to the seers, 'See not'; and to the prophets [preachers], 'Preach not unto us right things, speak unto us smooth things, preach deceits' " (Isa. 30:9-10).

Clergy Obey Men—Not God

In other words, the congregations say: "If you don't preach the lies we *want* to hear, we'll fire you and hire a pastor who will preach what we want to hear."

Continue Isaiah's prophecy: "Get you out of *the way*, turn aside from the path . . ."—that is, the people say to their pastors, "Get out of GOD'S WAY—tell us that SIN is good—proclaim a 'New Morality.' "

Now, complete the prophecy (Moffatt translation): ". . . trouble us no more with talk of Israel's Majesty! Well, here is the reply of Israel's Majesty [Christ]: Since you despise my warning and trust in wile and guile, and lean on *your own policy*"—the perverted morality—"this guilt of yours shall split you, like a high wall bulging to break, till swiftly, suddenly, down it crashes—as a man smashes a pitcher in pieces, so wantonly that not a shred remains" (Isa. 30:11-14).

I knew a certain minister of a large church in Eugene,

Oregon. A life-long friend said to him: "You *know* that God's definition of SIN is the transgression of God's LAW. Why don't you preach the TRUTH to your congregation?"

And he replied, "Why, Maude, *I wouldn't dare!* Some of the important men of our city sit in front pews in my church. Their contributions pay my salary. I have to preach what they want to hear, or be fired! And I have a wife and family to support."

About that same time—just prior to the beginning of *The* WORLD TOMORROW broadcast and the publishing of *The* PLAIN TRUTH—more than 30 years ago—I had been preaching on salary. Those who controlled the church treasury demanded I preach contrary to GOD'S WORD. Immediately I rejected the salary. I learned that if I worked for MEN, I would have to preach what MEN demand. But I was working for GOD. And from that moment I pledged that I would look to GOD ALONE, *in faith*, for all financial support. And God has demonstrated by more than 30 years' experience, that HE WILL PROVIDE FOR HIS OWN WORK! I have never been muzzled! This TRUTH now goes forth, in this book, to hundreds of thousands—whether readers like it or not—whether this world's (Satan's) clergy persecute or not!

To conclude the prophecy of Jeremiah 23: God says: "Behold, a whirlwind of the ETERNAL is gone forth IN FURY [the seven last plagues of Revelation 15], even a grievous whirlwind: it shall fall grievously upon the head of the wicked. The ANGER of the ETERNAL will not return, until He have executed . . . *in the latter days* ye shall consider it perfectly" (verses 19-20).

NOTE IT! This is a prophecy to be considered *in the latter days*—this 20th century—*NOW!*

Read God's stinging REBUKE against today's false clergy in Ezekiel 34. Read it in Ezekiel 20. Read God's pronouncement of their fate, now SOON to come, in Jeremiah 25:34-38!

Speaking of this latter half of the 20th century in prophecy, God says: "In those days, and in that time, saith the ETERNAL . . . My people hath been lost sheep: THEIR

SHEPHERDS [clergy] *have caused them to go astray!"* (Jer. 50:4, 6.)

WHERE does Almighty GOD pin the GUILT for this moral collapse? He pins it *squarely on the world's clergy*—the theologians—the priests—the rectors—the ministers—the preachers! They, who *ought* to be society's moral LEADERS, have forsaken the Creator God and have become society's FOLLOWERS!

WHY has God "opened the DOOR" of radio and the printing press—reaching a MASS AUDIENCE of nearly 25 million people *every week, on every inhabited continent* AROUND THE WORLD? Read it, in Revelation 3:8. Though we started *the smallest* of any ministry—though we had no financial backing—though we ourselves had *but little strength*— Christ OPENED THE GIGANTIC DOOR of radio and the printing press, to thunder HIS MESSAGE—*BECAUSE* WE HAVE KEPT HIS WORD *FAITHFULLY!* Even under every persecution and opposition from men, we have been preserved and prospered!

They Hate GOD'S LAW!

WHY do these pastors preach the fables—the deceits— the flatteries—instead of GOD'S TRUTH? Because human nature is HOSTILE to GOD (Rom. 8:7). Because THE PEOPLE are in REBELLION against obedience to GOD'S LAW (same verse). And because the preachers have been willing to FEED THEMSELVES—with salaries—instead of feeding the flock with TRUTH (Ezek. 34:2—*read it!*).

Remember, as pointed out earlier, the SUBTLE manner in which so many ministers today are injecting this so-called New Morality into a so-called Christianity. They *profess* to uphold a high standard of morals—but they "allow for the *exceptional* case." They put emphasis on the *compassion* of Jesus—and then they *twist* and *pervert* His *true compassion* by having "compassion" on the "exceptional" case of one who is the "victim" of homosexuality, or of a "problem" of sex.

In other words, they have "COMPASSION" on the sinner

who is committing SIN and in "compassion" they *approve* his *continuance in SIN!!!*

They say: "Jesus had compassion on the woman taken in adultery. He dealt with her UNDERSTANDINGLY, with LOVE, and MERCY and COMPASSION." They make it sound very sentimental—very "righteous." BUT THEY NEGLECT TO SAY THAT JESUS ALSO SAID TO THE WOMAN: "GO, AND *SIN NO MORE!*" (John 8:11.) They neglect to preach that Jesus said: "I tell you, Nay: but, except ye REPENT, ye shall all likewise perish." (Luke 13:3—and He repeated it in verse 5!) If this woman had not REPENTED, Jesus would have had no compassion with rebellion.

They NEGLECT to repeat what Jesus said about sex SINS: "Ye have heard that it was said by them of old time, Thou shalt not commit adultery: but I say unto you, that whosoever looketh on a woman to lust after her hath committed adultery with her already in his heart." And, *"Think not* that I am come to destroy the law, or the prophets: I am not come to destroy, but to fulfill [perform—obey]. For verily I say unto you, Till heaven and earth pass, one jot or one tittle shall in no wise pass from the law, till all be fulfilled" (Mat. 5:27-28 and 17-18).

Now notice this subtle, clever, cunning deception of Satan at work. Notice how words like "love," "compassion," "mercy," are used to TWIST God's truth and His WORD, into representing that sex SINS should be treated with "love" and "compassion." Notice how GOD'S LAW is rejected as evil —and how SIN is represented as GOOD to be condoned!

The Deceptive Twist

I have a book, by a minister who proclaims this "New Morality" and yet writes a book titled *No New Morality*, authored by Douglas Rhymes, Canon of Southwark Cathedral in England.

In the flap of the cover, it is stated about this book: "What is the 'new' morality? Is it new? Is it just about sex?

Is extramarital sexual intercourse [adultery] always wrong?

"These subjects are now under hot debate. Here *one of the leading exponents* of the mis-titled 'new' morality discusses the nature of *this way of thinking*, and its application to people's sexual difficulties. . . . the author refused to accept that Christian morality must be based on rules. [He means, on GOD'S LAW, which he rejects as a basis for Christian morality!!!]

"He believes it must be rooted in love, not in law."

In the book itself, the author says: "One group after another has questioned *the whole foundation* upon which morality is based—at first from outside the Church, with the questionings of writers, dramatists, psychologists, existentialist thinkers—and now from within the Church itself.

"From Cambridge Harry Williams and Donald McKinnon questioned *the very foundation* on which traditional morality has been built." (Emphasis added.)

This would lead most to assume that this FOUNDATION for "traditional Christian morality" is the BIBLE—and the TEN COMMANDMENTS. But, of course, as we have seen, that is not true. That foundation was pagan dualism, *contrary* to God's Word and His Law! Yet notice how that PAGAN foundation is made to appear to be GOD'S LAW.

First, he speaks of the foundation of *"traditional* Christian morality." This was neither Christian nor Biblical, but PAGAN. And it, of course, produced evil results. But, assuming this PAGAN concept to have been GOD'S LAW, he uses this twisted argument to condemn God's Law!

Next he quotes a few human "authorities": "Paul Tillich speaks of the moral law too intolerable to be borne. The Bishop of Woolwich criticizes the idea of moral laws which 'come down direct from heaven and are eternally valid for human conduct. . . .' "

Notice that play on words! It is *assumed* that this PAGAN sex dogma is the "moral laws which come down from heaven." Then he condemns, NOT the paganism which bore the evil fruit, but GOD'S LAW, which *he* labels "pagan."

Continue: "The group of Quakers who drew up the document, *Towards a Quaker View of Sex,* say 'we reject almost completely the traditional approach of the organized Church'"—meaning Roman Catholic and her Protestant daughters—" 'to morality. . . .' " Again, what they see as EVIL is *NOT* the Law of God, but paganism falsely cloaked as "Christianity."

Here again, what is objected to is HUMAN DEVISED codes, falsely represented to be THE LAW OF GOD—and thus he condemns God!

He says: "In fact, St. Paul found it quite impossible to live by the law." Now I am sure this clergyman should know better than that!

Paul Observed Mosaic Law

When Paul came to Jerusalem the Apostle James told him the Jews there had been falsely informed that Paul taught converted Jews to forsake Moses' law. To correct that, Paul took four men who had taken a Nazarite vow, as provided in Numbers 6:21. This vow was not commanded or obligatory, but might be taken voluntarily. The period of this vow was just ending for these four men, at which time they were to shave their heads.

Paul himself had, earlier, observed this Mosaic ordinance (Acts 18:18). And now, in order to demonstrate to Jerusalem Jews that the rumors were false, and that Paul *did follow Mosaic ordinances,* Paul took these four men, paid their expenses, and purified himself according to Mosaic directions with them—to show that HE KEPT THE LAW, even beyond what was directly commanded! See Acts 21:17-26. Also Acts 26:22.

This churchman joins so many others in arguing for "the exceptional case." He, like them, uses the argument of showing "love" and "compassion" and "having mercy" on those unrepentant, willingly in the grip of habitual SIN, in a manner to *approve* that sin. This is plain permissiveness!

Luther rebelled because the Catholic Church was selling indulgences for money: that is, granting *advance permission* for people deliberately to commit SIN! That is precisely what many modern clergymen are doing today. They simply use different terminology. They merely call it by another name.

In his appendix, on "The predicament of the homosexual," this Church of England canon argues for "compassion, understanding and concern" to APPROVE this revolting, soul-damning perversion.

He says: "Homosexuals are a minority group, but a considerable one (it has been estimated at about 10% of the nation), and they are a persecuted minority." Then he says the church should concern itself with the problems of persecuted minorities. "Should not the Church, for example make an urgent move to insist that Parliament implement the recommendations of the Wolfenden Report . . . ?"

He continues: "Ought we not to be working towards the kind of society in which we can learn to accept the homosexual so that he does not have to hide behind a mask?"

Now what kind of society would that be? What about the habitual criminal? Should not such a society release such from prison, encourage them to prey on society, stealing, robbing, slugging, murdering? Where would such ANTI-Christ policies lead?

Surely the time *has* come when the people will not endure sound doctrine—when they are heaping to themselves pastors who willingly turn their BACK TO THE BIBLE, and turn the people to fables, preaching the soft and smooth things— preaching DECEITS!

Let me tell you one thing—ON THE AUTHORITY OF JESUS CHRIST! Almighty GOD the Father will not compromise the millionth part of an inch on HIS LAW! His law does not BEND to fit our lusts. Jesus Christ never did and never will compromise the millionth part of an inch with God's LAW.

IF Christ had been willing to do that, He never would

have given His life for us! Instead of PAYING the FULL PENALTY of our transgressions FOR us, He would have merely stretched the Law to fit our wrong desires.

Jesus Christ gave HIS OWN LIFE to pay for our sins, *rather than CONDONE sin!*

Sin has caused every wail of human woe—every war—every bit of suffering and unhappiness!

God HATES sin!

His hatred of SIN proves His LOVE for the sinner! Sin is humanity's ENEMY! Christ came to SAVE US *from* sin—not to encourage sin. And "Sin *IS* the transgression of the law!" (I John 3:4.)

What Homosexuality Is

The way to show LOVE for the homosexual who is wallowing in a moral cesspool is to get him *out* of the cesspool—not to *approve* what he is doing. *"This* is the LOVE *of God,* that we KEEP his commandments: and his commandments are *NOT* grievous!" (I John 5:3.)

Homosexuals are not *born*—they are MADE! Homosexuality is a perversion of the MIND. It is a psychic and mental and spiritual DISEASE. Once "hooked" with it, true sex love for a wife or husband becomes impossible UNTIL the mind is *changed*—purified—straightened out!

A number of such men have come to me for counsel. How have I treated them?

That depends on *their attitude!* If they repent, acknowledge their transgression, will turn to God for HELP in being *freed*, accepting the blood of Christ to justify their filthy, revolting, guilty PAST, and really FLEE from it, I have shown them every consideration, given every help, as long as they remain truly repentant and flee *from* their sin.

But homosexuals, fornicators, adulterers, who have *not* repented, but continued wilfully in their sin—and, usually, even lied to me about it—have been dealt with in precisely the same way GOD deals with all such! "GOD HEARETH NOT

SINNERS" (John 9:31; Zech. 7:13); "Behold, the ETERNAL'S hand is not shortened that it cannot save; neither his ear heavy, that it *cannot* hear: *but your iniquities* have separated between you and your God, and *your sins* have hid his face from you, that HE WILL NOT HEAR!" (Isa. 59:1-2.)

Not long ago a 5-column-wide headline screamed across the top of the page of the London *Sunday Express:* "Commandments CAN be broken, vicar tells his parish." The news report said: "A VICAR has told his congregation that it is often right to break the Commandments—and sometimes it could be the 'height of wickedness' to keep them. . . . he calls them 'the Terrible Ten' " which "should not be regarded as absolute standards. . . . And in keeping the 'law of love' it would often be right to break the Commandments."

This man claims to be a minister of Jesus Christ—and therefore he professes to "know the Lord." WHAT DOES CHRIST SAY TO HIM? Jesus Christ calls him *A LIAR!* "He that saith, 'I know him,' and keepeth not his commandments, IS *A LIAR*, and the truth is not in him" (I John 2:4).

He talks of LOVE—meaning license to SIN! CHRIST says: "For *this* is the LOVE of GOD, that we keep His commandments." This vicar calls them the "Terrible Ten." Jesus says: "Whosoever therefore shall break one of these least commandments, and shall teach men so, he shall be called the least in the kingdom of heaven" (Mat. 5:19). And he did *not say* such will *be in* the Kingdom of God—DEFINITELY THEY SHALL NOT! But by those who shall be there, they will be called with contempt *"the least"*—the lowest—the most despicable—of the very dregs of degenerate humanity!

WHERE DOES GOD ALMIGHTY PIN THE *GUILT* for this moral debacle? He is going to mete out divine PUNISHMENT on these hypocrites who deliberately lead His people into the ways that bring on them unhappiness, suffering and death!

Today church attendance is at an all-time HIGH—but

so, also, is CRIME; and moral degeneracy is at an all-time LOW. This spells out just one thing—the CLERGY of this world is MISleading the PEOPLE!

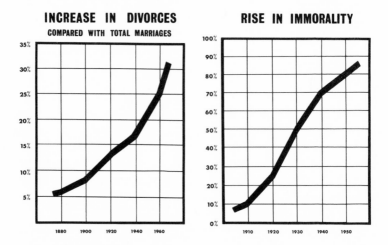

INCREASE IN DIVORCES
COMPARED WITH TOTAL MARRIAGES

RISE IN IMMORALITY

Today about one-third of all marriages end in divorce. This frightening trend, too often callously glossed over by clergy, psychiatrists, educators and scientists, has led to a tremendous rise in juvenile crime and immorality.

These men have joined the psychiatrists, the doctors, the educators, the scientists, in REJECTING the true FOUNDATION of all true KNOWLEDGE. In their smug complacency and intellectual vanity, they fancy they are the wise—the scholarly—the men of great intellect.

HEAR what GOD says of them!

God Brands Clergy GUILTY!

God says: "Professing themselves to be wise, they became fools. . . . Wherefore God also gave them up to uncleanness through the lusts of their own hearts, to dishonor their own bodies between themselves: who changed the truth of God into a lie. . . ."

"For this cause God gave them up unto vile affections:

for even their women did change the natural use into that which is against nature: and likewise also the men, leaving the natural use of the woman, burned in their lust one toward another; men with men working that which is unseemly, and receiving in themselves *that recompense of their error* which was meet.

"And even as they *did not like to retain God in their knowledge,* God gave them over to a reprobate mind, to do those things which are not proper; *being filled with* all unrighteousness, *fornication . . ."* (Rom. 1:22-29).

Does this mean that God teaches repression—or even nonuse except for reproduction? BY NO MEANS! But He teaches *right use for right purposes!*

This Biblical passage is both historic and prophetic. Much of prophecy is dual. It is a former application, which is merely the type and forerunner of that which is prophesied FOR OUR TIME, NOW.

This passage speaks literally of those pagan philosophers whom the Gentile-born Christians at Rome erroneously "looked up to" as the great of the world. They had set the system of education. It was their philosophy which was adopted by the great false Church that was to spring up from Rome. Socrates was the original exponent of these pagan philosophies. Yet, revolting though it be to mention, Socrates publicly masturbated for all to see! *Such* are the minds which set the philosophic standards to TODAY'S HIGHER EDUCATION!

Yet those perverted pagan philosophers were only the TYPE of the clergy of TODAY. They have absorbed the false and unfounded philosophies of those Gentile perverts. They profess to be ministers of Jesus Christ—yet they reject His teaching, and adopt the pagan perversions palming them off as "Christian."

They, too, have not liked "to retain God *in their knowledge.*" In the schools and colleges and universities in which they were "educated" God's knowledge had been rejected. In this world's theological seminaries, *God's knowledge is rejected.* Seminary students are taught little from the Bible. They study from textbooks written by *men*, contrary to the Bible!

I'm aware that most of my readers have never realized this! It is time you get your eyes opened to THE FACTS!

Now notice—these clergymen defending adultery, fornication, homosexuality—THEY ARE BRANDED AS GUILTY THEMSELVES in this passage in Romans 1! No wonder they attempt to justify it!

As Jude said, they are "ungodly men, turning the GRACE of our God into lasciviousness"—LICENSE to commit SIN— calling God's holy Law "The Terrible Ten!"

The GUILT has been pinned on the world's false and counterfeit clergy! God pins it squarely where it belongs!

"For," says God through Paul, "such are *false apostles,* deceitful workers, transforming themselves into the apostles of Christ. And no marvel; for SATAN HIMSELF is transformed into an angel of light. Therefore it is no great thing if *HIS MINISTERS* [Satan's] also be transformed as the ministers of righteousness; WHOSE END SHALL BE ACCORDING TO THEIR WORKS!"

As they sow, SO SHALL THEY REAP!

CHAPTER 8

The Sacred *Meaning* of Sex

Now you have the FACTS—as they existed from pagan times—as they continued through medieval "Christian" repression—as they are fast developing into the "New Morality" today.

Now you know the problem. And a sickening, tragic problem it is! It means—unless it is solved, *and soon*—the destruction of human society!

It will be solved!

The Costly Teacher

But the world will not do the solving. The world's "experts" and leaders—its theologians, its psychologists, its scientists, its doctors and its politicians—do not know THE WAY to solve it. They do not know THE WAY to peace—to human happiness—to abundant well-being!

History has been *written!* The more human leaders have tampered with moral codes, social regulations, forms of government, international movements for peace, the more they have plunged the world into wars and violence, the more they have increased human misery, and the farther they have driven humanity from mankind's true destiny.

Through six thousand long years the lesson *has been*

painfully written by cruel experience. But the LESSON of that most *costly* teacher—experience—*has not been learned!*

The problem *will be solved*—and very SOON!

In spite of man's efforts, the Almighty Creator will step in and solve it for us! God Almighty is now just about to *reveal* Himself to an astounded world that has lost all true knowledge of Him and His right ways. The ETERNAL will very soon *force* a rebellious humanity to enjoy peace, happiness, and universal prosperity! Jesus Christ is soon to return to this earth in all the supreme POWER, and GLORY of the Great GOD, to RULE mankind with divine POWER and FORCE—to bring us PEACE!

But *you* do not need to suffer on until you are *whipped* into receiving the blessings that are the rightful heritage of man. The WAY to happy living has never been inaccessible. God always has made it available. But mankind always has insisted in reaching out to partake of the fruits of the wrong tree!

The Poison in Both Moralities

Let's pin-point the pivotal CAUSE of the trouble. Then the SOLUTION will become clear.

What have we had? The "Old Morality" was, simply, a false *attitude* combined with sex *ignorance*. The "New Morality," just as simply, is an even more poisonous *attitude*, mixed with physical sex *knowledge*.

I have written, in earlier chapters, of *all this knowledge today*—and still NO HAPPINESS! WHY? This newly released flood of *knowledge* of the physical details of sex may not necessarily be false. Yet I have said it is false and soul-damaging, *because only half complete!* Now let me explain that point clearly.

WHY is the physical knowledge alone so poisonous?

Man is not a physical being *merely*, but a being with a spiritual attribute. And of the whole man, the MIND, with its spiritual aspect and potential, is the *all-important* factor. The body is merely the mechanism, or the vehicle, that the mind directs and uses. But how is mind connected with sex?

Sex anatomy and sexual functioning is connected directly with the mind through the system of nerves. There can be no use of sex apart from the mind. Every bodily action is directed, consciously or subconsciously, by the mind. And so it is, that ATTITUDE is an *all-important* factor of sex, and directly associated with its every function.

So there are TWO phases of any use of sex—the one, of first importance, the mental-spiritual phase; the other, physical.

Thus, as in almost every activity of life, ATTITUDE is of prime importance. Direction of mind!

Now let's UNDERSTAND what is so fatally WRONG with all this modern knowledge of sex. In both the "Old Morality" and the "New Morality" of this world's teachings and customs, IGNORANCE OF THE CREATOR'S INTENDED PURPOSES, and dissemination of diabolically evil *moral* teachings has poisoned human minds, and injected damage-causing ATTITUDES.

A mixture of half good food and half potassium cyanide will kill you as surely as the dose of potassium cyanide alone!

Not all of the purely *physical* knowledge published in this modern onslaught of sex books has been correct, by any means. But even if the dissemination of the physical details, of itself, were completely true, it is COMBINED, in every case —whether *in* such a book or from other sources—with a false and poisonous ATTITUDE OF MIND concerning sex PURPOSES and uses!

It thus becomes DEADLY MORAL AND SPIRITUAL POISON. And today's world is gulping down the fatal dosage!

The dictionary definition of poison is illuminating at this point. Here is Webster's: "Poison: Any agent which, introduced into an organism, may chemically produce an injurious or deadly effect. 2. That which taints or destroys moral purity, character, or the public welfare."

How descriptive! The false and evil concept of the PUR-

POSES of sex, both of the pagan dualism *and* the "New Morality," criminally *tainted and destroyed moral purity, character, and the public welfare!*

Now glance into the British Oxford Dictionary: "Poison: Substance that when introduced into or absorbed by a living organism destroys life or injures health."

Even if the pre-World War I society had been possessed of the *physical* knowledge of sex functions, the false *concept* being absorbed by the living *mental* organism would have destroyed happiness. But when this psychological poison was combined with biological ignorance, the effect was doubly disastrous.

Today, knowledge of physical details is abundantly available. Yet even among books disseminating biological information, I have not found a single volume I would want to recommend to our radio listeners and PLAIN TRUTH readers. And when physical information is combined with a poisonous mental attitude, it emphatically "destroys moral purity, character, and public welfare."

So WHERE NEXT?

So, we have the *facts!* Both past and present! But WHERE *NOW?*

A New York clergyman celebrity says he is not worried. He thinks we have hit bottom now, and there is no way to go but *up!* Perhaps he believes that when a man leaps over a thousand-foot-high precipice and hits bottom, that he goes immediately *up*—to heaven? Some *might* think he would go in the opposite direction!

But humanity has not yet quite hit bottom—it is on the downward plunge! And to quip that it automatically will propel itself back UP is just about the kind of "leadership" God Almighty attributes to this day's clergy!

We *can* find the way up out of the muck and mire of degradation here and now—if we are willing!

WHERE, then, for the SOLUTION?

WHERE, for the knowledge of RIGHT PURPOSES and USES?

WHERE, for the Supreme AUTHORITY for morals—WHERE for the right *attitude?*

In no field is the fact more positively demonstrated that the WORD OF GOD is the FOUNDATION OF KNOWLEDGE than in this area of sex!

HOW, and *from where*, and *when*, did sex originate? And WHY?

You shall see that there was great PURPOSE—great MEANING behind the origin of sex. There was intelligence, design, wisdom, in its planning. It was CREATED by the All-intelligent, All-powerful, All-HOLY Creator!

The answers are found in the Bible. And the place to begin is at THE BEGINNING!

Here is the beginning:

"In the beginning God created the heaven and the earth" (Gen. 1:1).

WHO—WHAT Is God?

I have quoted that passage in the English language. But when God inspired Moses to write it, originally, it was written in the Hebrew language. What I quoted is a translation from the Hebrew. And in the Hebrew, the word—or the NAME—translated into the English name, "God," was "ELOHIM." That is a uniplural noun. It is uniplural, like such words as *group, church, crowd, family,* or *organization.*

Take, for example, the word *church.* You will read, in I Corinthians 12:20, that the *Church* is only ONE CHURCH— the "one body" yet composed of "*many members.*" Even though it takes *many persons* to constitute the Church, it is not many churches—it is only the ONE CHURCH!

A family is made up of more than one person, yet only the *one* family.

And so, incredible as it may seem to those who do not rightly and fully UNDERSTAND the Bible—and only an infinitesimal minority does—GOD is not merely one Person, but GOD is a FAMILY. God is a KINGDOM—the Supreme divine FAMILY which RULES the universe! The whole GOSPEL Jesus brought to mankind is, merely, the Good News of the KING-DOM OF GOD—and that Kingdom *is* God. It is a FAMILY—a RULING divine Family into which humans may be born!

It is vitally necessary that we UNDERSTAND this truth—*if* we are to understand the MEANING and PURPOSES of sex!

There is only the ONE GOD! Because of false teaching nearly all of us have been reared from childhood to *assume* that GOD is *one individual Person*. It *is* true that each Person in the God FAMILY is an individual divine Person.

But "ELOHIM" is the divine FAMILY—only ONE family, but more than one divine Person. Jesus Christ spoke of His divine father as GOD. Jesus said He was the Son of GOD (as well as the Son of *man*). Jesus is called GOD in Hebrews 1:8 and elsewhere. All the holy angels are commanded to worship Jesus (Heb. 1:6; Ps. 97:7, 1)—and none but GOD may be worshipped!

So the Eternal FATHER is a Person, and is GOD. Jesus Christ is a different *Person*—and is GOD. They are two separate and individual Persons (Rev. 4:2; 5:1, 6-7). The Father is Supreme HEAD *of* the God Family—the Lawgiver. Christ is the WORD—the divine Spokesman.

But when Jesus was begotten within His human mother Mary, He was not, as all other men, begotten of a human father, but of GOD, by the agency and power of God's Spirit. He became the Son of God. He called God His FATHER. He prayed to His Father. So we have a *Father-and-Son* relationship. It is a FAMILY relationship!

But it goes further. Humans, in the *likeness* of God, may receive the gift of God's HOLY SPIRIT (Acts 2:38-39). Those thus converted become the begotten SONS of God—actually children of God (Rom. 8:14-17). Those thus *be-*

gotten of God are baptized into (that is, immersed into—
put into) God's CHURCH (I Cor. 12:13).

The CHURCH is the affianced BRIDE, to MARRY CHRIST
at His glorious return to earth (Eph. 5:25-27; Rev. 19:7).
So we have the Father-and-Son relationship; *and also the
Husband-and-Wife relationship!*

The CHURCH of God, now, is the begotten family of
God's children as yet unborn to spirit immortality. But, at
Christ's coming, when the begotten mortal *heirs* become the
BORN immortal *inheritors* of the GOD KINGDOM, *then* (and
not until) they shall enter into the KINGDOM OF GOD!

The KINGDOM of God, then, is merely the GOD FAMILY
as a RULING GOVERNMENT.

A KINGDOM is a government. God is CREATOR. God is
a FAMILY of Divine Persons. God *rules* His entire vast, limitless creation. GOD IS A KINGDOM!

Jesus preached one Gospel—one Message—the KING-
DOM OF GOD. The world rejected Him because it hated His
Message. The world appropriated His name, rejected His
Message, and proclaimed its false gospel—merely *about*
Christ, while rejecting His Message about the Kingdom of
God. That is why the world with its churches, wallowing
in the moral cesspools of confusion, *does not understand*
about either SEX *or* THE KINGDOM OF GOD!

Now let's UNDERSTAND! Genesis 1:1 In the beginning,
ELOHIM—*the* KINGDOM OF GOD—created the heaven and the
earth. . . . And ELOHIM—the God FAMILY—said, "Let us!"—
not "let ME!" Did you ever wonder why "GOD" said: "Let
US make man in OUR image"? God is a FAMILY—a ruling
KINGDOM.

Notice! Understand! We speak of the mineral kingdom
—the plant kingdom—the animal kingdom. Then there is
the *human* kingdom—for humans are *not* animals, and did
not descend from animals. There *is, truly,* a "missing link"!
But the "missing link" does not link man to the dumb animals. The "missing Link" is JESUS CHRIST—the true Link

between MAN and GOD—and through whom *we may be born into the GOD Kingdom!*

The First Man and Woman

Now consider the first man.

Adam was *not born:* he was *created,* suddenly, a full-grown adult man. His wife, Eve, was created, suddenly, a full-grown adult woman.

But we must not suppose that they were created with a full storehouse of knowledge implanted automatically in their minds. Perhaps you never thought of it in this light before—but consider:

How did we, the adults of today, come into possession of the knowledge we have? We were not born with it. A newborn babe knows nothing at birth. He is born with a mind capable of absorbing knowledge—a very little at first, but cumulatively additive. Humans must be taught—must learn. That is one of the *vital reasons* why marriage and family life are necessary for humans, unlike animals. Human babies start out very helpless. They need parental care, protection, teaching, training, and love. They need the warmth and companionship of family life.

What was the difference between Adam, at the instant of his creation, and a baby at the instant of birth?

Within a portion of a single day, AN ADULT MAN was miraculously created, *suddenly,* out of the dust of the ground! Adam was created with a MIND, *as yet unfilled with knowledge,* but capable of receiving knowledge, reasoning from it, acting on it.

And *it was a mind free from defect or degeneration!*

What, then, was the difference between Adam at the instant of his creation, and a baby at birth? He was started off as an adult—his mind had adult capabilities—but he was as much without knowledge, and therefore as helpless, as a newborn babe! He was created with adult *capacity,* but not with adult knowledge!

The *very first need* of the first man and the first woman was to be given essential KNOWLEDGE!

The Great Educator

And here enters a basic TRUTH long ago forgotten by the world!

The Almighty is *not only* the Creator! He is also the Great Educator!

The ETERNAL instructed the first man and woman. And He instructed them about SEX! The Great Designer, Creator, and Lawgiver revealed for mankind the basic FOUNDATION of ALL KNOWLEDGE! From the time of our first parents that foundation of necessary knowledge—not otherwise discoverable by man—has been accessible. It is available today in the Bible.

Yet our first parents rejected that knowledge, rebelled against God and His Law for man's welfare! And their children have been rejecting and rebelling ever since!

Now consider! The very last act of God's creation by work, was the creation of MAN. It was on the sixth day of that first week. Earlier that sixth day God had created cattle, the other mammals, the creeping animals. The creation of Adam was the very final act of the *work* of creation. That day, by God's order, ended at sunset.

As that day's sun set, and the seventh day of the week arrived, "God ended *His work* which He had made" (Gen. 2:2). Notice what God ended. *Not creating!* He ended *His work* which He had made. God did not end *creating!* Only His *work*—those things made by *work*. Now He created His Sabbath by *rest—not by work!* He blessed that day, and sanctified it—that is, set it apart from other days as HIS, for holy use and purpose. He established the Sabbath as the day for assembly and spiritual instruction.

Just as this first Sabbath came on, there was the man Adam—suddenly formed, shaped, created as an adult MAN —needing instruction! And there, beside him, was his Creator, ceasing from the *work* phase of creation! Did the Creator walk off, or vanish out of sight, leaving the man helpless with an empty mind, to stumble and bungle around aimlessly into trouble and harm?

The record shows that the Eternal God began *speaking* to the man—communicating knowledge—giving instruction.

It was on another Sabbath day, some 4,000 years later, that Jesus preached and instructed His followers. God is consistent—never changing (Mal. 3:6; Heb. 13:8). As that first Sabbath came on, God set the example—teaching the Gospel to the first man—giving that man, so far sinless, HIS FELLOWSHIP on His Sabbath day!

The historic record says: "And the ETERNAL God took the man, and put him into the garden of Eden to dress it and to keep it. And the ETERNAL God *commanded the man, saying . . .*" (Gen. 2:15-16). The ETERNAL immediately began *speaking to,* TEACHING, INSTRUCTING, the man.

Understand, now, two points: 1), *Which* Person of the God Kingdom spoke to man; and 2), the brevity of this record, as the very briefest SUMMARY.

WHO Is Yahweh?

It has been explained that in Genesis 1:1 the word for "God" in the Hebrew—the language in which it originally was written—is "ELOHIM"—meaning more than one Person forming one GOD—the *one* God FAMILY or the God KINGDOM—for GOD *is* a KINGDOM.

But now, when the historic account first begins to record the fact of God speaking to the man He created, a *new* and different Hebrew name is used. In Genesis 2:15 (and previous verses beginning verse 4) the English words "LORD God" (in the A.V.) are translated from the Hebrew *Yahweh Elohim.* The Hebrew Elohim already has been defined as a uniplural. It is the plural of *El,* or *Eloah,* meaning GOD, Strength, Might, Deity.

But *Yahweh* is a name meaning *the Everliving,* or the

ETERNAL. There is no one word in the English language that translates it exactly. God always NAMES things or people *what they are*. Actually *Yahweh* means the Self-Existent, Everliving, Eternally Living Creating One. Personally, in the English, I prefer the name "the ETERNAL" as most nearly translating the Hebrew name into modern idiom.

This is not the place for a long, technical, theological explanation. It would require a long chapter or more on the one subject. But in many places in the New Testament you may find quotations from the Old Testament referring to Jesus Christ, where, on turning to the Old Testament passage from which it is a citation, it speaks of Yahweh—translated as "the LORD" (in capital letters) in the King James Version.

In other words—and you may write in for a free article giving proof—the "LORD" (*Yahweh*) of the Old Testament, in nearly every case, is the Jesus Christ of the New—but as He was prior to His birth as a human of the virgin Mary.

In John 1:1-3, this same Personage is spoken of as *the Word*—the Greek word (the New Testament was originally written in Greek) is *Logos*, meaning Word, or Spokesman, or Revelatory Thought. Jesus the Christ (Messiah) is, and always has been, the individual Person of the GOD KINGDOM who is the Spokesman. But He said that He had spoken nothing of himself—the Father which sent Him had instructed and commanded Him what to say.

The FATHER of the God Family is the HEAD—the Lawgiver—the Creator. Yet He created everything *by* Jesus Christ (Eph. 3:9). Christ carried out the Father's orders, *by speaking*, as the Father had directed. In the creation, *"He spake*, and it was done" (Ps. 33:9; Gen. 1:3). The HOLY SPIRIT is the POWER that produced what He commanded (Gen. 1:2). Thus, in John 1:3: "All things were made by him"—by the Logos or Word, who is Jesus Christ (verse 14).

The specific *Person* of the Godhead who spoke to Adam,

then, was *Yahweh*—the ETERNAL (often falsely translated
Jehovah)—*who became Jesus Christ.*

Genesis Hits High Spots

The second important point I wish to stress at this
juncture is the fact that God has not seen fit to give us
the full details of all that was said and done in these first
few chapters of Genesis. The inspired record, in these chapters, reveals to us *only the briefest* SUMMARY.

Yet this abbreviated account does *summarize* what was
said and done. It does tell us that God, in and through the
Person of Christ, immediately began to teach, instruct and
command the first man and woman. It hits the high spots.
And even though the record omits the details, *it spans
the fields covered.* Much of the detailed instruction,
therefore, may be accurately filled in from other parts
of the Bible.

What fields, then, did God cover, in teaching our first
parents?

He gave them all essential *spiritual truth*—*He revealed*
to them the TRUE GOSPEL. And He also instructed them in
all necessary *physical* knowledge—including knowledge of
the marriage institution and of SEX.

The two trees in the Garden of Eden were SYMBOLS
representing vitally important truths. Actual literal trees
though they well may have been, they were symbolic, and
of tremendous significance.

Notice! One of many trees in the Garden was "the
TREE OF LIFE also in the midst of the garden" (Gen. 2:9).
This tree symbolized God's GIFT of the HOLY SPIRIT. Freely
God (in the Person of Christ) offered this supreme gift.
"The ETERNAL God commanded the man, saying, 'Of every
tree of the garden *thou mayest freely eat: but....*' "—
excluding the tree of *the knowledge of good and evil.*

In other words, God offered him FREELY His Holy Spirit!

" 'But,' " continued God, " ' of the tree of the knowledge

of good and evil, thou shalt not eat of it: for in the day that thou eatest thereof thou shalt surely die' " (verses 16-17).

Here, in briefest condensation, we find the teaching of the GOSPEL—that "the wages of SIN is death; but the GIFT of God is eternal life" (Rom. 6:23).

The Bible says *all* have sinned—and Adam sinned first of all (Rom. 3:23; 5:12). God could not have allowed Adam to sin, without first having taught Adam *what* sin *is*. The Bible definition of sin is: "Sin is the transgression of the law" (I John 3:4). And again, sin is the conscious, *knowing* transgression, for "to him *that knoweth* to do good, and doeth it not, to him it is sin" (Jas. 4:17). Adam *knew* about God's Law—for Adam SINNED! Therefore, definitely, God instructed Adam and Eve about His great basic spiritual Law, God's *WAY OF LIFE!* And that instruction was given *immediately*—of necessity *before they sinned!*

On the physical plane, God instructed them in regard to food (Gen. 1:29; 2:9).

And He also instructed them in regard to SEX.

Original Sex Education

So here, once again, we begin at the beginning:

"In the beginning God created the heaven and the earth. . . . And God said, 'Let us make man in our image, after our likeness' . . . So God created man in his own image, in the image of God created he him; *male and female* created He them. And God blessed them, and God said unto them, 'Be fruitful, and multiply, and replenish the earth' . . . And God saw everything that he had made, and, behold, it was VERY GOOD!" (Gen. 1:1, 26, 27-28, 31.)

GOD made mankind *male*, and *female*. God created SEX in humans. And GOD said it was *VERY GOOD—not* evil, shameful, degrading, or sinful *of itself*. Only *wrong use* becomes sinful.

God created sex for USE. Had He not intended sex to be

used, He would not have designed it. In the angel family God did not intend sex to be used—so He did not design angels to be male and female. Angels have no sex apparatus, perform no sex function, do not reproduce.

If the Creator designed human sex anatomy, and set in motion human sex stimuli and capacity for functioning, He did it for definite PURPOSES. And God most assuredly did not neglect His responsibility of *revealing* to that first man and woman the right PURPOSES this functioning within their bodies and minds was to serve. The Genesis account, I repeat, is the briefest SUMMARY. Yet the basic nature of the Creator's original instruction is plain. And the full details are brought out for mankind through other portions of the Bible.

Remember, before proceeding, God's over-all PURPOSE for humanity. God said: "Let us make man in OUR IMAGE." Man, as previously stated, was created physical, out of MATTER, in the likeness of God. But, as of now, man is merely the raw CLAY, out of which the Master Potter is— with man's yielding—forming and shaping the final IMAGE— the spiritual CHARACTER of God.

CREATION IS STILL GOING ON! The New Testament reveals that, once man has *surrendered*, repented of his rebellious past, and through Christ been reconciled into contact with GOD, he BECOMES A NEW CREATION (II Cor. 5:17).

This creation of right spiritual CHARACTER in us demanded free moral agency—that man must intelligently CHOOSE the right as opposed to the wrong—that he exercise free choice, develop self-discipline.

God designed and created SEX for right, wholesome, and holy functions. But, in the process of CHARACTER development, God *allows* man, if man rebels and so wills, to pollute, besmirch, befoul and pervert that which God intended to bring rich BLESSINGS. But *wrong* uses impose CURSES!

God made His TRUTH available. God instructed the

first man and woman. He *commanded* that they travel the RIGHT ROAD. But they, and their children universally ever after them, rebelled and chose to travel the WRONG road— the WAY that somehow *seems* better to a man, but which leads him into pain, suffering, sorrow and DEATH (Prov. 14:12; 16:25).

So God *did* instruct the first man and woman in the intended right, wholesome, happiness-producing, uplifting PURPOSES of SEX!

In the passage quoted above, God commanded sex to be used FOR REPRODUCTION! He said, "Be fruitful, and multiply, and replenish the earth" (Gen. 1:28).

SPECIAL Meaning of HUMAN Reproduction

So one of the purposes of sex, *in humans*, is *reproduction.*

But that is far, far, from the *only* purpose—as we shall see later!

Now reproduction, merely as such, is, of course, common to animals and plants, as well as humans.

BUT, IN HUMANS, REPRODUCTION HAS A SACRED AND GOD-PLANE MEANING NOT APPLICABLE TO ANY OTHER KIND OF LIFE!

We shall see, later, that the birth of a human baby differs in striking manner from that of animals. Animals are not born to become the very HEIRS of God!

In humans, there is TREMENDOUS, AWE-INSPIRING MEANING and significance to begettal and birth that is entirely nonexistent with animals or plants. And God intended—had man been willing to heed God's instruction—that the very KNOWLEDGE of these deep and wonderful MEANINGS should bring man dynamic JOY!

So far as the purely *physical* functions of the process are concerned, reproduction is the same in mammals as in humans. That is a mere PHYSICAL process. But there is deep, spiritually transcendent MEANING in human begettal, gestation, and birth that raises it to an altogether and incomparably higher plane than mere animal reproduction.

Human children are begotten through sex. And that very begettal, period of gestation, and birth of a human baby gives us the very PICTURE of the SALVATION made possible through Jesus Christ!

This is *another* reason Satan seeks to deceive his world regarding the purposes and right attitude toward sex!

By this very BLINDING of the world to GOD's *purposes* of SEX, Satan has HIDDEN from his world the true KNOWLEDGE about *GOD*—that God is actually a FAMILY—a divine KINGDOM into which we may be born! He has HIDDEN from the world the real TRUTH of SALVATION—what it *is*, where it *leads*, how we receive it!

This FALSE MORALITY—both the so-called old and the so-called new—has been a far more potent weapon for the destruction of humanity than has been realized!

Now see and UNDERSTAND how human reproduction pictures SALVATION!

All human life comes from a tiny egg, called an ovum, produced inside the human mother. This ovum is about the size of a pin point. Inside it, when highly magnified, can be seen a small nucleus. But this ovum has a very limited life, *of itself!* Some doctors believe it has a life of some 24 hours, unless fertilized by a male sperm.

But human life may be imparted *to* it by a sperm cell, produced in the body of the human father. This male sperm cell is the smallest cell in the human body—about one-fiftieth the size of the ovum. The male sperm—technically named a spermatozoon (plural, spermatozoa)—on entering an ovum, finds its way to and joins with the *nucleus*. This imparts *life—human* life—to the ovum.

But it is not yet a born human being. Human life has merely been *begotten*. For the first four months it is called an *embryo*. After that, until birth it is called a *foetus*. This human life starts very small—the size of a tiny pin point—and the sperm that generates it is the *smallest* cell in a human body!

Once begotten, it must *be fed* and nourished by physical food, through the mother. From this physical nourishment it must grow, and *grow* and GROW—until physically large enough to be born—after nine months. As it grows, the *physical* organs and characteristics gradually are formed. Soon a spinal column forms. Then, gradually, a body, a head, legs, arms. A heart forms and begins to beat. Other internal organs form. Finally hair begins to grow on the head, fingernails and toenails develop—facial features gradually shape up. By nine months the average normal foetus has grown to a weight of six to nine pounds, and is ready to be born.

The Type of Salvation!

Now notice carefully the astounding comparison!

Each adult human is, spiritually, an "egg" or "ovum." This spiritual "ovum" has a very limited life span, of itself— an average of 70 years. But spiritual, *divine immortal* life may be imparted *to* it by the entrance into it of the HOLY SPIRIT, which comes from the very Person of GOD the Father. This divine Spirit of GOD imparts to us also the *divine nature* (II Pet. 1:4). Heretofore we have had only human, or carnal nature.

As the human sperm cell is the very *smallest* of all human cells, even so, many newly begotten Christians start out with a very *small* measure of God's Holy Spirit. Many may still be, at first, about 99.44% carnal! Apparently those in the Church of God at Corinth were (I Cor. 3:1-3). The Apostle Paul said he still had to feed them on the spiritual *milk*—not yet adult spiritual "food."

Now, as the physical male sperm finds its way to, and unites with the *nucleus* in the ovum, so God's Spirit enters and combines with the human MIND! There is, as explained in an earlier chapter, a *spirit* IN *man*. This human spirit has combined with the brain to form human MIND. God's Spirit unites with, and witnesses with *our* spirit that we are, now, the children of GOD (Rom. 8:16). And God's Holy Spirit, now combined with our human spirit in our MIND, imparts to our mind power to comprehend SPIRITUAL KNOWLEDGE (I Cor. 2:11).

Now we have the presence of ETERNAL LIFE—God life—through God's Spirit, but we are not yet immortal beings—not yet BORN of God—not yet inheritors, and possessors, but HEIRS (Rom. 8:17). But *IF* God's Holy Spirit dwells in us, God will, at the resurrection, "quicken" to immortality our mortal bodies *BY* His Spirit that "dwelleth in us" (Rom. 8:11; I Cor. 15:49-53).

Now see how the astonishing analogy continues!

As yet we are not *born* divine beings. The divine life has merely been begotten. This divine CHARACTER starts so very small it is doubtful if much of it is in evidence—except for the glow of that ecstasy of spiritual "romance" which we may radiate in that "first love" of conversion—spiritually speaking. But so far as spiritual KNOWLEDGE, and developed spiritual CHARACTER goes, there is not much, as yet.

So now, once spiritually begotten, we must be fed and nourished on SPIRITUAL food! Jesus said man shall not live by bread (physical food) *alone*, but by EVERY WORD OF GOD (spiritual food)! This we drink in from the BIBLE! But we drink in this spiritual knowledge and character, also, through personal, intimate, continuous contact with God through PRAYER, and through Christian fellowship with God's children in His Church.

Now the physical embryo and foetus is fed physically through the mother. God's CHURCH is called Jerusalem *above* "which is the MOTHER OF US ALL" (Gal. 4:26).

Notice the exact parallel! The CHURCH is the MOTHER of its members. God has set His called and chosen ministers in His Church to FEED THE FLOCK—"for *the perfecting* of the saints, for the work of the ministry, for the edifying of the body (CHURCH) of Christ: TILL we all come in the unity of the faith, and of *the knowledge* of the Son of God, unto a perfect man, unto the measure of the stature of the fullness of Christ" (Eph. 4:11-13).

It is the duty of Christ's TRUE ministers (and *how scarce today!!!*) to PROTECT the begotten but yet unborn saints from false doctrines, from false ministers.

The HUMAN mother carries her unborn baby in that part of her body where she can best PROTECT it from *physical* harm; and that protection is part of her function, as well as to nourish the unborn child! Even so, the CHURCH, through Christ's ministers, instructs, teaches, counsels with, advises, and PROTECTS from *spiritual* harm the unborn members! What a WONDERFUL picture is human reproduction of spiritual SALVATION!

Continue further! As the physical foetus must grow *physically* large enough to be born, so the begotten Christian must *grow* in grace, and in the knowledge of Christ (II Pet. 3:18)—must overcome, must develop in spiritual CHARACTER during this life, in order to be BORN into the Kingdom of GOD!

And as the physical foetus gradually, one by one, develops the physical organs, features, and characteristics, even so the begotten Christian must gradually, continually, develop the SPIRITUAL character—love, faith, patience, gentleness, humility, kindness, temperance. He must live by, and be a DOER of the Word of God. He must develop the divine CHARACTER!

Then, in God's due time, by a resurrection, or by instantaneous CHANGE to immortality at Christ's coming, he shall be BORN of God—into the KINGDOM OF GOD—because GOD *is* that Kingdom!

How WONDERFUL is the TRUTH of GOD!

Yet, by his dastardly perversion of sex attitudes and purposes and the true sex knowledge of GOD's Word, Satan has DECEIVED THE WORLD—has blinded humanity to the fact that God *IS* this KINGDOM Jesus proclaimed—and that WE may be *born* as part of that divine FAMILY—as part of the GOD KINGDOM!

How precious, pure and wholesome is GOD's TRUTH!

And God designed SEX to picture, and in physical manner, to KEEP US CONSTANTLY IN THE KNOWLEDGE OF HIS WONDER-FUL PLAN OF SALVATION!

Let us, then, allow the living Saviour to CLEAN UP our minds, and open them to HIS TRUTH!

CHAPTER 9

The Divine *Purposes*
of Sex

Now comes the *BIG* Truth! Sex was designed and created in *humans* for purposes *other than* reproduction —for purposes totally foreign to animal or plant life!

But the world has continued in unhappy and wretched IGNORANCE of these glorious and God-bestowed purposes! The paganized "Christianity" that dominated the western world after 100 A.D. was either ignorant of these God-intended purposes, or else it suppressed them!

AND WHY?

The Only Authority for Morals

This brings us again to that striking truth, that THE WORD OF GOD IS THE FOUNDATION OF ALL KNOWLEDGE! The Bible is far, far, from the *sum-total* of knowledge. It is the BASIS—the FOUNDATION—the *starting point*, and the foundational *approach* to the acquisition of discoverable knowledge!

God, through the Maker's Instruction Book, reveals *what man cannot otherwise learn!* Full TRUTH comes from the Biblical revelation, PLUS acquired and discoverable knowledge approached through the CONCEPT revealed in the Bible.

Man, without divine revelation, has been able to observe that plant life reproduces; animal life reproduces; and human life reproduces. From this, IGNORANT of the divine revelation, man has formulated erroneous and happiness-destroying concepts about purposes and uses of sex.

The Roman Catholic Church has always taught that the *only* purpose of sex is reproduction—and it has viewed even that purpose with suspicion! That Church, *not understanding* the real meaning and true purposes of marriage, and inheriting from the Babylonian Mystery religion its sacraments, has made marriage a sacrament. But it placed marriage on a LOWER PLANE than celibacy or lifelong virginity!

The Catholic Church has been blinded to the glorious truth in this area, as in others, because it rejects God and the Bible as Supreme Authority. It sets *itself* up in place of God, as the one and only Supreme Authority!

Today educators, scientists, psychologists, doctors, and those who set the moral standards, rely on the evolutionary concept as their approach to knowledge. *They* do not know the origin or PURPOSES of sex. THEY do not know how, why, or when MARRIAGE originated.

The Bible reveals knowledge *otherwise unacquirable!*

So once again, let us go to that SOURCE of knowledge!

Remember, the ETERNAL (Heb., *Yahweh*), who literally spoke to and instructed Adam and Eve was the very Person of the Godhead who later became Jesus Christ.

The Second Purpose

Jesus taught the Pharisees precisely the same thing about sex that He had taught Adam and Eve. To the Pharisees, He said: "Have ye not read, that he which made them at the beginning made them male and female, And said, 'For this cause shall a man leave father and mother, and shall cleave to his wife. . . . What therefore GOD hath joined together, let not man put asunder'" (Mat. 19:4-6).

Sex did not evolve, without intelligence or purpose! It was GOD, by miraculous creation, who made man *male and female!* And God always has a purpose for what He does!

So *because* God created sex, He ORDAINED THE MARRIAGE INSTITUTION. And it is GOD who binds together, as husband and wife, a man and woman.

MARRIAGE, then, is the *second*-named PURPOSE of sex!

Marriage is a physical union, but a divine institution. Almighty GOD ordained it! It did not evolve. It is not of MAN'S devising.

Notice, in the scripture quoted above, Jesus said to the Pharisees, "Have ye not read, . . .?" He quoted an already written passage of Scripture. He said the Pharisees should have read it! *Where* is that scripture found? It is found in the second chapter of Genesis. It is part of the brief SUMMARY record of the ETERNAL'S original instruction to the newly created Adam and Eve. The creation of Eve had just been described, and God then said: "Therefore shall a man leave his father and his mother, and shall cleave unto his wife" (Gen. 2:24).

So the Almighty revealed the sacred MARRIAGE institution to the first man and woman.

WHY Marriage

Now stop and think for a moment. WHY did God ordain the human relationship of MARRIAGE?

The old repressive, dualistic morality taught that the *only* purpose of sex was reproduction. But if merely reproducing their kind were the *only* purpose of sex, NO MARRIAGE WOULD BE NECESSARY! God made *animals* male and female. Animals reproduce—BUT THEY DO NOT MARRY! Marriage is not necessary to procreate.

Realize this! UNDERSTAND this Truth! We can, through sex, have reproduction without marriage! Indeed, that is one of the world's greatest evils today—there is entirely too much reproduction without marriage!

Animals reproduce. But *animals do not marry!* Animals are born with *instinct.* They need little or no teaching.

Ever see a little calf born? The mother cow does not

need to call an obstetrical physician or go to a hospital for the delivery of her calf. As soon as it is born, the calf will begin to stagger to its feet, while the cow just stupidly stands waiting. She does not need to teach her calf how to walk, how to take its food, how to do anything. A little wobbly and unsteady the first thirty, sixty or ninety seconds, the calf is up and walking in just a minute or two.

Now how long does it take a *human* infant to learn to walk? Usually a year—and often more. But the newborn calf walks almost immediately. No one teaches it. THE CALF HAS INSTINCT. And where does it start walking? It has no instruction from anyone. It starts walking for its first "dinner." It *knows* where to go. And the mother cow just stands dumbly still while her calf sucks its milk.

And where is "Daddy cow"—the bull? That's hard to say. Perhaps miles away. He probably is nowhere around. And soon the calf will not even need the milk from its mother—and will be on its own.

There is no marriage—no FAMILY LIFE—no HOME!

But with humans all this is different. The purely *reproductive* process is the same in all mammals. But beyond this, *all is different!* The *only* purpose for sex in animals is reproduction. But HUMANS ARE DIFFERENT! In humans reproduction is *not* the only purpose of sex. A second purpose is MARRIAGE—and there is yet another!

The newborn human does not get up and walk immediately to its food. The tiny baby is absolutely *helpless*. It has no instinct, in the strict sense of the word. It has MIND —but at birth there is NO KNOWLEDGE as yet in its mind. It knows virtually *nothing* at birth. It must be *taught!* It needs parents to teach it! It matures so very much more slowly than animals! Yet its potentiality is *infinitely higher!* And for this higher purpose, parental guidance and FAMILY LIFE are NECESSARY!

For God had said: "Let us make man in OUR IMAGE."

God made cattle "after their kind"—after the *cattle* kind. He made "every winged fowl after his kind"—after the winged fowl kind! But He made MAN *after the GOD kind!*

MAN'S Destiny

Now, incredible as it may sound to those who do not UNDERSTAND the revelation of God's TRUTH—and only an infinitesimal minority does—GOD is a FAMILY! This we have explained in Chapter 8.

And in MAN, God is reproducing HIS kind! Man has the supreme potentiality of being actually born into the very divine GOD FAMILY!

Do you realize what that means? Of course, God is *composed* of immortal SPIRIT—while man, like animals, is composed in *this* life of FLESH—matter! But the transcendent *essential* factor is that GOD is PERFECT SPIRITUAL CHARACTER! It is the supreme intelligence, combined with holy and righteous CHARACTER of MIND that most importantly distinguishes GOD from every other living creature. No animal has this potential—but it is the true destiny of MAN. Of course God, too, possesses supreme ALL-mighty POWER. But without right CHARACTER, this power would be destructive and dangerous!

What *is* this righteous spiritual character?

It is that controlled ability, in a separate independent entity, to come to a *right knowledge* of the TRUE from the false—the RIGHT from the wrong—and, by free choice, to CHOOSE the right and the true; and, further, to use the self-discipline to *will* and to actually DO the right.

This necessitates that each individual human be an independent entity, with a mind of his own—with freedom of choice (free moral agency)—and it requires MIND power—intelligence—intellect—ability to absorb KNOWLEDGE, to reason, to think, to plan, devise, to draw conclusions, to *will*, and to act.

Inanimate objects have no mind, make no decisions, have no character. Animals have instinct installed in *brains*. But animals do not absorb knowledge from which they reason, make choice, and will to act even to enforcing self-discipline. Animals do not comprehend such things as art, literature, music. Animals do not imagine, and by thought and reasoning processes design creatively. Animals do not acquire scientific knowledge. They develop no character.

Humans are born with MINDS. Humans must be taught, or learn. But the human mind can absorb knowledge and reason from it—think creatively, formulate plans, make decisions, render judgments, and exercise self-discipline. Man has the POTENTIALITY of developing CHARACTER.

So the human baby is born without knowledge, but with capacity for acquiring it, and of developing CHARACTER. The human has the supreme potential of receiving God's own HOLY SPIRIT, to impart the divine nature, to equip the MIND to comprehend revealed *spiritual* knowledge!

Human babies are born helpless! They need the tender care, the loving instruction, the patient training and discipline of a father and a mother. They need the warmth and protection and security of family and of home life. And they are of supreme importance—for they are the potential HEIRS OF GOD!

This righteous CHARACTER is not created instantaneously. It develops through *experience*, and experience requires TIME. Instinct in animals is automatic, *set* in the animal brain from birth. But divine righteous CHARACTER must be developed, over a span of years.

All this is *one reason* for marriage and the FAMILY relationship.

But there are more! There are other reasons for marriage—for FAMILY—and for HOME!

WHY should humans marry?

Well, the educators today *do not really know!* The scientists do not fully comprehend! They suppose that somewhere along the evolutionary trail, perhaps millions of years ago, man himself started it merely as a custom. They do not know *when* the marriage institution started, by whom, or for what purpose! Of the tremendous MEANING of this institution they are ignorant! The Communist U. S. S. R. even experimented on abolishing marriage and producing humans outside marriage.

Angels Are Sexless

The real TRUTH about sex and marriage in humans goes deeper still! Its overwhelming significance and meaning seems to have become lost by man.

We have seen that animals have sex; that animals reproduce; but MARRIAGE is not required for reproduction, and animals do not marry. They do not establish the HOME and the FAMILY RELATIONSHIP.

Now consider angels. The skeptic doesn't believe it, but the Bible reveals that angels do exist. Angels are on a higher level of life than men. It is written that man was made "a little lower" than the angels—that is, during this mortal, fleshly, human life, *now*.

Yet angels, on a higher plane than physical man, *do not marry!* (Mat. 22:30). Each angel was individually and separately *created*, not born. Among angels there is *no marriage—no home life—no family life!*

And NO SEX!

Then what is the function of angels?

Angels are *spirit beings*—composed, not of material flesh, but of spirit—immortal. "And of the angels he saith, 'Who maketh his angels *spirits*, . . .'" (Heb. 1:7, Ps. 104:4). GOD is immortal, and composed of SPIRIT. Then are angels on the same level with God? *Not at all!* They are mere spirit *creations* of God, created to be His servants, messengers, representatives in the administration of God's UNIVERSE-RULING GOVERNMENT.

The Heritage of MAN

Angels, on a plane far lower than God, are higher than mortal man, now. But consider man's ultimate heritage— *if* he chooses it!

Speaking of the relative difference between man and

angels, in the first two chapters of the Book of Hebrews, we read:

"For unto the angels hath he *not* put in subjection the world to come [The WORLD TOMORROW!!], whereof we speak. But one in a certain place testified [Ps. 8:4-6], saying, '*What is man*, that thou art mindful of him?' . . ." (Heb. 2:5-6).

UNDERSTAND THIS! The earth *was* once put in subjection to angels, with the archangel Lucifer on that world throne as God's administrator to administer God's government over the angels that then populated the earth. But Lucifer became proud, filled with vanity, and decided to become an aggressor, attempting to dethrone God and place himself on the throne of the UNIVERSE! He was cast back down to earth, his name changed to Satan, meaning Adversary. The angels which joined his mutiny became demons.

Satan and his demons still sway, invisibly, this world. But Jesus Christ conquered Satan, and qualified for WORLD RULE. He is coming again to earth—soon, now, as KING of kings to set up and re-establish on earth GOD'S GOVERNMENT.

Now what of MAN? Those truly converted before Christ returns shall RULE the WORLD TOMORROW, under Christ (Rev. 3:21; 2:26-27). Yes, but ultimately even *more* than that!

Notice, now, this passage in Hebrews 2. The statement is made that *angels* will not be ruling The WORLD TOMORROW. But what of MAN? Yes, insignificant flesh-and-blood mortal MAN! Why should the Great GOD consider *him?* And here comes the stupendous answer few humans, blinded by Satan's deceptions, have ever noticed:

"Thou madest him a little lower than the angels; thou *crownedst him* with GLORY and HONOR, and didst set him over the works of thy hands: thou hast put ALL THINGS in subjection under his feet. For in that he put ALL in subjection under him, he left nothing that is not put under him . . ." (Heb. 2:7-8).

You won't quite grasp that at first. It is too overwhelming! To be *crowned* means to be given kingly RULE. To be crowned with GLORY and HONOR is to be given such rule as Christ has, NOW—and that is described in chapter 1 of Hebrews as being the Administrating, Ruling Executive over the ENTIRE UNIVERSE! Christ is now ruling over "ALL THINGS"! The Moffatt translation renders this, properly, from the Greek as THE UNIVERSE—that is, *all that God has created!*

Christ rules it all *now!* The FATHER of the God Kingdom has placed the resurrected, everliving CHRIST as Chief Executive over the GOVERNMENT OF GOD over the entire, vast, limitless UNIVERSE. And converted humans are HEIRS of Christ—JOINT-HEIRS *with* Him to inherit *with* Him, in due time, all that HE has now inherited! (Rom. 8:17—which *read!*)

But continue the passage in Hebrews 2: ". . . But now we see *not yet* all things put under him" (verse 8). Oh, then the rulership over the universe is NOT YET under man—not while he is human—mortal! But what do we already, *now*, see? Continue the passage:

"But we see Jesus, who was made a little lower than the angels [even as we, now] for the suffering of death, CROWNED WITH GLORY AND HONOR . . ." (verse 9). And verse 10 shows that Jesus Christ is the captain—the Leader, the Pioneer who goes on before—of our salvation!

Christ already is CROWNED with this HONOR and GLORY. Christ ROSE from the dead! He is ALIVE—and He is DIVINE! He has been GLORIFIED—and in His glorified SPIRIT condition His eyes are like flames of fire, and His face shines as bright as the very SUN—FULL STRENGTH! (Rev. 1:14-16.)

And mortal man, if he repents, surrenders unconditionally to God and God's government, accepts in living FAITH Jesus Christ as personal Saviour, can receive God's gift of His HOLY SPIRIT—the very *life*, essence, nature, mind and power of God—thus BEGETTING him, now, as God's own (yet unborn) son! If he then GROWS spiritually (II Pet. 3:18), overcomes, and endures, he shall—at Christ's soon coming, be changed (or resurrected if he dies) from mortal to immortal (I Cor. 15:44-54).

And then—IF the very CHARACTER of God has been developed within him—his vile material body will be instantaneously *changed* (converted) into one "like unto his [Christ's] GLORIOUS body!" (Phil. 3:21.) But your vile *character* will not then be instantaneously changed—THAT change must take place NOW, in *this* life!

So THAT is the supreme heritage of MAN—*if* he is willing!

Man, now lower than angels, has a destiny far higher!

A GOD-PLANE Relationship!

So GRASP this colossal TRUTH, if you can!

Here is the greatest TRUTH you can ever know! MAN, and man *only*, of all life forms God has created, can be born into THE GOD FAMILY—the KINGDOM OF GOD! The family relationship is a GOD-PLANE relationship—not an angel-plane relationship. And God bestowed it on MAN!

Of all life forms—whether plant, animal, or angel—in all God's creation, *MAN ALONE* was created for MARRIAGE—for HOME, and FAMILY LIFE!

Read that again! Try to comprehend it! THINK of the significance! This pivotal truth has been *hidden* from a deceived world!

Man is, now, composed of matter. Yet in man—and in MAN ONLY, is God's CREATION still going on! Humans, by repentance, surrender to God, and acceptance of Christ, may be in mind and attitude *converted*—may receive God's Holy Spirit. Thus they are actually *begotten* as God's *children!* They may have direct communion with God, and call Him FATHER! They are brought into a FATHER-AND-SON relationship with GOD!

This is possible for no other creature—not even angels! Angels were not, never can be, begotten and BORN of God! Each angel is a separate creation. *No angel can ever become a part of* the DIVINE FAMILY OR KINGDOM OF GOD!

Notice! Of angels, God says: "For unto which of the angels said he at any time, 'Thou art my son, this day have I begotten thee'? And again, 'I will be to him a Father, and he shall be to me a Son'?" (Heb. 1:5.)

Neither animal, nor angel, nor any other being, except MAN, can be literally begotten by *spiritual reproductive process*, and then actually BORN into the divine GOD FAMILY!

What a matchless, supreme, awe-inspiring, breath-taking potential!

The Function of Angels

Angels, higher than man is now, are the *ministering servants* of God in the administration of His universe-ruling government! And, in relation to MAN, angels are "ministering spirits, sent forth to minister for them who shall be heirs of salvation" (Heb. 1:14). Invisible angels actually minister to, and serve the human children of GOD. Begotten humans are the actual *heirs* of God—and joint heirs of CHRIST (Rom. 8:17).

Notice! "And because ye [converted Christians] are sons, God hath sent forth the Spirit of his Son into your hearts, crying, 'Abba, Father.' Wherefore thou art no more a servant, but a SON; and if a son, then an HEIR of God through Christ!" (Gal. 4:6-7.)

A young son of a wealthy man, while still a child, may be under the care of an adult servant. The servant is older, farther advanced in knowledge, on higher status physically and mentally—but far lower *potentially*. For when the son is mature, he will inherit his father's wealth and power. Therefore the servant, temporarily older and farther matured, is *servant*, ministering to the young HEIR! That illustrates the fact of angels ministering to humans!

Humans are, if converted through Christ, the *heirs* of the GOD FAMILY. They are to enter the divine FAMILY. They are, even now, *the begotten children of God*. Therefore God ordained the *family relationship* for human beings.

No OTHER BEINGS—whether angel or animal—HAVE THIS RELATIONSHIP.

But it goes further!

The FAMILY relationship demands the HUSBAND-AND-WIFE relationship! And that demands MARRIAGE, and *faithfulness* to that matrimonial bond! The CHURCH of God is merely that BODY composed of the begotten *children* of God. And the Church, as a BODY, is the affianced BRIDE OF CHRIST —to MARRY Christ at the time of the resurrection and His second coming!

So there is also the divine MARRIAGE relationship!

Now UNDERSTAND! The *husband-and-wife* relationship, and the *family* relationship, *are God-plane relationships!*

These are NOT animal-plane, or angel-plane relationships!

Since humans were put on earth for the very PURPOSE of being begotten, and then BORN into the GOD FAMILY— which is the KINGDOM OF GOD—the ETERNAL has endowed this GOD-PLANE relationship for HUMANS—and for *humans only!* What a WONDERFUL PRIVILEGE to be HUMANS—to be given the MARRIAGE relationship now—to marry Christ and become part of the GOD-FAMILY!

The Affianced Bride

Here is another vital REASON for the institution of MARRIAGE in the human family. It is to teach us—to constantly remind us—of our sacred relationship to Jesus Christ!

Here is the vital teaching:

"Wives, submit yourselves unto your own husbands, as unto the Lord. For the husband is the head of the wife, even as Christ is the head of the church: and he is the saviour of the body. Therefore as the church is subject unto Christ, so let the wives be to their own husbands in everything.

"Husbands, love your wives, even as Christ also loved

the church, and gave himself for it; that he might sanctify and cleanse it with the washing of water by the word . . ." (The Word, if obeyed, washes away error.) "That he might present it to himself a glorious church [GLORIFIED—DEIFIED], not having spot, or wrinkle, or any such thing; but that it should be holy and without blemish. So ought men to love their wives as their own bodies. . . . For we are members of his body, of his flesh, and of his bones. *For this cause* shall a man leave his father and mother, and shall be joined unto his wife, and they two shall be one flesh.

"This is a great mystery: but I speak concerning Christ and the church" (Eph. 5:23-32).

Notice! *For this cause*—because of the coming MARRIAGE (spiritually) between Christ and the Church—because the Church is, now, the affianced bride, engaged to marry Christ—FOR THIS REASON, God ordained the MARRIAGE institution for humans! But not for animals! Not for angels!

Notice Revelation 19:7—speaking of the second coming of Christ in GLORY: ". . . the MARRIAGE of the Lamb [Christ] is come, and his WIFE hath made herself ready." ONLY those made ready in righteous CHARACTER will be presented to Him then!

WHY Home and Family!

So, in addition to the FAMILY relationship, there is also the divine MARRIAGE relationship.

So UNDERSTAND! The *husband-and-wife* relationship, and the *family* relationship, are *God-plane relationships!*

These are *not* animal-plane or angel-plane relationships!

Humans are free moral agents. God never forces one to be truly converted—to become His very begotten son. Yet the PURPOSE God is working out here below is to reproduce Himself—to bring, through Christ, "many sons unto GLORY" (Heb. 2:10) in the divine KINGDOM OF GOD!

And since humans were put on earth *for the very purpose* of being begotten, and then BORN into the GOD FAMILY, the Eternal has endowed this God-plane family status for humans, now—and for humans ONLY!

What a WONDERFUL PRIVILEGE to be given the MARRIAGE and FAMILY relationship—that we may be prepared for the spiritual marriage to CHRIST and the divine family status, *for eternity*, in THE KINGDOM OF GOD!

CHAPTER 10

But Was *Sex* Really Necessary?

W<small>E HAVE COVERED</small> two vital <small>PURPOSES</small> relating to sex in humans—procreation, and marriage. And these mean a <small>GOD-PLANE</small> *family* relationship.

But did these really require <small>SEX</small>?

Could not God have devised some other means of generation than <small>SEX</small>? And would not the marriage and family relationships be happier without <small>SEX</small>?

The "Chaste" Severity of Catholic Fathers

The formulators of Roman Catholic thought would have answered the above two questions in the affirmative.

Referring to these founders of Catholic teaching, Gibbon says, in his famous Chapter XV (*The History of the Decline and Fall of the Roman Empire*): "The chaste severity of the fathers in whatever related to the commerce of the sexes flowed from the same principle—their abhorrence of every enjoyment which might gratify the sensual, and degrade the spiritual nature of man."

Their favorite opinion, continues Gibbon, was that if there had been no "fall," Adam would have lived forever in a state of virgin purity. Paradise might have been peopled, not by "degrading" sex, but by some harmless mode of vegetation.

Apparently God made a terrible mistake when He created sex. That is, in the "chaste severity" thinking of those Catholic fathers!

"By them," continues Gibbon, "the use of marriage was permitted only to the fallen posterity, as a necessary expedient to continue the human species."

Gibbon speaks of these men, as "unwilling to approve an institution (marriage) which they were compelled to tolerate." And, further, "Since desire was imputed as a crime, and marriage was tolerated as a defect, it was consistent with the same principles to consider a state of celibacy as the nearest approach to the Divine perfection."

Poor souls!!

Ignorant of the Biblical revelation that God—(Hebrew, *Elohim*) is a FAMILY—ignorant of the truth of the KINGDOM OF GOD—these men condemned the very GOD-PLANE relationship of the Eternal! The fruits of that teaching have been an indescribably enormous MOUNTAIN of human woe and misery!

Views of Augustine and Aquinas

Two men, Augustine and Thomas Aquinas, largely defined into dogma the Roman Catholic teaching on sex. Their history and interpretations have been covered in an earlier chapter. But certain additional facts are pertinent at this point.

Neither man claimed that the original sin was the use of sex. The original sin, they reasoned, must have been pride. But the use of sex—regarded by them as degrading—came as a result. Aquinas reasoned that all sex desire is concupiscence, and is transmitted hereditarily by the "corrupting" sexual act. Entirely at variance from God's revelation, they reasoned that begettal through sex is the carrier, by heredity, of original sin. WHY could not God have created bodies out of human flesh, or by some sexless means, untainted by the "degrading" act of coitus, they asked.

Thomas Aquinas was ignorant of the fact that we humans can receive salvation only by *spiritual* begettal— of which *physical conception* is the type!

Of course, neither Augustine nor Aquinas would go so far as to directly accuse God of wrong. Marriage, they acknowledged, was instituted by God. It had to be accepted —reluctantly—as good. What was wrong about marriage, they reasoned, was not the ceremony or the *state* of marriage —but the use of sex *in* marriage! How much better would marriage have been, *without sex!*

And that is the BIG QUESTION to be settled once and for all in this present chapter! Was SEX necessary for the God-plane marriage and family relationships? Could we not have had these without SEX?

WHY was sex necessary, anyway?

Why not some intellectual way, free from passion and sex, of producing offspring?

What They Never Understood

The highest estate of man, according to Augustine and Aquinas, was mental reasoning and philosophic contemplation. These leaders of religious thought never understood that the human mind, naturally, is limited to the sphere of MATERIALISM. It is capable of grasping knowledge of intricate mathematics, physical sciences, and of indulging in philosophical reasonings—but always limited to the materialistic plane.

Of course man was put on earth to *become* a spiritual being, entering the divine FAMILY. The very PURPOSE of life, and the existence of TRUTH involve spiritual knowledge. Yet, this spiritual knowledge can come only through divine revelation—and Biblical revelation can be understood ONLY by a mind opened to spiritual knowledge by God's Holy Spirit—and God gives His Spirit *only* to them that OBEY Him (Acts 5:32). Just as animal brain, devoid of human *spirit*, cannot know the things an educated human may comprehend, so, devoid of God's Holy Spirit, a human mind *cannot* grasp SPIRITUAL KNOWLEDGE (I Cor. 2:11).

The true spiritual revelation is barred, completely, from natural minds. It even appears as foolishness to the rational, intellectual, yet natural man. Until God's Holy Spirit impregnates the mind, it is cut off, utterly, from real TRUTH. God's Spirit is given after surrender—*unconditional surrender*—to GOD! It does not come by meanderings through one school of pagan speculation after another. This trail may appeal to intellectual vanity, but it leads only down the blind alleys of error, fable, superstition, and nonsense.

This was the dilemma of men like Augustine and Aquinas.

In their carnality, neither taking the Bible as their authoritative SOURCE of knowledge, nor having the Spirit to understand it—trusting rather in their own intellectuality—these men nevertheless tried to square their ideas with certain Biblical statements.

They had to face the statement that God ordained the marriage institution. Therefore it could not be rejected. Even so, they regarded asceticism and celibacy as higher verities.

All sexual desire, in their carnal speculation, was corrupted by concupiscence—tainted with evil. Since God caused procreation to be brought about by use of sex, they were unable to condemn reproduction in marriage. But for *any* purpose within marriage, except to beget children, the use of sex was branded SIN—though only venial, which the priest could forgive.

Even the good of conceiving offspring to be converted to Christ was on a plane far lower, in their thinking, than the "blessing" of lifelong virginity, or the "virtue" of celibacy.

Satanic Origin

This pagan concept, falsely labeled "Christian," was Satan-inspired (I Tim. 4:1-3). It simply means this:

Satan is an *individual being*, with NO POWER TO REPRO-
DUCE HIMSELF. Satan is deprived of FAMILY RELATIONSHIP.
God, on the other hand, *IS* the divine FAMILY. God's whole
PURPOSE in man is to spiritually REPRODUCE HIS OWN KIND,
begetting us, through Christ, to be born into His FAMILY—
the universe-ruling KINGDOM. God has bestowed on mankind
the privileges of FAMILY, and of reproducing our kind, bringing our *human* offspring into our human FAMILIES.

Satan resents this!

So Satan palms himself off as the GOD of this world
(II Cor. 4:4).

The *true* God—the Eternal CREATOR—pictures Himself,
in His Word, as the divine FAMILY, and bestows on man
the privileges of reproduction and family. But the god of
this world—the counterfeit god—represents GOD as putting
a spirit, called an "immortal soul," *into* a man—just as
Satan causes his *demons* to enter into and possess those
humans who will yield. Satan represents God's system of
reproduction as being wrong. He deceives the world into
believing marital LOVE through sex is a corroding, contaminating thing. He exalts celibacy, because it is most like HIM
—single—no sex—no family. This, teach HIS followers, is a
HIGHER ESTATE—more noble—than that which the true God
ordained—marriage—LOVE—reproduction—FAMILY!

Marriage, thought Augustine, is at its best when a man
and his wife live wholly without sex. Best of all, is the SINGLE
life, however! Can't we see the diabolical sway of Satan in
all this?

But one of the fruits of this false concept which became
fixed Catholic dogma is seriously plaguing the present pope,
Paul VI. In December, 1963, he came out in strong terms
against any artificial means of contraception—in line, of
course, with this fixed Catholic teaching. But within six
months this "New Morality" was sweeping the western world
and bringing such pressure that Pope Paul was forced, in
late June, 1964, to make a public statement that the matter

would be seriously restudied at Vatican Council II!

The "New Morality" Concept

Will even the Roman Church, which has boasted that Rome never changes, be forced to see its dogma on sex and marriage crumble before the "New Morality" onslaught?

Worldwide REVOLT has set in against the repressive "chaste severity of the fathers."

The formulators of the modernistic perversion see only one thing—that Catholic repression, passively adopted but not practiced by Protestants, became intolerable. The sex-is-evil attitude had to go.

The medieval concept downgraded the God-plane MAR-RIAGE and FAMILY relationships *below* asceticism. The "New Morality" threatens to *abolish* these divine institutions!

Instead of coming to the true MEANING and PURPOSES and right USES of sex, they blindly swung to the opposite extreme of declaring ANY USE OF SEX IS GOOD—NOT EVIL! Therefore, says the modern revolt, "Let's USE IT—freely—in or out of marriage—perverted or otherwise—DOWN WITH ALL RESTRAINTS! Let's LIVE IT UP!!!"

So, in the present moral rebellion, labelling IMMORALITY *"The New Morality,"* marriage has lost whatever meaning or sanctity it had under the straight-laced prudery. Its very existence is threatened.

Now we have seen, in the preceding two chapters, that there is vital and deep-rooted MEANING to the MARRIAGE institution, and to the establishment of HOME and FAMILY life.

But the BIG question of the present chapter is: Was SEX really necessary for these high and noble God-plane relationships of the marriage state, and the institution of home and family? Could not these have been more enjoyable, more pure and clean, more righteous—and better for humanity—*without sex?*

Has not sex brought only suffering, frustration, and unhappiness to marriage, and to family life?

They Are LOVE Relationships

To answer this BIG question about sex, we need to look further into the FAMILY relationship that constitutes the KINGDOM OF GOD, and the betrothal relationship between CHRIST and the CHURCH.

God has given mankind the institutions of *marriage*, and *family*, to *prepare* us for an ETERNITY of happiness and joy in His Kingdom—His FAMILY!

Just WHAT, then, is the very basis and foundation of the FAMILY RELATIONSHIP of the Kingdom of God? That basis is LOVE!

Of all the CHARACTER ATTRIBUTES of God—of the GOD FAMILY—the very first, greatest, and most important is LOVE!

Above all, GOD *IS* LOVE! (I John 4:8, 16.)

The very first of the attributes of God—expressed in the fruits of His Holy Spirit in man is LOVE (Gal. 5:22). When this very God-life is infused within us, by His Spirit, it is "the LOVE OF GOD . . . shed abroad in our hearts by the Holy Spirit" (Rom. 5:5).

Thus, in first begetting us, to prepare us to enter HIS FAMILY, God infuses within us the divine GIFT of *His Love!* The divine FAMILY RELATIONSHIP is a LOVE relationship. The tie that holds the divine Family together is the tie of LOVE!

To those thus begotten of God, converted by His Spirit, Christ says through John: "Behold, what manner of LOVE the Father hath bestowed upon us, that we should be called THE SONS OF GOD . . . Beloved, *now* are we the sons of God [begotten], and it doth not yet appear what we *shall be* [when *born*]: but we know that, when he [Christ] shall appear, we shall be like him; for we shall see him as he is" (I John 3:1-2).

Even now, converted begotten sons of God have spiritual FELLOWSHIP with the FATHER of the God Family, and with the Son, Christ (I John 1:3).

So the FAMILY relationship, both on the divine plane, and in the human type, now, is a LOVE relationship—and GOD implants within His begotten children *His divine love* to equip them for that divine LOVE relationship.

Likewise, the betrothal Husband-and-wife-to-be relationship between CHRIST and THE CHURCH is a LOVE relationship.

Notice, again, God's teaching that MARRIAGE on the present human level is to be a LOVE relationship, just as is Christ's relationship to His Church:

"Husbands, LOVE your wives, even as Christ also loved the church, and gave himself for it . . . that it should be holy and without blemish. *So* ought men to love their wives as their own bodies. . . . For *this cause* shall a man leave his father and mother, and shall be joined unto his wife, and they two shall be one flesh" (Eph. 5:25-31).

For *what cause* shall a man marry a wife? For what PURPOSE? For that of LOVE!

The betrothal relationship between Christ and the Church—of which marriage between humans is the type— is a LOVE relationship. Husbands are to love their wives "even as Christ also loved the church, and gave himself for it."

But notice again! To Adam and Eve in the Garden in Eden, God gave SEX as the cause for marriage—as did Jesus in Matthew 19: "He . . . made them *male and female*, and said, '*For this cause*' " shall a man and woman marry (verses 4-5). Because of SEX they shall marry.

So we have the two Scriptural reasons for marriage—for LOVE, and because of SEX. These are not two contradictory reasons. They blend into ONE—to express LOVE through SEX! This will be made far more plain in the chapter to follow!

Sex was created, not only as the means of reproduction and bringing about a FAMILY, but, in humans, as a means of expressing LOVE in marriage.

So again I ask, *just what* IS *Love?*

And again I answer, the world does not know!

Three Kinds of Love

There is more than one kind of love. The Greeks had *three* words for it—each with a different shade of meaning.

In today's modern world, the meaning of LOVE has been all but lost. It has been so romanticized, so confused with LUST, that people carelessly call any sex desire or sex use "love." Usually this is LUST.

Today nearly all popular songs are falsely supposed to sing about love. Motion pictures, television, novels—all confuse and eroticize "love" and induce society to accept lust in the name of "love."

The Greeks are more definitely expressive. They use three words which define love more accurately.

First, is *agape*, which is moral or spiritual love. This is the love GOD expresses toward humanity. It is the divine, spiritual love, supplied by God's Holy Spirit. The natural and unconverted man *does not have this love!* But God *longs* to fill him with it—if he will surrender and believe!

Second, is *philia*, or *philadelphia*, in two of its forms. This is the love of friendship—brotherly love—love of parent, or child.

Third is *eros*, which refers to sexual love between husband and wife. But it means *love*, not lust. The Greek language uses a different word for lust. *Eros*, however, is a love expressed physically, not spiritually.

Just what, then, *is* love?

If I had to define love in four words, I would say "Love is *an unselfish outgoing concern*" for the one loved. Love is primarily on the *giving, serving, sharing* side of the fence —not on the *getting, taking*, factional, striving side. It is not selfish.

God *is* Love. Consider how God expresses love toward us who are humans. Yes, even those who are *hostile*, and rebellious toward God: "God *so loved* the world, that he *gave* his only begotten Son, that whosoever believeth in him should not perish, but have everlasting life" (John 3:16).

Jesus Christ is God—one of the divine Persons who compose the God Family. Notice how Christ manifested love: "God commendeth his love toward us, in that, while we were yet sinners, *Christ died for us. . . .* when we were enemies, we were reconciled to God *by the death of his Son*" (Rom. 5:8, 10).

How did Jesus Christ express His love for the Church? The Scripture has been quoted above—*He gave Himself for it!*

Love is UNselfish. It is not an emotion, though it may be expressed with an emotional content. True love *combines* the rational aspect of outgoing concern—desire to help, serve, give or share—along with sincere affectionate *feeling.*

William Graham Cole, in his book, *Sex in Christianity and Psychoanalysis,* gives an excellent analysis of love. He draws an interesting distinction between true mature love and infantile love. The latter is primarily emotional, thoughtlessly selfish, seeking its own gratification. Like "puppy love," it does not love another as he is, or for what he is, but as he is imagined or romantically desired to be.

"Illusion," says Cole, "is the standard diet of infantile love. It is, as the poets say, blind. . . . Cupid appears appropriately enough in diapers." (For our British readers, "nappies.")

Mature love, says Cole, is not blind. "It has progressed from pabulum to porterhouse."

Jesus said: "It is more blessed to *give* than to receive." That is a true statement, of which nearly all humans are ignorant. Carnal humanity is bent on getting, taking, having. The average person, selfishly, is primarily interested in gratifying the desires of his five senses—with no concern for others.

ALL Sense-Enjoyment NOT Sin

The five senses do cry out for gratification. We humans are composed of FLESH—mortal flesh—MATTER. We can receive pleasurable sensations through these five senses. In their "chaste severity" the Catholic fathers deemed *any* pleasurable sensation or experience, through the senses, to be sinful.

THAT IS EMPHATICALLY NOT TRUE!

God even tells us, in His Word, that our senses *should be exercised by use*, so that we can distinguish good from evil (Heb. 5:14). Our senses were put within our bodies *to be used—but not misused!*

God created us so that we must eat food to live. He equipped us with the sense of taste. God gave us this sense so that we might *enjoy* the necessity of eating. We should, therefore, exercise our senses to distinguish true, natural, health-building food from those false foods which destroy health—and then *give God thanks*, and really ENJOY the eating!

In like manner God made it possible for us to receive great pleasure and enjoyment of the most upbuilding and wholesome kind from the sense of sight. He gave us the faculty for appreciating the *beautiful*. But a man can *misuse* his sense of sight by looking *lustfully* at a woman.

God equipped humans with the sense of *hearing*. How much inspiring, uplifting, pleasurable enjoyment we receive from beautiful MUSIC! But of course, this sense, too, may be used for good, or for evil. Glorious music was actually created in the archangel Lucifer. But when, in pride and greed, his whole character changed, and he FELL from his estate of perfection to become Satan, he became corrupted and perverted in all his ways (Ezek. 28:13, 17). Satan is the author of perverted, discordant, degenerated modern music.

IN LOVE, God equipped humans with the five physical senses, to supply man with wholesome ENJOYMENT AND PLEASURE! But the *use* of these senses can be turned in the wrong direction! The *privilege* carries with it the obligation of responsibility. This is part of the character-building process.

I repeat! Sin is not the *thing*—but the WRONG USE of the thing!

God *intended* man to be HAPPY! It is God's will that

we ENJOY life—that it be pleasurable, satisfying, wholesome, rewarding! But God gave us *minds*—and made HIS WORD available—to distinguish the TRUE values from the false! The *right* use of the five senses brings enjoyable, pleasurable sensations that are uplifting, constructive, beneficial—not only to the self, but to others. The *wrong* and sinful use of the senses also may produce pleasurable sensations, but these wrong uses are destructive and harmful—not only to the self, but often also to others.

It is a matter of RIGHT or WRONG direction.

How may we humans *know* which use is right, and which is wrong?

BY THE LAW OF GOD!

RIGHT Use of Senses

God's Law is A WAY of life. It guides actions and uses in a definite direction—always constructive, upbuilding, beneficial. That WAY always is THE WAY of LOVE—the way of *unselfish, outgoing concern.*

SIN is the transgression of THAT WAY! Sin travels in the direction of vanity, greed—INflowing selfish gratification. It wants to *be served,* not to serve. To *be helped,* not to help. To *get,* not to give.

The WHOLE LAW OF GOD is summed up in one word— *LOVE!* And it requires love *expressed in action* to fulfil the Law (Rom. 13:8, 10).

But this Law-*principle* of LOVE is subdivided into the two Great Commandments—LOVE toward God, and love toward neighbor. The first four of the Ten Commandments define love toward GOD. The last six tell us *how* to love neighbor. Love toward neighbor is *not altogether* outgoing concern. It is also a *sharing with* neighbor—"Thou shalt love thy neighbor *as thyself.*" Of course that is *a lot of love!*

It is human to love your own self. That requires no effort—no character. But what is *not* human nature is to love your neighbor EQUALLY! That requires recognition by an intelligent mind of the TRUE VALUES—and it requires the exercise of WILL and self-discipline and CHARACTER!

The Love Man Doesn't Have

Now we are approaching the real ANSWER to the BIG question of this chapter.

Consider! The Law allows you to love yourself equally with your neighbor. But NOT GOD! It requires you to love GOD with ALL your heart, mind, soul, and strength!

How, then, may a person LOVE GOD?

Actually, the natural unconverted man *CANNOT!* Take, at random, any man—any woman—you might meet on a busy street—or out on a country lane. Has he the ability to love GOD far more than SELF—with *ALL* his heart, mind, soul, and strength? DOES the average person love God that much?

What's the answer?

God's Word answers: *"We* love him, *because he first loved us"* (I John 4:19). The "we" here is addressed to converted Christians.

A human can only really and truly love God with *the very love* which we first must receive *from Him!* This is the spiritual divine Love God GIVES us by the Holy Spirit! But we must first REPENT—surrender unconditionally to live GOD'S WAY—and truly BELIEVE in Christ, accepting Him as personal Saviour.

When we love GOD, it is merely HIS OWN LOVE, on a return circuit, flowing on back to Him again! GOD'S SPIRIT is *active—flowing!*

So the first Great Commandment—to be kept in its complete and true spiritual sense—requires a love MAN SIMPLY DOESN'T HAVE! Of course, God *longs* to GIVE every man that love, and *fill* him with it! But mighty few are willing!

Now consider TWO EXTREMES:

1) Love toward your NEIGHBOR *farthest* from any natural affection—a recognized *enemy.* Here is Jesus' teaching of fulfilling the Law toward him: *"Love* your enemies, bless

them that curse you, do good to them that hate you, and pray *for* [not against] them which despitefully use you, and persecute you . . ." (Mat. 5:44). Does the natural, unconverted man have *that* kind of love? The world doesn't consider *that* teaching of Jesus very practical—because the world is empty of *that kind* of love.

2) At the other extreme, two categories of neighbor *closest* to you are singled out in the New Testament for SPECIAL LOVE. One of these categories is one's neighbors *closest* to him *spiritually*—his *brethren in Christ.* Many scriptures put emphasis on a SPECIAL LOVE for these. Here again, a love is required which is totally absent in unregenerate man. But, in this case, they are not brethren in Christ UNLESS both they and you are IN Christ—have received God's Holy Spirit! Otherwise you are *none of His!* (Rom. 8:9.)

The other of these, singled out in the New Testament for *special love* is the neighbor *closest* to you *physically—* your *husband or wife!*

And right here is the BIG POINT, vitally important, that probably never before entered your mind!

Four categories have just been cited—*love to GOD*, and (of love to neighbor) *your enemy*, your true *fellow Christians*, and your *marital mate.*

Man simply is not born with—does not have—the divine SPIRITUAL love required for the first three of those four categories!—to love God, enemy, and fellow Christian SPIRITUALLY, in the manner the Law requires!

But when we come to the fourth category—MARRIAGE—we find an altogether different situation!

Even here, when, in the New Testament, the command is given to those IN THE CHURCH: "Husbands, love your wives," the word "love" in the original Greek in which the Apostle Paul wrote it, is not *eros*, but is *agape*, which is the divine love which emanates from God!

The true Christian husband loves his wife, not only in the physical and natural sense possible for a natural, yet unconverted, person—but *also* with a special *spiritual* love!

But God well knew that an infinitesimal percentage of humans, from Adam and Eve to now, would yield themselves to receive that divine love of God. And, even so, it is *then* mingled with the physical love God has made possible through sex!

Now we are ready for the ANSWER to this chapter's big QUESTION:

We need, now, to understand some of the FACTS OF LIFE which few ever grasp!

Marital LOVE

GOD is a Spirit. But God *did not create humans out of spirit!* To have done so would have defeated God's whole grand PURPOSE! So MAN is physical *flesh*—made from matter —the dust of the ground!

Of the three kinds of love, expressed by the three Greek words *agape, philia,* and *eros,* the natural man is capable of expressing only the last two types of love. There is a certain selfish element in the *philia* love—love for children, parents, or family. We may have this love for those of "our club," "our team," "our group." That often is a factional-type love —one of the "works of the flesh" of Galatians 5:19-21 (see especially Moffatt translation).

WHY did not God design things so that married humans would love each other with God's SPIRITUAL LOVE—*without* the *physical* love of SEX? Simply because it would have defeated God's whole PURPOSE. Simply because God found it necessary to make MAN, for now, of physical matter.

In His divine wisdom, God knew that His supreme PURPOSE required that man be made, first, on the material level—a physical being!

Being physical, we were made with the five physical SENSES.

It was God's PURPOSE that humans, unlike animals, angels, or any other living beings, enjoy the blessings of MARRIAGE and FAMILY relationships—actual *God-plane* relationships—to fit us for the *spiritual* marriage relationship with CHRIST—and an eternity of happiness in the very GOD Family! The marriage relationship, as explained, had to be a LOVE relationship. But human, fleshly man is not born with *spiritual love*. Man's comprehension of MIND—his expression of LOVE—is confined, naturally, to the physical level, through the senses. Unconverted man can express only *physical* love —and, in marriage, through sex. But to become a begotten child of God, man must CHOOSE! The decision is HIS! Otherwise there could be no character.

Man is given a CHOICE! So he has full ability to turn physical sex love in the *wrong direction* of LUST. God equipped him with MIND. He has capability to discern—to CHOOSE—and what he sows he shall reap!

Making man a physical being, it was still God's design to make possible our greatest HAPPINESS.

It was God's PURPOSE that man should learn that HIS WAY brings happiness and joy. It was God's PURPOSE to make great happiness and joy possible for us now—in this physical life—and that we might enjoy it forever, in His Kingdom! It was God's PURPOSE that we humans *learn*, through experience if we will not learn otherwise, that GOD'S WAY produces every happiness, while the *other way* imposes every curse.

Mankind has WRITTEN the lesson. But, as previously stated, he has refused, as yet, to LEARN it!

Of all the truly ENJOYABLE experiences received through the five senses, perhaps the most intense and supremely gratifying is that received in the sex act of expressing LOVE for the one who is dearest of all people on earth, and to whom one has been joined in blessed and holy wedlock by GOD HIMSELF!

I remember when I was a young unmarried man, some of us young men had a good argument for resisting fornication. *IF*, we reasoned, a man might get a momentary sensual thrill and gratification out of an act of fornication, *how much greater* would be the satisfaction of waiting, to share that act with the one sweetest, dearest, loveliest girl in all the world—as a matter of LOVE with clean conscience. With a harlot or a girl loose and immoral enough to permit fornication, it could not be real LOVE—and, besides, it involved a guilty conscience—and it could involve premarital pregnancy or venereal disease.

Even in carnality, we realized it was better—BETTER FOR US—to *wait* for marriage.

God made us so that we may really ENJOY the taste of delicious food—the sound of beautiful music—the sight of a beautiful landscape or flower garden—the fragrance of beautiful roses. The RIGHT exercise of our senses is RIGHT. God *intended* this pleasure and enjoyment. God is LOVE, and God expressed His love toward us by making these delights possible. Yet, probably the most intensely delightful of all physical joys God's love has made possible, is that of sexual LOVE between husband and wife.

It was GOD who created these five senses, and set them in such dynamic action, with their various stimuli. And God beheld everything that He had made, and pronounced it VERY GOOD!

God wants us to ENJOY LIFE! God made us so we can find true happiness, here and now—we can simply *radiate* HAPPINESS AND JOY! His LAW is the guide to the RIGHT USE of these powers which can produce joyous blessings, or terrible curses. *And He gave us the CHOICE!*

God gave us the blessed MARRIAGE relationship, and the *God-plane* FAMILY relationship!

LOVE is God's WAY. But natural man can express it only *physically*.

So, since humans can express naturally only a human and physical love, we come to the answer of the question of this chapter:

THE CREATOR, IN HIS WISDOM, KNEW THAT SEX *WAS* NECESSARY TO PRESERVE THE MARRIAGE AND FAMILY RELATIONSHIP, IN REAL LOVE!

God knew what He was doing!

If I could talk to those stern and unhappy "fathers,"

I would ask them: "Who are YOU to question your Maker, on how or why He made you?" GOD's answer to them and His critics is: "WOE unto him that striveth with his Maker! . . . Shall the clay say to him that fashioneth it, 'What makest thou?' " (Isa. 45:9.)

And again: "Surely your turning of things upside down shall be esteemed as the potter's clay: for shall the work say of him that made it, 'He made me not'? or shall the thing framed say to him that framed it, 'He had no understanding'?" (Isa. 29:16.)

SEX was created, in God's loving wisdom, to make possible these sacred God-plane institutions of Marriage, Home, and Family!

Sex was created to stimulate pure romantic love between a young man and a young woman properly mated for marriage; to inspire them with desire to share their lives, their problems, their trials and troubles, their hopes and successes TOGETHER; to enjoy the planning and building together of a happy HOME; and to rear a happy FAMILY.

God designed SEX to produce pure, righteous, clean, holy and rich BLESSINGS! He made it to be the loving BOND which not only would inspire a properly mated couple to marry, but which would PRESERVE that marriage in love. Sex should be the energizing magnet to draw constantly closer and closer together with increasing LOVE a husband and wife— to heal over those little irritations, disturbances, or misunderstandings which do occur.

Yet, this very bond which should bind the marriage tightly together is also the cord which, misused and perverted, *severs* more marriages than all other causes combined ten times over! *Mis*used, it can bring nightmarish divorces, wreck homes and lives, leave children without parents, spawn juvenile delinquents!

Let's save sex for MARRIAGE. Let's turn to the WAY of all the blissful joys and blessings God made possible, and intended!

CHAPTER 11

Recapturing the True Values
of Sex—the Commanded
Functions

*I*T ASSUREDLY is evident by now that sex was designed neither as something evil, filthy and degrading— nor, on the other hand, to be used in premarital, extra- marital, homosexual, or other manner of perversion.

Beyond Comprehension

Sex did not aimlessly evolve without purpose. It was designed by the Creator, and is to be held in sacred and holy honor. It was created for man's GOOD, not his destruction.

When God Almighty created sex in humans, there was PURPOSE so high and wonderful it transcends human ability fully to comprehend. It was designed directly to reflect our relationship with the HOLY GOD! Man's destiny is to be *born into* the very God Family—to become a member of the divine KINGDOM OF GOD.

What an incomparable destiny! Think of it! To be privileged to enter the DIVINE FAMILY—to be enabled to know and experience the blessings of FAMILY relationship— a God-plane relationship allowed to no other species or kind of life—to be given the joys of the LOVE relationship of marriage and family here and now—in this present mortal life!

All this is beyond the comprehension of those deceived by repressive prudery, and those contaminated by the modern sweep of IMMORALITY being falsely labeled "The New Morality."

God, in His wisdom, knew the necessity of *preparing* potential members of His divine Family, during *this* life, for that peaceful, happy, loving *family* relationship. Man should be boundlessly GRATEFUL, instead of polluting, profaning, perverting these blessings of God!

God Commands Sex Love

Now back once again to God's original instruction to our first parents!

Because, after creating Adam, God created the female Eve, He said: "Therefore shall a man leave his father and his mother, and shall cleave unto his wife: *and they shall be one flesh*" (Gen. 2:24).

Now what does *that* mean—a husband and wife *"shall be one flesh?"*

Remember, this Genesis record is the most abbreviated *summary* of God's instruction to the first man and woman. *Man* must not try to interpret Scripture. The Scripture *interprets itself!* One scripture interprets another!

What, then, is the *Bible* explanation of what is meant by being "one flesh"? It is explained very plainly in I Corinthians 6:16. There we find this very passage of Genesis 2:24 quoted and explained.

Condemning fornication between a man and a harlot, this passage says: "Now the body is not for fornication, . . . Know ye not that your bodies are the members of Christ? [the temple of the Holy Spirit—verse 19] shall I then take the members of Christ, and make them the members of an harlot? God forbid. What? know ye not that *he which is joined to an harlot is one body? for two, saith he, shall be one flesh*" (I Cor. 6:13, 15-16). And verse 18 adds: "FLEE FORNICATION."

The words in this passage: "for two, saith He, shall be one flesh," is a direct citation from Genesis 2:24!

That is PLAIN SPEAKING!

A man and a woman—*any* woman, even a harlot— become "one flesh" through the sexual act! A man and a harlot *are not married*—but in coitus they are *one flesh!*

In I Corinthians 6:16 this act between a man and a harlot is condemned as a capital SIN! But in Genesis 2:24—and also in Jesus' quotation from it in Matthew 19:5—this same act is *commanded* between husband and wife! God says a man and wife SHALL—a direct command!—*"be one flesh."* A man and a woman (I Cor. 6:16), become "one flesh" in sexual intercourse.

So, translated into frank and plain words, God says that, because God made humans male and female—a man shall marry a wife, and they shall have sexual intercourse!

And the Bible also commands: "Husbands, *love* your wives!

And Jesus added, "What therefore GOD hath joined together, let not man put asunder" (Mat. 19:6).

MARRIAGE was ordained of GOD! Marriage has *God's blessing!* God commanded the first humans to have sexual intercourse—and so this relationship is directly commanded by God, *and has God's blessing!*

But ONLY IN MARRIAGE!

Sex in marriage, far from being a sin, is "what GOD has joined together." It is *a holy and sacred relationship!*

All through the Bible, God condemns lust. Fornication— the sex act committed *prior* to marriage—is a SIN and breaks the Seventh Commandment. Homosexuality is condemned in the Bible as SIN—Sodomites shall not inherit the Kingdom of God! ANY use of sex, except as an expression of LOVE in MARRIAGE, and for the purpose of procreation in marriage, is a SIN, and breaks the Seventh Commandment! That includes masturbation, bestiality—any perversion—*any use* except that of love and reproduction *in marriage!*

The marriage relation is the very type of Christ's relation to the Church! The family relationship is a sacred GOD-PLANE relationship!

Now UNDERSTAND this entire passage in the 6th chapter of I Corinthians—for you probably have never looked at it closely enough to fully comprehend it before.

"Glorify God in Your Body"

This chapter continues the thought of the preceding 5th chapter. It is, of course, part of a letter written by the Apostle Paul to the Church of God at Corinth. These people, as a whole, were converted Christians—they had really *repented* of the former life, and had received God's Holy Spirit. But of course that does not remove *human nature.* Those of this Church were still spiritual babes. Paul's letter was corrective. Some were being enticed into fornication and immorality. One, in particular, had been indulging in a sex relationship with his stepmother.

It seems the Church at Corinth was adopting the attitude of some ministers today. They showed "compassion" on this fornicator by condoning and approving his sin. Paul sternly commanded them, by authority of Jesus Christ, to put this evildoer out of the Church (chapter 5, to verse 13).

In chapter 6, some church members were taking their disputes before the civil courts. Paul condemned this, saying they should bring such matters before Church officials for settlement.

"Do ye not know that the saints *shall judge the world?*" he asked. He was speaking of the time, after Christ's coming and the resurrection, in the coming "millennium," when the begotten children of God shall have been BORN into the world-ruling Kingdom of God! Here Paul reminded the Church (for his epistle was inspired as God's Word for God's WHOLE Church, even of our day) of man's tremendous DESTINY! "Know ye not that we shall judge angels?" he continued (verse 3). "How much more things that pertain to this life?"

He continues, verse 9: "Know ye not that the unrighteous shall *not* inherit the kingdom of God? Be not deceived: neither fornicators, nor idolaters, nor adulterers, nor effemi-nate, nor abusers of themselves with mankind [homosex-uals], nor thieves . . . shall inherit the kingdom of God."

Then Paul shows that, even though one has led such a life—committed such sins—HE CAN BE FORGIVEN, if he re-pents and turns from them—and STILL CAN INHERIT ETER-NAL LIFE. In the next (11th) verse, he continues:

"And such were some of you: *but ye are washed . . .*" (forgiven and cleansed of such things, through Christ).

This MORALITY subject is continued in verses 13-15: ". . . Now the body is not for fornication, but for the Lord; and the Lord for the body. And God hath both raised up the Lord [Christ's resurrection], *and will also raise up us* by his own power. Know ye not that your bodies are the mem-bers of Christ? shall I then take the members of Christ, and make them the members of an harlot? God forbid!"

Then follow the verses first quoted above: "What? know ye not that he which is joined to an harlot is *one body?* for two, saith he, shall be *one flesh*" (verse 16). Then verse 18: "FLEE fornication. . . . What? know ye not that *your body* is the TEMPLE OF THE HOLY SPIRIT which is in you, which ye have of God, and *ye are not your own?* For ye are bought with a price [by Christ's DEATH!]: therefore *glorify God in your body . . .*" (verses 18-20).

Look at that carefully! The BODY is the temple of the Holy Spirit. The BODY does not belong to the individual— we are not our own—Christ bought and paid for us! There-fore glorify GOD—*HOW?* It does not say with "your mind" —but "in your BODY!"

All through this passage, even from the preceding chap-ter, the theme has been SEX. These two chapters forbid and condemn the MISuse of sex through fornication, adultery, homosexuality, masturbation. But GOD established MARRIAGE. Marriage is honorable—marriage has God's blessing—it is GOD who joins the husband and wife in a GOD-PLANE rela-tionship. And GOD has said a man and wife shall "be one flesh"—shall express marital LOVE in sexual intercourse!

This GLORIFIES GOD—because God ordained it—because God actually joined the husband and wife. You thus glorify God in your BODY by this God-ordained use of sex.

This is a direct command thus to glorify GOD by *using* the body in this GOD-ORDAINED use.

Minds Unknowingly Perverted

If a husband and wife approach the sexual union in LOVE, as an expression of LOVE, comprehending the divine *significance* and God-ordained *meaning* of this use of sex—and giving God thanks—they are glorifying GOD with their bodies!

But have our *minds* become so perverted by this satanic teaching that even God-ordained MARRIED LOVE seems shameful, degrading, and leaves us with a sense of guilt? One of the tragedies of all time is the fact that some actually *have* been thus *branded!*

What a catastrophe in human experience! What a cunning, diabolical deception of Satan!

God blessed mankind with the holy GOD-PLANE institution of *marriage*—the very *picture* of the Christ-Church relationship. God made possible this expression of marital LOVE, by which two whom GOD has joined for life may glorify GOD in their bodies! God endowed mankind with the God-plane institution of the FAMILY and the HOME—the very type of the KINGDOM OF GOD into which we may be born. Thus God ordained that even in *this* mortal life we may *experience* the blessing of FAMILY life, to *prepare us* for life in the Kingdom of GOD!

But humanity has *lost* the knowledge of these glorious truths!

A clever, subtle devil has instilled in human minds these false attitudes toward SEX. By this very means he has blinded men's eyes to these truths. He has robbed potential heirs of God of these blessings!

Today the new IMMORALITY calling sex GOOD—even in promiscuity—is sweeping the world. Nevertheless, a large portion of girls being drawn into mental acceptance *still* FEEL a sense of shame and guilt. It's a psychological hangover from the agelong "old morality."

I know, too, that thousands of wives will read this book —accept this TRUTH with gratitude to God—and *still* find themselves unable to eradicate false convictions. They are simply victims of this agelong "moral" teaching of Satan.

Many of today's women have been taught from early childhood by well-intentioned parents that sex is some kind of "animal instinct"—that sex is "not nice," but shameful, degrading, sinful. This attitude has been so deeply embedded they now find themselves unable to free their minds.

Coming to know the truth intellectually, a wife may really want love and a good physical relationship with her husband. Yet she finds that she just somehow can't "let herself go." Love-making, which a benevolent God formed her to enjoy with her husband, just somehow seems to be contaminated. It leaves her with a sense of shame and guilt. She *knows better*, in her mind—yet this false sense has been inculcated so deeply, it seems still to hold her in its clutch.

Do you know why?

"Seared with a Hot Iron"

Do you realize that one can be taught a thing so intensively, so repeatedly, that the false concept has become literally *burned in* to the extent he (or, usually *she*) is unable to root it out?

It becomes a scar that can never be removed.

It is like a woman—some thirty-seven years ago—who was chief librarian in the Science section of a large city library. I had been making a critical study of the theory of evolution, side by side with my first study of the Biblical account of special Creation. I had found the "trunk of the tree" of the evolutionary hypothesis. Every argument—

every purported "evidence"—was merely a branch off that main trunk. If it fell, the whole tree fell with it. I had written a brief thesis setting forth the facts, and since I knew this librarian was well schooled in science I asked her to read it and give me her evaluation.

"Mr. Armstrong," she said, with a sharp but half-puzzled gleam in her eye, "you have an uncanny knack of getting to the very heart and core of a subject. You have reduced it to comparatively few words. You have, beyond question, felled the trunk of the tree of evolution. With my mind, I can recognize that you have *disproved* the doctrine. Your argument is correct. Your facts are true. Yet, in spite of your positive PROOF that evolution has no foundation— that it is false—I could never in all my life cease to believe in it. I am simply too steeped in it. All my life I have been associated in scientific circles. I have devoted years doing graduate work at Columbia, the University of Chicago, and other universities. Everything I have always read, been taught, and accepted in every field of science *is based on evolution.* You force me to admit evolution is false by your paper—yet I am unable to put evolution out of my mind."

A person's conscience may be "seared with a hot iron" (I Tim. 4:2). We can have a false teaching so deeply *burned into* our minds that we are "given over to BELIEVE a lie."

We read, in II Thessalonians 2 of those who have been indoctrinated with Satan's delusions, that "God shall send them strong delusion, that they should *believe a lie*" (verse 11).

Because of this ungodly teaching that sex, even in marriage, is degrading and shameful, countless wives, even after coming to a knowledge of God's TRUTH, are utterly *unable* to bring themselves to *feel right*—as God intended—about the marriage relationship. This is actually a form of incurable *perversion*—mental perversion in which the mind has been *trained* to reject what is holy and good and God-ordained as if it were something *evil!* It is incurable by human means—

incurable except by divine miracle! It takes God's power!

Most assuredly some who will read this book will find themselves in this category. With their minds, they will now see the TRUTH. Yet, in the marriage relationship, they will automatically freeze up in dread. They will, in spite of true KNOWLEDGE, feel dirty, with a sense of condemnation and guilt. This has been "brain-washed" into their subconscious minds—*burned in*—as if cauterized; and cauterizing deadens sensation.

To enjoy the rich BLESSINGS a loving GOD wishes to *lavish* on every true wife who follows HIS LAWS and is led by HIS SPIRIT, God's *TRUTH* must be not merely recognized by the mind—it must be *acted upon!*

Every victim of this foul satanic mind-branding should pray earnestly, prevailingly with the whole heart, to the Holy GOD to remove root and branch that false concept. Pray, as did David, "Create in me a *clean* heart, O God; and renew a *right* spirit [attitude] within me" (Ps. 51:10).

When David, filled with remorse and emotion, prayed this prayer, he was in brokenhearted repentance because of his SEX sin with Bathsheba, wife of Uriah. He was repenting of his wrong attitude toward sex. He was beseeching God to take this *dirty* attitude of lust out of his heart—to create in him a *clean* heart, and to restore a *right* spirit—or attitude —a *right concept* toward sex—in his mind.

Read again and again this and the preceding three chapters. Read all the Bible passages. Learn to OBEY God gladly, wholeheartedly, in love and loving anticipation, when He commands: "Wives, submit yourselves unto your own husbands, *as unto the Lord*" (Eph. 5:22; Col. 3:18). Even as husbands are commanded to *love* their wives, so wives are commanded to give *love* to their husbands (Tit. 2:4).

God's LAW—God's WAY to every happiness—safeguards this holy, pure, righteous, personal and intimate loving marriage relationship. It has GOD's BLESSING!

Travel *this way*, in prayer and thanksgiving, in love,

and in deep gratitude to a benevolent and loving GOD!

Frank New Testament Teaching

Now study the 7th chapter of I Corinthians.

The BIBLE—as originally inspired—SPEAKS OUT in plain and frank language, not only *against* every misuse and perversion of sex, but just as frankly *instructing* us in God-ordained right uses!

Remember we read the Bible as it has been translated into the English language. Some translations—especially the Authorized (King James) version—were made at a time when sex was universally regarded as shameful and evil. The King James translators tried to cover up the true meaning, feeling it was "not nice" to speak so plainly. But every original word was inspired by God's HOLY SPIRIT! And it is time we throw off Satan's false accusations that some of the Word of God is "not nice." It is holy and sacred!

For this reason, the Moffatt translation will be used, as well as the King James, in expounding this crucial New Testament chapter on SEX. The Moffatt translation renders the inspired original Greek in the English words of its TRUE MEANING.

This was written originally as a letter from the Apostle Paul to the Church of God at Corinth. But it was inspired through the Holy Spirit. It is part of GOD'S WORD for us today.

We have seen, earlier in this chapter, that in his 5th and 6th chapters the Apostle was writing about SEX. There were sex abuses—sex misuses—in that Church, which God through Paul *condemned*. But we have seen how Paul, in the latter part of the 6th chapter, taught that husbands and wives, through God's sacred MARRIAGE institution, should GLORIFY GOD in their bodies—by giving LOVE through sex.

Chapter 7 continues the instruction from GOD of the true God-intended use of sex.

Notice verses 1 and 2: "Now concerning the things

whereof ye wrote unto me: It is good for a man not to touch a woman. Nevertheless, to avoid fornication, let every man have his own wife, and let every woman have her own husband."

NOTICE THAT! *Get its real meaning!* Every man and woman should marry—but *WHY?* Because it is a sin to remain single? No—verse 1 says it would be good for "a man not to touch a woman"—that is, to remain free from sex, and unmarried. It is not WRONG to remain single.

Then WHY does this passage teach that men and women should marry? Does it say "marry in order to beget children"? No, it says nothing here about the purpose of sex being reproduction.

WHY, then? This scripture answers: *"To avoid fornication"!* Paul has just been condemning premarital sexual intercourse—FORNICATION—as a SIN, which breaks the 7th Commandment.

The plain teaching here is that, to avoid sexual intercourse *out of* marriage, a man and woman should marry! Have sexual intercourse IN marriage! This has God's blessing. This is commanded by God!

To avoid the SIN of fornication—unmarried sex—and to have the sexual relationship with God's blessing in TRUE LOVE, let men and women marry!

The PURPOSE here given is *not* reproduction, but lawful and righteous sexual intercourse instead of unlawful and sinful fornication. This becomes even more plain as we proceed.

Plain Speaking

Now verse 3: "Let the husband render unto the wife due benevolence; and likewise also the wife unto the husband." The King James translators in the year 1611 tried to translate this in "modest" language, and this largely covers up the true meaning. However, "benevolence" does mean disposition to do good; charitableness; love.

Now read it with the false modesty stripped away, in the

Moffatt translation: "The husband must give the wife her conjugal dues, and the wife in the same way must give the husband his . . ." And the word "conjugal" means sexual or marital.

Notice, in this verse these points. The sexual relation in marriage is a *command*: "The husband *must* . . . and the wife . . . *must.* . . ." Notice, next, God's principle of *giving, sharing*. Each is to *GIVE* this sexual-intercourse love to the other. God does not speak of it in terms of carnal *taking*, or *receiving* sensual gratification—but in terms of *giving love*.

Continue, verse 4—Moffatt: ". . . a wife cannot do as she pleases with her body—her husband has power; and in the same way a husband cannot do as he pleases with his body—his wife has power."

Notice how the principle of God's Law—that of LOVE—of GIVING—of outgoing concern rather than selfish gratification, is stressed. It is a command: "a wife *cannot.* . . ." It does not say "ought not," it flatly forbids, as contrary to the Law—and consequently SIN—for either husband or wife to use his or her body *selfishly*. The wife made frigid by false concepts must not withhold sexual intercourse from her husband. Her sex organs do not belong to her—they belong to her husband!

In the same way, a husband cannot withhold participation in coitus from his wife—or, conversely, neither shall a husband make inconsiderate demands on his wife, so that *he* may use *his* sex organs as *he* pleases for *his* selfish gratification. His sex anatomy does not belong to him. Christ bought both husband and wife with the price of His very life.

Actually our bodies belong to HIM—but He, here, gives the right and power of the husband's body over to the wife; and the right and authority over the wife's body to the husband. Yet the teaching of God—the WAY of His Law—denies selfish *taking*, and demands considerate *giving*.

The motive and intention are here involved. Actually, it devolves down to direction of mind and intent—to attitude. The man who argues that this verse of God's teaching gives him the *right* to make inconsiderate and selfish demands on the use of his wife's body—arguing that her body belongs to him—overlooks the fact that his motive and purpose is merely to use his own sex organs for his own sensual gratification without any consideration or outgoing *concern* for her wishes.

There are times, in the life of any married couple, when it would be cruel, totally inconsiderate, utterly selfish on the part of a husband to demand his own satisfaction and gratification by use of his wife's body. At such times, God's teaching, when understood, says the husband's sexual apparatus *does not belong to him*—he has no right to use it selfishly at cost of pain, suffering, or mental harassment to the wife. God commands husbands to be considerate of their wife's feelings—to be tender, gentle, as much concerned for *her* desires and comfort and pleasure as his own.

On the other hand, there are times when sexual union is a definite *need* for a husband. At such times, the wife must be considerate, and *not* defraud her husband. At such times she must not claim her body belongs to her and deny it to him.

Then again, the selfish "frigid" wife who deliberately denies love in coitus to her husband, merely because she "isn't in the mood," is violating God's command which says "a wife cannot do as *she* pleases with her body—her husband has power"—her body belongs to him.

God's Law, at all times, is THE WAY of LOVE—which is concern and consideration for the other at least equal with that for the self. Selfishness becomes lust. LOVE flees when the whole concern is for *self*.

Verse 5 of this 7th chapter of I Corinthians becomes still more plain: "Do not withhold sexual intercourse from one another, unless you agree to do so for a time, in order to devote yourselves to prayer. Then come together again. You must not let Satan tempt you through incontinence."

And "incontinence," of course, means lack of sexual control.

Now notice that same verse in the King James version. It shows that abstaining from sexual intercourse in marriage —except by *mutual* agreement at infrequent intervals—or, for either one to selfishly *deny* coitus to the other—is actually DEFRAUDING the other!

In other and plainer words, to practice what falsely called "Christian" teaching has demanded for 18½ centuries —withholding sexual intercourse *except* for begetting children—is a *direct violation of God's teaching*—is ITSELF SIN AND DISOBEDIENCE TO GOD—and is *DEFRAUDING* one's mate!

This dualistic paganism piled up a mountain of human woe and frustration through these 18½ centuries higher than all the geological mountains of earth piled one on top of the other! It taught millions of husbands and wives to disobey God's commands—to commit SIN—and the human suffering is the evidence. Obedience to GOD's Law brings happiness and joy. SIN brings suffering and misery. The very fruits of this medieval prudery demonstrate that it has been the WAY of SIN!

Here, then, is that same verse 5 in the King James translation:

"Defraud ye not one the other, except it be with consent for a time, that ye may give yourselves to fasting and prayer; and come together again, that Satan tempt you not for your incontinency."

Painful Experience SPEAKS OUT!

Not only does ALMIGHTY GOD, through the Bible, *speak out* in plain language against this pagan and medieval teaching. The VOICE OF CRUEL EXPERIENCE also cries out!

This stern teaching that sex must be used *only* to beget children has put marriages beyond count into an injurious, impossible situation.

Augustine, Aquinas, and the church "fathers" who preceded them in their "chaste severity" could see no LOVE in the marital union. Marital sex, *except* for procreation, was viewed always as lust, concupiscence, degrading and sinful self-gratification. And, even if a husband and wife mated in coitus for the express PURPOSE of begetting a baby, they viewed it with suspicion.

Of course those men—at least Augustine, and those Catholic priests after him including Aquinas—never *experienced* the happy joys of married LOVE. Augustine's conscience was racked with guilt over his fornication and sex vices contrary to the Seventh and Tenth Commandments. He NEVER MARRIED. He largely influenced the establishment of priesthood celibacy. He was not without quantitative sex experience. But all that experience was motivated by concupiscence. He never experienced the GIVING of love *in marriage*. He knew NOTHING of its happy and blissful joys. All he knew, by experience, was inordinate *self*-desire, followed by the conscience-stricken pangs of self-condemnation and guilt. Such men never experienced that clean, wholesome, LOVE of a pure wife, mingled with respect, admiration, high regard, esteem and honor.

Yet thousands of intelligent victims of that repressive teaching have come to see—in spite of that teaching—that the expression of pure LOVE between husband and wife through coitus is every whit as vital a purpose as producing children. Of course, probably the overwhelming majority, blinded by the false teaching, never discovered this. But where did it leave those who did?

Thousands of case histories—and I know of enough to be sure of what I am saying—have found that this repression robbed their marriage of spontaneity and joy. There are times when circumstances dictate either the spacing of the next child, or else that there should be no more children. Even in the case of couples who have *discovered* the true, clean and beautiful happiness of *giving* and *bestowing*

LOVE in the sexual union, where does this teaching leave them?

They have been sternly taught that "they must hear the CHURCH!" To disobey this teaching, they have been led to believe, will mean an *eternity* of indescribable torture of burning forever and ever in hell! This has been made REAL to them! They are filled with fear and the terror of it! They *dare not* disobey their church teaching. And, usually, they *want* to obey it—because they have been made to believe it is right! So what happens? They strive to live *without* sex. Sex comes to carry the hateful meaning of FEAR that *destroys* love!

Many, in their desperate dilemma, have gone tearfully to their parish priest for counsel and help. When they are told that the only difficulty is lack of self-control, they are really frustrated.

They may struggle and wrestle with the one allowance of the church—resorting to the "rhythm method." In desperate determination, they restrain themselves for what is calculated (often erroneously) to be the prescribed period. Then, often, they find this method simply DIDN'T WORK!

Today many doctors admit that this "rhythm method" is a faulty theory. There is no part of the month during which all women are for a certainty immune from conception. There may be a decrease in probability—but the matter is only relative. Medical charts show conceptions occurring at any or all times of the month.

And so millions, under the whiplash of this UNscriptural teaching, even if they had once found the joys of true marital love, find their marriages twisted. Wives become frigid. Husbands become frustrated.

Case histories by the uncounted thousands PROVE that the Biblical way, once rightly understood, is RIGHT and its FRUITS are abundant happiness and joy. But *man's* way, whether of medieval prudery or modern promiscuity, produces only the bitter grapes of wrath!

CHAPTER 12

The Biological Differences

*N*OW YOU HAVE, in brief, the missing half of
sex knowledge. In all books pretending to impart information
about sex, the half from God's revelation *should have* come
first, as, indeed, it has been placed first here.

The Foundation

It has, in this book, been emphasized that the Holy
Bible is the FOUNDATION of all knowledge. Especially is this
true in the subject of sex. Also, it provides the right *approach*
to acquirable, experimental and discoverable knowledge.

Now we have the FOUNDATION *on which* knowledge of
the physical details of sex ought to be built. We have, now,
the true, wholesome, clean and God-directed attitude as
our approach to the biological facts. Now you may view the
physical facts with right attitude, clean mind, and profound
respect and awe for the wisdom of God for having designed
SEX for man's highest GOOD!

God's ways are PERFECT! They are the bestowal of HIS
LOVE!

We are ready, now, to proceed in receiving the necessary
BIOLOGICAL knowledge. And even in this physical area, the
true WAY is the WAY OF LOVE!

There are *two* biological *differences* we need to understand. First is the difference between *human* and *animal* FEMALES.

So far as reproduction itself goes, the physical process is the same in humans as in mammals. But *beyond* the purpose of reproduction *there are vital differences.*

All reproduction—plant, animal and human, comes from a union of male and female elements or cells. *All physical life* is carried on by reproduction *through sex.* Walt Whitman wrote that we see "everywhere sex, everywhere the urge of procreation." Flowers, plants, vegetables; the whole of the animal kingdom from smallest insect to largest mammal; and humans, too—all are male and female.

There is an old Latin phrase, *Omne ex ovo,* meaning *everything comes from an egg.*

The beginning of reproduction—in mammals and humans—is from an egg, or *ovum.* The ovum always is produced by the female. Yet every ovum—human or animal—is infertile of itself. Life must be imparted to it by a sperm cell, called a *spermatozoon* (plural, *spermatozoa*), produced within the body of the male. Within the ovum is a nucleus, or dormant germ. After a sperm cell enters an egg cell, it unites with the nucleus, and then a new human or animal has been begotten, and is well on its way to developing into the same kind, or species, as its parents.

This fertilization of the ovum is called *conception,* or begettal. A woman in whom such conception has occurred is said to be pregnant. The growing state, from conception until birth, is called *gestation,* or period of the mother-to-be's pregnancy. Its birth is called *parturition.*

This physical process of reproduction is the same in mammals as in humans. But, aside from the reproductive process, there are extremely important *biological differences* between human and animal females.

Women Different from Female Animals

In both women and female mammals, the ova are produced within the body, by germinal glands called *ovaries,* of which there are two. In women, an egg cell, or ovum, is produced approximately every four weeks. If the ovum is not fertilized, the uterus discharges a little blood. This is called menstruation, and will be explained more in detail later. Menstruation occurs normally in women about thirteen times a year.

But in ANIMALS, *there is no menstruation* in the sense and manner it occurs in women.

Female animals have, instead, a rutting period. It does not occur with the frequency of humans. In dogs, for example, females have a rutting time about every six to eight months. In other animals, this occurs less, and in some more frequently. They produce an ovum only once in that period. At all other times, female animals are virtually *sexless!* The female does not allow the breeding act, and the male animal seldom attempts it. If one does, the female will fight him off with all her strength.

But at this rutting time, commonly spoken of by farmers as being "in heat," the sexual organs secrete substances which release an odor. This excites the animals automatically (instinct) to sexual intercourse for breeding.

In the animal world, SEX SERVES NO PURPOSE EXCEPT REPRODUCTION! No expression of love, in the human sense, exists. The female sex organs in animals are absolutely DORMANT at all times, *except* the rutting period. It would be utterly IMPOSSIBLE to arouse a female animal, sexually, during all this long time from one rutting period to the next. Experiments in artificial insemination have proven that animals *cannot* be impregnated during the long periods between rutting times.

With animals there is no marriage—no home—no family relationship. No husband-and-wife sexual LOVE relationship. Females are sexless between rutting periods!

Female humans *do not have a "rutting period,"* or a mating period when they are "in heat." Between the age of puberty and the time of menopause—roughly between ages 14 and 44, or a duration of approximately 30 years—

women have the monthly period (approximately each 28 days) when they menstruate. *Female animals do not menstruate.*

But when "in heat," the female animal is beside herself with desire for mating. And until she is relieved, by the fertilization of the ripe ovum from coital breeding by the male of her kind, she knows no rest. Actually, unless the female animal is soon bred, she will make every effort—run any risk—to obtain pregnancy.

But in women, such things are *utterly different!* Women are never "in heat." The presence of an ovum in a Fallopian tube (when it is ready to be fertilized) makes little or no difference in either a woman's desire for, or reluctance against sexual intercourse. The Kinsey reports and other surveys including findings of doctors, have shown that in many, if not most women, no difference whatever is noted. In the minority, the difference in either desire or abhorrence is slight and merely relative.

What does all this MEAN?

It means that, except for purposes of producing progeny, the functions and responses of sex in women are *entirely different* from sex in animals. Although marital coitus should never, of course, occur during menstruation (see Ezek. 18:6 and parallel scriptures), there is NO TIME during the month when a woman is virtually sexless—when sex functioning goes dormant—when she is *unable* to engage in coitus with her husband. She is as much capable of coitus at one time as another.

God made WOMAN, as well as MAN, on a plane infinitely higher than animals! He created SEX in HUMANS as a means of bestowing reciprocal LOVE. He created women so that their sex organs may be used for the purpose of sharing LOVE—when pregnancy is virtually IMPOSSIBLE. (At least, when the "rhythm method" advocates say it is.)

Animals DO NOT MARRY. The use of sex for breeding purposes, in animals, *is not a matter of love-making!*

Can you *imagine* a big bull and a cow in passionate embrace, with their "arms around each other"—that is, trying to wrap their front legs, with their hoofs, around each other, trying to hug and kiss, and caress, and make LOVE?

If a circus could ever train a bull and a cow to put on such an act, it would be *sure* to bring the house down with side-splitting laughter. You may be sure the circus people would have thought of that—and done it—long ago, IF IT WERE POSSIBLE to train a bull and a cow to go into a LOVE embrace!

Sex SERVES NO PURPOSE OF LOVE with animals!

With mammals, *reproduction* is brought about by the same process as in humans. But animals DO NOT MARRY. Animals do not have either the *"philia"* or the *"eros"* love. Animals cannot receive the *"agape"* love from God. With animals, sex does not stimulate desire for LOVE—or, for that matter, for lust.

WHY do people refer to human LUST as "animal passion"? Why do some women say: "Men are BRUTES"? WHY INSULT THE ANIMALS? They do only what God set their brains to cause them to do BY INSTINCT!

In women, sex is a LOVE stimulant. Women *can*, and usually do, engage in sex as a LOVE embrace, *even at times when pregnancy is impossible!* Female animals cannot.

When a female animal is served by the male, there is NO LOVE EMBRACE—no love-making. The male mounts on the back of the female, imparts the fertilizing spermatozoa, and departs.

Human *bodies* were deliberately designed BY GOD *in a different manner*—so that sex in humans becomes an embrace of love.

What Evolutionists Don't Know

The evolutionists, in willful and inexcusable ignorance, classify MAN within the ANIMAL kingdom. There was no intelligent Creator. There was no rational, thoughtful and wise planning and designing, with PURPOSE. In their stubborn, *irrational* rebellion against revelation, they formulate and religiously embrace in blind faith ridiculous and vanity-inspired fables. They cling defiantly to the postulate that MAN descended, over millions of years, from animals similar and ancestor to the anthropoid ape. All this by hereditary reproduction, brought about by natural processes and resident forces.

How, WHEN, and WHY, then, did animal instinct disappear, and human MIND with its human SPIRIT, arrive on the scene? And if no intelligent GOD designed and created sex for definite PURPOSES, just how do we explain these amazing sex *differences* between animals and humans? And WHY such a *total* gap in fossil findings? WHY no intermediate species?

There is yet one other amazing factor the evolutionist will have difficulty in explaining. And that is what happens after human menopause.

Women have been given a duration of approximately 30 years of fertility, during which they may become mothers. At an age averaging 13 or 14, girls reach the age of puberty. At that age their breasts develop, for the purpose of supplying milk to newborn babies. Their sex organs mature, and their ovaries begin to produce ova.

These egg cells usually are produced at the rate of one every 28 days, alternating from each ovary. If the ovum is fertilized in the Fallopian tube, a new human life has been begotten. It then continues on into the womb, or uterus, where it is protected, nourished, and gradually developed ready to be born after approximately nine months.

But if the ovum is not met by a sperm cell and fertilized —and some doctors say it has a life of only 48 hours after leaving the ovary—it dies. Meanwhile, with the releasing of each egg cell from an ovary, the uterus has been prepared to receive a fertilized embryo. But if fertilization did not take place, then the womb discharges a little blood through the vagina, gradually, over a period of about 5 days. This is called *menstruation*.

Although the menstrual period occurs generally about

every 28 days, many if not most girls experience irregularity beginning at the age of puberty. Sometimes this irregularity persists for some years before a regular rhythm is established. Unless this irregularity is quite excessive, it need cause no alarm.

As soon as a girl begins her menstrual periods, she is *physically* capable of becoming a mother. But she is not yet, for some years, mentally and emotionally mature enough for motherhood.

This physical capacity for reproduction continues for approximately 30 years. Then a woman reaches the "change of life" period, called *menopause*.

After Menopause

Some women reach this period of change at about age 40—some, rarely, as late as age 50. The average will be somewhere around 45.

This *menopause* is a more or less trying experience. There will be nervousness, often complaint of "hot flashes," and sometimes neurotic disturbances. The discomforture depends largely on physical, mental, and emotional health. Some women foolishly have internal sex organs removed by surgery at this time, only to discover later that they obtained temporary relief at cost of greatly *increased* mental problems, as well as physical.

But *WHY* this menopause stage?

Here again the wise *design* of a loving, all-intelligent Creator is emphasized. After this stage of life, women simply *should no* longer carry the responsibilities of caring for babies and training young children. Children begin to "get on their nerves."

Neither women nor men ever reach the age where they no longer *enjoy* children. You see, *this* is the age when they usually become grandparents. God has designed things so that all grandparents find their own grandchildren are just as sweet, lovely and dear to them as their own. They now have the privilege (barring geographical separation) of EN-

JOYING the grandchildren—*on occasion*.

It is a real JOY to see the little tots come scampering into the grandparents' home. But after an hour, or two or three, it is somehow a welcome relief when their parents take the kiddies home. Grandma just simply ought not be burdened down too often with the *care and responsibility* of the children.

So there was intelligence, wisdom, loving *concern*, in the designing hand of the Creator. When a woman reaches this stage of life, her ovaries cease manufacturing ova.

No SUCH CHANGE TAKES PLACE IN MEN. There *is* a mild sort of menopause in men—more mental than physical. But men may become fathers into a very ripe old age.

BUT WHAT ABOUT EXPRESSING LOVE THROUGH SEX?

The Creator *designed* HUMAN sex (but not *animal* sex) as a means of expressing pure, righteous, and undefiled LOVE. And God commands: "Husbands, LOVE your wives!" And also for women "to LOVE their own husbands."

Now should a husband and wife stop LOVING each other, after age 45 or 50? *NEVER!*

And so a benevolent, loving GOD, designed women so that they are freed from exposure to pregnancies after this stage of life—BUT THEIR PARTICIPATION IN SEXUAL LOVE WITH THEIR HUSBANDS *DOES NOT CEASE!*

Actually, most women are either less reluctant (if inhibited by the dualistic repression), or else *more desirous* of sexual intercourse with their husbands after this period than they were before!

It is true that, after this age, sex drives in both sexes *begin to slow down gradually*. The act of coitus will not be desired quite so often. But if the wife slows down, so also does her husband. So a God who had great outgoing concern for us—His own potential children—designed humans so that husband and wife continue to be endeared to each other by coitus all through life.

MARRIAGE is ordained "until *death* do us part." One purpose of marriage is sexual LOVE. When the *other* purpose—childbearing—ceases, sexual LOVE continues to draw husband and wife ever closer in the bond of true LOVE—until *death* parts them!

Can anyone contemplate these wonderful facts of the Creator's wisdom and love and power, without an emotional feeling of awe, reverence, respect, and gratitude?

How WONDERFUL are the works of GOD's hands!

So we have these *marked differences* between *human* and *animal* females.

These physical, biological differences, as well as God's WORD, prove that sex in HUMANS was designed for a PURPOSE not applicable to animals. It was designed for MARRIAGE—for FAMILY relationship—for *expression of* LOVE between husband and wife. And sex provides the means for this bestowal of LOVE "until death do us part," even into old age!

CHAPTER 13

How God Designed Sex

*M*AN has produced many highly complicated mechanisms out of matter he has appropriated from the ground.

The huge, intricately designed modern newspaper and magazine presses bring exclamations of amazement from visitors seeing one for the first time. I am reminded of this, because we have just installed one of these big magazine presses in our new enlarged printing plant in Pasadena, California.

Awe-Inspiring Mechanism

But the largest, most complicated machines man has designed pale to insignificance beside the most wonderful of all mechanisms—the HUMAN BODY AND MIND!

This awe-inspiring mechanism *also* was formed from matter out of the ground. It was the supreme MASTERPIECE of God's great creative handiwork! The Almighty formed man after His own likeness! And his SPIRITUAL CREATION is still in process!

God reveals much about *Himself!* He is composed of Spirit—not matter. He is a God of supreme MIND. He tells us He has eyes, ears, nose, mouth. He has arms and legs—feet and hands! He wrote the Ten Commandments on stone tablets with His own *finger!*

The marvelous human body is formed and shaped like

God, unlike any other creature! Yet God, being Spirit, possesses inherent eternal life. He has endowed MAN with only a limited physical existence, sustained chemically, in principle, much like the motor in your car.

So God designed in the human body two basic types of systems.

One is the *life-sustaining* apparatus. This includes the highly complicated digestive, circulatory, respiratory and other systems. These are coordinated in functioning by the nervous system, which, in turn, is directly connected with the mind.

The other basic system is the genital, or sex system, making humans male and female. This has no direct part in sustaining the individual's existence. It serves to perpetuate, *not* the individual, but the *race*. But it also generates love and a desire to marry a certain one, and stimulates marital love to preserve the home and family. This genital system, too, is connected by the nervous system directly with the mind.

These two general systems serve different purposes, yet there is a connection between the two. The genital apparatus exercises a considerable influence on the life-sustaining functions. The female sex hormones cause a woman's body and mind to be feminine. The male sex hormones cause a man's body and mind to be masculine.

Also there is a closer analogy between male and female sex organs and sex functioning than is generally understood.

It is the genital system that we need here to describe.

We shall use, in this description of sex anatomy and functioning, the medical, or scientific, terminology. I strongly urge all parents to learn these terms, and to use them in teaching their children.

If it were not entirely too embarrassing, a social gathering could be given a hilarious evening by each, one at a time, saying right out loud the *names* for sex organs and functions —especially the eliminative functions—which *their mothers* taught them! Probably no two people at the party would reveal the same terminology. Every young mother seems to think up some new outlandish names for such things. It becomes a sort of secret language.

If I might, at this point, be permitted one digression intended to be humorous, I should like to mention the cute saying of a year-and-a-half-old little girl. Her mother had tried to break her of bed-wetting by making a shaming face and uttering a sound something like "kh— kh— kh—." In her baby talk this little girl soon began to call this particular means of elimination by a term she pronounced "kuh"— almost like "koo." Then one day, for the first time in her life, the little girl saw an ocean. She was tremendously impressed by its magnitude.

"O Mommie!" she exclaimed, excitedly, "Ocean kuh pang!" "Pang" was her baby talk for panties. The adults present haven't stopped laughing since.

The moral is, children should be taught the proper professional terms rather than some weird terminology of your own devising.

Three Functional Categories

We humans cannot live the clean and happy lives the Creator intended and made possible, unless we understand His PURPOSES, and the laws regulating sex functions. This is true, regardless of age, sex, or marriage status. It applies to all from the age of puberty. And there are many things about sex which parents *need* to teach children as soon as little minds begin to become curious about little bodies.

This book is not intended to be a technical scientific textbook to educate professionals—though certainly every doctor, psychiatrist, or other professional dealing with sex *ought* to know what has been covered in this book.

It *is*, however, the purpose of this book to reveal not only God's PURPOSES, and the *right attitude* toward sex, but those basic though somewhat elementary biological facts which ought to be known by teen-agers as well as the marriageable and the married.

Man, utterly unlike animals, arrives at sexual maturity

several years before he achieves mental, emotional, and social maturity. Boys and girls are capable of becoming parents years before they are qualified for the responsibilities of parenthood.

Teen-agers *need* this knowledge for their own protection. In this age of pressures toward promiscuity, blinded by false teachings, adolescents cannot be expected to resist premarital sex unless their minds are opened to intelligent acceptance of GOD'S PURPOSES and LAWS.

Also, all married people *need* this knowledge if their marriages are to be preserved in happiness. It is the *lack* of this knowledge which has caused 90% of all marital unhappiness, contention, separation and divorce.

None can understand what he *needs* to know without an elementary knowledge of the anatomy of sex organs, as well as some knowledge of sex stimuli and sex functioning. And so we approach, here, the necessary knowledge of anatomy and functioning in a manner quite different from that which has been commonly used.

The genital system is composed of three functional categories. These are

1) *Glands.* These produce the germinal cells and the hormones. In the male these glands are called *testes*, or testicles; and in the female, *ovaries.*

2) *Ducts.* These tubes transport the germinating cells from testes and ovaries, and render possible fertilization. In the male they are the *vasa efferentia*, the *epididymis*, the *vas deferens*, the *ejaculatory duct*, and the *urethra*. In the female, they are the *Fallopian tubes*, or oviducts, through which the ovum is carried from the ovary to the uterus.

3) *Organs of copulation.* Through these the male germinating cells, called spermatozoa, reach the ovum for fertilization. These organs are, in the male, the *penis*, and in the female, the *vagina.* The fertilized ovum remains in the female *uterus* or *womb*, where it is nourished and developed sufficiently to be born.

The Body Like the Church

No book I have procured on sex anatomy and functions makes any mention of the Great Architect who planned, designed, and produced it. Sex is viewed coldly merely as something man finds he has—not knowing WHY, or anything of the Designer's *purposes*—knowing only what he sees, and, in his self-centered concupiscent human nature, experiences.

But The ETERNAL, in His INSTRUCTION BOOK for mankind, compares the marvelous human body to God's CHURCH, which is the "Body of Christ."

The various members in God's Church have various functions, and God provides them with various spiritual gifts for performance of these functions. This is found in the chapter devoted to the "spiritual gifts," the 12th of I Corinthians.

The human body—like God's true Church—is not composed of one member, but MANY. It is the same with GOD. As explained previously, the Biblical INSTRUCTION BOOK reveals God as a divine FAMILY—only the ONE God, but composed of *more than one* divine Person.

So with the Church. And so, likewise, with the God-designed human body, made in the likeness of GOD. Here, then, we see still *another* manner in which MAN is made in the likeness of GOD—*one* God, more than one Person; *one* human body, more than one member. Also *one* Church, more than one member.

Notice! "If the foot shall say, Because I am not the hand, I am not of the body . . . and if the ear shall say, Because I am not the eye, I am not of the body; is it therefore not of the body? If the whole body were an eye, where were the hearing? If the whole were hearing, where were the smelling? But now hath GOD set the members every one of them in the body, *as it hath pleased him*" (I Cor. 12:15-18).

It was GOD who designed and set the sex apparatus in the physical human body—"AS IT HATH PLEASED HIM!"

Then let us learn what we *need to know* about them,

without false modesty or foolish prudery—but as God would *have* us know!

Follow this 12th chapter of I Corinthians a little further. The stern, harsh prudes who formulated a false so-called "Christian" ethic about sex said of the genital system: "We have no need of thee!" God rebukes them—and they should, even in those early centuries, have read His rebuke!

Here it is—beginning verse 21: "And the eye cannot say unto the hand, I have no need of thee: nor again the head to the feet, I have no need of you. Nay, much more those members of the body, which seem to be more feeble [Moffatt: rather delicate—or dishonorable], are necessary: and those members of the body, which we think to be less honorable [sex], upon these we bestow more abundant honor; and our uncomely parts have more abundant comeliness."

When we come to consider the human body from the MIND OF GOD—we see it, not as something shameful and evil, but as something WONDERFUL, to be understood with clean and healthy minds, in AWE of the handiwork of the Great Designer. For *this* is what God beheld, when He had formed it, and pronounced "VERY GOOD."

The Psalmist was inspired to cry out: "I will praise thee, for I am fearfully and wonderfully made: MARVELOUS ARE THY WORKS!"

God has given each of us a marvelous human body— to *use* as He has directed in His INSTRUCTION BOOK. The possession of such a body imposes on each individual a SACRED RESPONSIBILITY! It is something you may use to God's honor and glory—and to your own great happiness; *OR* you may misuse and abuse it to *dis*honor the Creator, and bring degradation, shame, and curses on yourself.

The Male Genital System

First, then, we examine the masculine genital organs.

God says, through Paul: those physical organs of the body which humans regard as more uncomely, He has made very necessary, with HONOR. And He continues: "Yet God has tempered the body together, with a special dignity for the inferior [uncomely] parts, so that there may be no disunion in the body, but that the various members should have a common concern for one another" (I Cor. 12:24-25). And all this is compared to GOD'S CHURCH—the Body of Christ!

It may seem to many that the most "uncomely" parts of the male body are those organs we now explain *first*— the germinal glands, called *testicles*. That is, until the truth about them is learned. And then one should stand in AWE at the divine MIND and HANDIWORK of the Great God who designed and produced such a marvelous mechanism!

See the matchless Mind and Hand of the Creator in these extremely necessary glands! Actually, they are the most important organs in the male generative apparatus.

The testes are a pair of oval-shaped glands. They are enclosed in a cutaneous sack, or bag, called the *scrotum*. It is made up of several layers, and is divided into two compartments, each containing a testicle. Each testicle is about the size of a hickory nut, approximately 1½ inches long, and 1 inch thick.

The testes, with the scrotum, hang between the thighs, forward, underneath the base of the penis, by the spermatic cord. The testes are located *on the outside of the body*. Did you ever wonder WHY? The Creator had a very good reason! This will be explained.

Many men themselves do not realize it, but the left testicle hangs a little lower in the scrotum than the right. There is an important *reason*. Could blind evolution, without intelligence, have thought this out and made it thus? There is perhaps no pain a boy or man can suffer that is as excruciating as a crushing of or injury to the testicles. Did blind "nature" know this? Or did an All-intelligent Creator, concerned for our welfare, design it so that, in case the thighs are crowded together, one testicle will slip over the other, thus avoiding any crushing. No evolution here!

Miniature "Colossal" Laboratories

When we understand what science tells us about these glands, we ought to be struck with amazement. Small as they are, still they are "laboratories" performing a colossal work, going on day and night! They perform an astonishing dual activity. They produce both the germinal or reproductive cells, which impart *human life* to an otherwise infertile ovum; and also the hormones which cause the body to be masculine in shape, the voice to be masculine in tone, and *the mind* to be masculine in its thinking! And that's an incredible job to be performed by two small "factories" weighing less than an ounce each!

Let's take a quick inspection of these "laboratories" that generate human life. Each small testicle contains a very large number of convoluted tubules, sometimes called seminiferous tubes—infinitely tiny. There are about 300 of them, intertwined in a tiny but vast network of coils. If stretched out straight, the length of these tubules, in the two testes, would be approximately *one mile in length!* And all within "factories" only 1½ inches in length! Astonishing? I should say!

These tiny coils of tubules produce the male reproductive cells at an astounding rate—actually millions an hour, *any one of which* could impart a human life to an ovum!

These male reproductive cells are called *spermatozoa* (singular, *spermatozoon*)—and are quite generally, in professional circles, called *"sperm cells"* for short—or, sometimes, just *sperm*. These sperm cells are unbelievably infinitesimal—the smallest cells in either male or female body. They are very different from any other cells in the human body. Each has a minute egg-shaped head, an intermediate segment and a tail comparatively long. They look, under a microscope, like tiny tadpoles. These infinitesimal cells cannot be seen with the naked eye, but are visible and measurable under a high-powered microscope. Each sperm is approximately one four-thousandth of an inch in length. Even the female egg cell, or ovum, is only about the size of a fine pinpoint—just barely visible to the naked eye—and a sperm cell is not more than about one-fiftieth as large as an ovum.

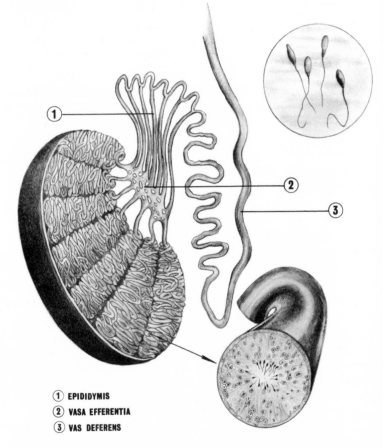

① EPIDIDYMIS
② VASA EFFERENTIA
③ VAS DEFERENS

This drawing shows the interior of a testicle. Arrow points to a greatly enlarged section of tubule, as if sliced open—to illustrate how millions of spermatozoa are produced within a single hour within the mile length of these infinitesimal tubules. Inset at top shows sperm cells, greatly magnified.

Think of it! Every human being starts his existence in so miniature a size!

Spermatozoa of animals are much larger than those of humans.

The scientific "authorities" now claim the discovery that each spermatozoon contains twenty-four chromosomes —and that it is through these that the characteristics of the father—and also of grandparents—are transmitted, by heredity, to the child. Of course the mother's characteristics also are passed on, through the nucleus within the ovum.

The tiny intertwined tubules within each testicle, in which the spermatozoa are produced, are so narrow that a hair could not pass through them. This book is not intended, as mentioned before, to be a technical or professional scientific work. But I do feel that certain of these more technical facts are important, for the reader should come to a realization of the awesome mind and purpose of the Creator!

This vast, intricate network of intertwined canals, or convoluted tubules, unite near the top to form a set of larger ones—the so-called *vasa efferentia*, and these in turn unite to form the *epididymus*. All this is encased within the scrotum. And finally, the tubules forming the epididymus converge into one seminal duct or tube, called the *vas deferens*. The vas deferens continues up into the body, carrying spermatozoa to the seminal vesicle—which will be explained later. As there are two testicles, there are also the vasa efferentia, the epididymus, and the vas deferens for each—terminating into the *two* seminal vesicles located beside, or just under, the bladder within the body.

The Male Hormones

But before we leave the description of these tiny yet colossal "laboratories"—the testicles—there is still another most important function they perform.

They produce also the male hormones. These are of vital importance, and deserve a brief description.

Scattered among these seminiferous tubules are microscopically tiny islands of cells. In these infinitesimal islands the male hormones are produced. These are not carried through the vas deferens, as are the spermatozoa, but pass directly into the bloodstream, and thus circulate through the body.

These male hormones cause changes in the shape of the body. Thus, from age of puberty, a boy's body develops into the masculine form—narrow hips, wider shoulders for masculine strength; beard on the face, hair on the chest and other parts of the body more than is common to females; the deeper voice.

And these hormones directly influence the MIND. There are certain pronounced differences between male and female minds, some of which will be explained later—although many of these are generally recognized by all.

For example, little girls are interested in dolls and feminine things; little boys in machines and masculine things. Boys and girls are not sex conscious before the age of puberty in the same manner they become after puberty—bodily changes become pronounced after puberty—yet there are noticeable MIND differences in young boys and girls.

Tremendous Importance

Let me illustrate further the ENORMOUS IMPORTANCE of these "uncomely parts" which humans too often regard as "less honorable," but on which the Great Designer has bestowed "more abundant honor."

Certain experiments made in the interests of "science" should teach us an impressive lesson. Perhaps, in the sight of the Eternal, such experiments ought not be made. But men have made them, and the results are both intriguing and enlightening.

As far back as history records, men have practiced castration. It is widely practiced today on animals—removing testes before male animals reach sexual maturity. You probably eat steer beef often, and capon occasionally—to name just two examples.

Of course castration destroys reproductive capacity. No spermatozoa are produced. But also the male hormone production is destroyed, and that is the striking thing revealed by certain experiments.

Of course, the castration practice in modern stock raising is not done primarily to destroy breeding capacity. It is done to alter the appearance and behaviour of the animal.

The stock-raiser does not need a bull for every cow. One bull can take care of the breeding requirements for a number of cows. But steers make fatter and more tender steaks, and if the steer is not butchered for meat, the animal which, uncastrated, would have grown into a wild bull, will, as a result of castration, become a docile ox, willing to work. The castration causes changes in bodily form, and in the horns. Roosters and pigs are castrated to increase the poundage and thereby the profits.

In the Bible you read of castrated humans, called eunuchs. Middle East sultans and other rulers used eunuchs to serve in harems. The eunuch lost all sexual desire —the harem women offered no temptation. They were once used at the papal court—said to be employed as singers because of their high-pitched voices. Eunuchs become obese, without beard or normal male hair growth on the body.

However, even though castration is an age-old practice, much of the true importance of male testes and female ovaries was unknown until the experiments of Berthold in 1849.

It had always been known, of course, that the comb of a castrated cock degenerates. But Berthold experimented further. He removed the testes of cocks and then regrafted these testes on the cocks' backs. The combs remained the same as in all uncastrated roosters. All bodily appearances remained the same. But of course all reproductive capacity was lost!

This proved that the testes serve a DUAL purpose. Many similar experiments have been made since. They prove that the testes and ovaries not only serve to reproduce one's kind, they also determine the sex characteristics of the individual.

Some astonishing experiments were made by the scientist of Vienna, Professor Steinach. First, he castrated *both* male and female animals of the same species. They both acquired a neutral appearance—neither male nor female. But this professor went further. He *exchanged* ovaries and testes. Into castrated males he grafted female ovaries; and into the females the germinal glands removed from the males. The former males now took on female characteristics, and the former females acquired those of males. The former females now behaved as males toward the former males—and the males now took on the behaviour of females. Former males even developed mammary glands, and nursed the young!

Of course there is much more to the hormone story than this. Other glands in other parts of the body have their coordinating relation to bodily characteristics—such as the pituitary, pineal, thyroid and suprarenal glands. It is not our purpose to discuss them here. But what little has been covered about the hormones, it is hoped, will be of interest.

Marvelous Temperature Gauge

The question has been asked, WHY are the testes located *outside* of the body? The Great Architect had a very good reason—but men never learned this reason until quite recent times. The earliest account of it I have been able to find dates from 1950.

Scientists, it seems, stumbled onto this in making tests on animals to learn how long spermatozoa retain both their motility and their fertility at various temperatures.

Then, in these experiments, the testes of rabbits were kept in a refrigerator. The sperm cells remained alive much longer than when kept at body temperature.

So next, they made tests on live animals to determine what happens in testes at various temperatures. They discovered that the temperature inside the scrotum was several degrees *lower* than body heat.

They made an experiment on male mice, in a hatching

oven at 110 degrees. They found fertility drastically reduced, and soon nil.

Test now followed test. They were learning things!

So next they tried heating the testes alone, with bodies at normal temperatures. This experiment was made on sheep, goats and pigs. The same thing happened—fertility rapidly reduced, until there were no fertile spermatozoa!

Finally a Dutch scientist determined that the temperature inside the *human* scrotum is actually six to fifteen degrees lower than body temperature!

It took man thousands of years to learn what the Creator planned and designed! Finally men learned that these colossal, yet miniature "laboratories" are so designed that they require this slightly *lower* temperature to produce fertile life-imparting cells for the reproduction of the race!

Then they discovered additional proof. It is claimed that, in the foetal stage of development before birth, the testes first develop inside the body, and then descend into the scrotum some considerable time prior to birth, through the inguinal canal. In all normal cases male babies are born with the testes already in the scrotum. But it sometimes occurs that one or both testicles remain in the abdomen at and after birth. These infants are born with either a half-empty or wholly empty scrotum. Doctors today bring down the testes with a minor operation.

Yet, when this was not known, there were cases where the testes remained, after puberty, and after marriage, inside the body. Formerly, neither these men—nor, for that matter medical "science," could understand WHY such men appeared in every other way normal MEN—they could marry—they had normal desire and ability for coitus—*yet they could not become fathers!* Their testes were normal—they did manufacture spermatozoa. But not *fertile* sperms. They were sterile! Today it is known that the cause was, simply, that these marvelous and mighty little "factories" generating human life do *not* perform their wonderful operation of producing *life-imparting* sperm cells at bodily temperature. They must be kept at a temperature several degrees lower!

So now the "scientists" have at last learned something else!

The scrotum—the sack which houses the testicles and epididymides—is made up of a kind of skin *different from any other* in man or woman! It is a nonconductor of heat! It is made up of folds. In cold temperatures, or if the man is bathing or swimming in cold water, these folds shrink up, and draw the testes up tight against the body—almost partially into it! In such cases, the temperature becomes *too cold* for these marvelous little "laboratories."

But, in very *warm* weather, they stretch out, until the testes are dropped down a considerable distance farther from the warmer-than-normal body.

Thus, this scrotum *not only* needed to be on *the outside* of the body—it also acts as an AUTOMATIC TEMPERATURE GAUGE, to keep these little life-germinating "factories" producing at temperatures proper for their work!

If you think "mother nature," blindly, and without mind, intelligence, or knowledge, planned and worked all this out, you are welcome to your ridiculous opinion! It was not dumb and stupid "MOTHER nature"—it was the Supreme *FATHER—GOD*—who instructed CHRIST, who "spoke" and commanded, and the Holy Spirit was the POWER that brought it into being. If you think the evolutionary fable sounds more rational as a means of accounting for such wonders—well, of course you are allowed your opinions, however far from FACT!

The "Authorities" Speculate

These experimenting scientists deduce something further from their experiments. Their tests indicate that male sperm cells gradually lose both vigor of motility, and also fertilizing power, under the normal bodily temperature once deposited within the female body. Some experimenters insist spermatozoa retain power for fertilization only 48 hours, and that ova must be fertilized within 24 hours, in the Fallopian tube.

Thus, if this were true, there is only a period of a few hours in any month when human conception is possible. This "discovery" led to the "rhythm cycle" theory. But this so-called method of planned parenthood has, in fact, produced quite a bumper crop of babies!

However, the doctors and scientists *do not agree* among themselves! A European "authority" says: "This period of time is variously estimated. Some authorities think it is only from twenty-four to thirty-six hours. Others assume eight or even fourteen days. Taking into consideration the analogy of various animal species and practical experience rather than experimental research, I am inclined to believe in a long continuance of seminal vitality."

Notice these expressions in the above quotation—typical of "scientific" language, as I have expressed in an earlier chapter: "Variously *estimated*"; "Some authorities *think* . . ."; "Others *assume* . . ."; and "I am inclined to *believe.* . . ."

We are dealing, here, not with the AUTHORITY of revelation, but with the speculations, opinions, and guesses of "science."

Personally I claim no authority, save that of God. I have seen charts in medical books generally available only to doctors—and I have read many statements of *experience*, which do indicate that pregnancy is possible at any time of the month.

And so we have now covered the most important organs in the male generative apparatus.

Female Generative System

We come next to the equivalent system in the female.

I am departing altogether from the method followed almost universally in the flood of books on the subject of sex, in covering essentials of the sex organs. Instead of grouping the organs as to external and internal—male, and then female, it seems more logical, for our purposes here, to describe them according to functional classification.

The most important organs in the generative system of the female are the *ovaries*. There are certain similarities between the female ovaries and the male testes—yet in other ways they are quite dissimilar.

The ovaries are located on the *inside* of the body. They do not, like the male generative "laboratories," require a lower-than-bodily temperature to do their work.

They are, like the testes, a pair, located within the pelvis, in the lower abdominal region, one on each side of the upper portion of the uterus. Also, like male testes, each ovary is about 1½ inches in length, but they are more almond-shaped. They are connected to the uterus by a pair of ducts called Fallopian tubes.

The ovaries produce the egg cells, called *ova* (singular, *ovum*). When an ovum is fertilized by a sperm cell, it is the start of a new human life.

In each ovary, many egg cells (ova), between the age of puberty and menopause, are in various stages of development. But ova are produced very much more slowly than spermatozoa. The mature ova is released from the ovaries about every *four* weeks—alternating every other month, so that *each* ovary produces a mature ovum approximately every *eight* weeks.

Each ovum is an almost round, or globular cell, about the size of a pinpoint, just barely discernible by the naked eye—if your eyes are really sharp. Yet, tiny as they are, each ovum is about fifty times larger than a spermatozoon.

As they are produced inside the ovary, each ovum is surrounded by, and enclosed in, a sort of very tiny bladder, called a Graafian follicle. This follicle is filled with fluid. As each ovum matures, enclosed in its follicle, it is developed in the outer layer of the ovary. This causes the outer ovarian wall to bulge. Then the Graafian follicle bursts, or rather explodes its contents out into the abdomen. The ovum is caused to bounce out, like a ball, into the fringed, or near funnel-shaped end of the Fallopian tube. This fringed end of the Fallopian tube, shaped something like a carnation flower, seems to open like an outstretched hand, to receive the ovum, which is virtually shot into it. It opens only when an ovum is mature and ready to be released into it. This

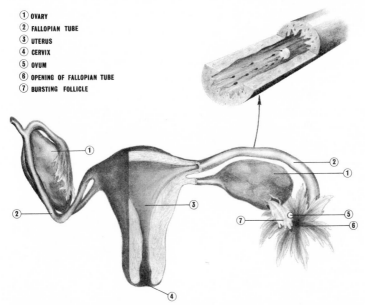

① OVARY
② FALLOPIAN TUBE
③ UTERUS
④ CERVIX
⑤ OVUM
⑥ OPENING OF FALLOPIAN TUBE
⑦ BURSTING FOLLICLE

Illustration of ovulation, showing bursting follicle, with ovum being shot into opening of Fallopian tube, together with uterus. Upper inset shows greatly enlarged cut-open section of Fallopian tube, with sperm cells attacking ovum.

discharge of the ovum from the ovary into the Fallopian tube is called *ovulation*.

The Female Hormones

At this same instant something else, quite interesting and very important, happens.

The female sex hormone is called follicular hormone, because it is formed within this membranous envelope or follicle. When the follicle bursts, only the infinitesimal round ovum is shot into the oviduct (Fallopian tube). The follicular hormone is then released into the abdomen, absorbed into the blood stream and thus carried by the blood to do its work in various parts of the body.

So the hormone production in females is unlike that in males. It is formed in the female germinal cells—the ovaries —but not in tiny islands among tiny tubules. Ova are not formed in tubules, as sperm cells are formed in testes. Instead of being developed in a system of coiled tubules, both ovary and hormone are formed near the outer surface of the ovary.

In a sense, this membranous envelope formed around the ovum compares to the shell covering a hen's egg. When the follicle bursts and the ovum is bounced out of the ovary, it would quickly perish if it were not, in a fraction of a second, shot directly into the oviduct, where an albuminous substance immediately protects it.

And that, in brief, is the story of the sexual *glands* in both men and women. They are, indeed, miniature "laboratories," or tiny "factories," where, in a sense, human beings are manufactured—or, at least the germinating cells which *start* every human life!

It is, when seen from the *approach*, and through the eyeglasses of the *revelation* of the Creator, a fascinating and awe-inspiring bit of knowledge.

CHAPTER 14

"Fearfully and Wonderfully Made"

*P*EOPLE SPEAK of "the dignity of man." But *how little* do they know, usually, whereof they speak!

As humanity generally conducts itself, little of that dignity is apparent. Yet the true *potential* of man is utterly and incredibly beyond his ken.

DIGNITY of Man?

Ringing silently in my ears, as I write, are those strains from one of the lively choruses of Handel's *Messiah:* "All we, like sheep, have gone astray; we have turned every one to his own way" (quoted from Isa. 53:6). Yes, as Paul was inspired to write, *"all* have sinned."

Man, by his own thoughts and actions, has contributed only conversely to any commendable dignity. He has polluted, contaminated, perverted, abused, ruined, misused everything a benevolent God has placed within reach of his hands. He has rejected and rebelled against his Maker.

WHY, then, should the Great GOD be concerned about MAN? The Psalmist asked that question (Psa. 8:4-6). David's answer was, "Thou madest him *to have* dominion over the works of thy hands" (verse 6). But the WHOLE TRUTH is not revealed in that Old Testament passage. David merely included the dominion God gave Adam and his descendants

—dominion over the animals and the land; over the fish and the seas; and over the fowls and the air—as far as earth's atmosphere extends.

That is all the dominion God has given mortal man— YET! And man has polluted and misused it all! Not satisfied with that, man is now seeking to extend his dominion *beyond* the jurisdiction God assigned. Today man is venturing OFF-LIMITS. He has shot rockets to the moon, and boasts that he is going to land *himself* on the moon by 1970 or before!

But man is simply getting in too big a hurry! He is striving to "take over" what he has not fitted himself to manage, and before it has been made lawfully his!

For what man does not know is that —IF he first qualifies for the trust—it has been God's intention all along to place not only the moon and Mars, but THE WHOLE VAST, LIMITLESS UNIVERSE under his jurisdiction!

The WHOLE answer to David's question was not given in the Old Testament. It *is* revealed in the New! But the religious leaders of MAN have never caught the overwhelming truth. To minds hostile to God's authority, it would seem too incredible to accept. So they read right over the glorious revelation of the true *potential* DIGNITY OF MAN!

Even though explained in Chapter 9, this answer NEEDS REPETITION!

Here, then, is the full answer to the Psalmist's question:

Repeating the *question*, God inspired, through Paul, "What is MAN, that thou [God] art mindful of him? . . ." And the answer: "Thou hast put *all things* in subjection under his feet" (Heb. 2:6-8). Just what do those words, "ALL THINGS," mean? THEY MEAN JUST WHAT THEY SAY— *ALL THINGS—the entire vast, limitless UNIVERSE!* Read the next words! "For in that he put *all* in subjection under him, HE LEFT NOTHING THAT IS NOT PUT UNDER HIM" (verse 8).

But how about the fact that, to Adam, God did limit

man's dominion to the land, the seas, and the atmosphere
OF THE EARTH?

The last sentence of this same 8th verse explains: "But
now we see NOT YET all things put under him. BUT WE SEE
JESUS . . . CROWNED WITH GLORY AND HONOR" (verses 8-9).
In verse 10 Jesus is called the "captain"—the LEADER—the
PIONEER who has gone on before—of OUR salvation!

And just HOW, and in WHAT CAPACITY do we now see
Jesus?

We see HIM (chapter 1:2-3) in POWER and GLORY, "up-
holding ALL THINGS by the word of HIS POWER." Look at
the plain English translation of "ALL THINGS" in the more
modern Moffatt translation: "sustains THE UNIVERSE with
His word of POWER."

Yes, Jesus Christ, the "firstborn among many brethren,"
is now on the very throne that governs the entire UNIVERSE
—He now controls every POWER, every FORCE, every ENERGY
that exists! And He has merely pioneered the way! We, IF
we yield to God and HIS GOVERNMENT, may, *through Christ*,
be reconciled to the Great GOD, and become *co-heirs with
Christ*, to inherit, after OUR resurrection, EVERYTHING HE
ALREADY HAS INHERITED!

And THAT is the true potential DIGNITY OF MAN!

Truly, most men who prate around in their vanity about
"the dignity of man" little comprehend the REAL meaning
of those words! Man must first turn around and GO THE
OTHER WAY—he must REPENT—for he has been traveling
in the wrong direction! He must go GOD'S WAY. He must
first *qualify*, before God will entrust him with the government of the universe!

HOW Wonderfully Made?

But Isaiah, who said we were now stray sheep, did point
to the Great Shepherd, Christ, who shall rescue all sheep
who are willing, when he finished the citation above quoted
thus: "and The ETERNAL hath laid on HIM the iniquity of
us all." Jesus Christ paid the full PENALTY for man's rebel-

lion—if only man will repent and TURN THE RIGHT WAY!

For this mortal life, the Creator made us out of PHYSI-
CAL substance, and confined us to this PHYSICAL earth. But
He made us in His likeness—even though now merely the
CLAY to be re-fashioned, shaped, and molded into His own
SPIRITUAL CHARACTER!

Of course the MOST fearfully and wonderfully made
part of man is his MIND. That is something the brute animals do not have!

Yet the mind requires a BODY to keep it functioning,
that man may fulfil his tremendous destiny. He requires
legs and feet to transport him. He needs arms and hands
to *make* and *do* what his mind directs. He needs the *life-
sustaining* apparatus—the digestive, circulatory, respiratory
systems. He needs the nervous system. And he also needs
the genital or sex system.

Of course man has gone astray in this area of sex, as
he has in every other possible way. But the fact that man
has, by wrong CHOICE of mind, misused, abused, and perverted this genital system does not alter the FACT that what
God designed was VERY GOOD. And it was intended to be—
and indeed CAN be, if we are right-minded—put to most
honorable and glorious USE.

We can, as mentioned before, GLORIFY GOD in our
BODIES—by preserving them for God-intended uses and
functions. Young people glorify God by keeping their bodies
undefiled as God *made* them, until a right and proper and
God-joined MARRIAGE. And the married—by the uses God
intended and instructed for the very great joys of love in
marriage, and the happiness of home and family!

We have covered, in an elementary way, the generating
glands God fashioned in both male and female bodies. Truly,
they are WONDERFULLY and fearfully made!

The Female Ducts

So now we come to the ducts, or tubes, which transport both ova and spermatozoa from their "laboratories"

for conception and gestation of humans who may be the very heirs of God.

Since we have just finished explaining about the marvelous manner in which the infinitesimal ova are literally shot from the ovary into the open funnel of the oviduct, we shall continue, now, with this duct connecting the ovary with the uterus.

This oviduct, which transports the ova, is called the *Fallopian tube*. As there are two ovaries—one on each side of the uterus, there are also two Fallopian tubes.

Ova do not possess, in themselves, power of motility, as do spermatozoa. Once the carnation-shaped funnel, at the entrance of the oviduct, opens to receive the ovum shot into it, the ovum travels very slowly on its journey through the Fallopian tube. This tube is made up of a three-layer wall, with fine "feelers." When the ovum bursts out of its follicle and into the entrance funnel of the tube, it is like a hen's egg *without a shell*. Not according to size, of course. It is smaller than the period at the end of this sentence. But uncovered by its membranous envelope it would soon perish if it were not immediately covered and protected by an albuminous substance in the Fallopian tube.

The infinitesimal "feelers" along the interior membrane of the tube very slowly propel this human egg cell on its way toward the womb. This journey through the Fallopian tube is said by the doctors and scientists to require approximately *eight days!*

Consequently, since most "authorities" believe the life of the ovum is limited—some say to only 24 hours—unless met and fertilized by a sperm cell, all scientific opinion today asserts that impregnation must take place in the Fallopian tube. And that, before the egg cell has proceeded far on its passage through the tube.

The Womb

The two Fallopian tubes lead to the *womb*, or *uterus*. In medical parlance, this organ is still called by its ancient name, *womb*, about equally with the use of the more modern term, *uterus*. It is a pear-shaped organ, with the wider end at the top, and the Fallopian tubes enter it at this wider top portion. It is suspended by cords and muscles from above, and its downward-hanging neck, called the *cervix*, enters into the vagina.

The urinary bladder is located just in front of the uterus. The normal position of the womb is to incline or tip slightly forward from the bottom—almost at a right angle from the vaginal canal.

The purpose of the uterus is to receive, house, protect and nourish the fertilized ovum, or *embryo*. After four months it is called a *foetus*. At approximately nine months, it is born as a human baby—with all the overwhelming POTENTIALITY to which he may become heir!

In its quiescent state, the uterus is hard and muscular, its walls so close together that actually there is no real uterine cavity.

In nonpregnancy the uterus is about two inches wide at the top, one inch thick, and three inches long.

Menstruation

Once each 28 days (on the average), a congestion occurs in the uterus preparing for reception of a fertilized ovum. If the ovum is not fertilized in the Fallopian tube, then, about 14 days after ovulation (discharge of the ovum from the ovary), the uterus sheds the special mucous lining prepared in readiness for the embryo. This slight hemorrhage then escapes through the cervix and the vagina.

This monthly process is called *menstruation*. It begins at the age of puberty—average around age 14—though sometimes a little later or earlier. Menstruation continues until the menopause.

This monthly emission of blood in females was formerly supposed to be a periodic purging of poisonous accumulations. That, of course, is not the fact at all.

If the ovum is fertilized, then the mucous lining specially formed in the womb receives the embryo and performs its important function.

The average menstrual cycle is about 28 days. However, it may vary from 21 to 35 days—and occasionally there are much wider variations. The average duration of the menstrual flow is about five days—but it may vary from three to seven.

The Male Ducts

We now return to the male seminal ducts.

As previously described, the tiny convoluted tubules of the testes converge ultimately into the epididymus, where all tubules unite into the one seminal duct, termed the *vas deferens*. The vas deferens, then, is a continuation of the epididymus. Passing from the scrotum into the body, the vas deferens runs alongside lymphatic vessels and nerves, arteries and veins, and these combined form the spermatic cord.

Spermatozoa are transported through the vas deferens to the seminal vesicles. This is done by repeated contractions.

Immediately under the bladder, and surrounding the urethra, is the *prostate gland*. It is between 1¼ and 1½ inches in diameter, globular-shaped. The *urethra*, the urinary tube or duct, passes through it. This gland secretes the *prostatic fluid*—milky-white and alkaline.

Formerly the so-called "authorities" thought that the entire seminal fluid was produced in the prostate. More recent speculation of the "experts," however, tends toward the belief that a certain fluid is formed in the epididymus, assisting in transporting the spermatozoa through the vas deferens. In any event, it is claimed that sperm cells do not possess their full motility until they reach this alkaline prostatic fluid, which serves both to preserve spermatozoa and stimulate motility.

The vas deferens enters into the prostate gland, and through it into the urethra. Of course they are a pair, one entering on each side. Also at this point of entry into the prostate is a sort of reservoir, or elongated bladder. There are also two of these, called *seminal vesicles.* Each vesicle joins as one tube with the vas deferens at the point of entry into the prostate gland. They then form a single tube through the prostate, entering the urethra. The urethra is the tube through which urine passes from the bladder, and on out through the penis.

Until the last decade or two, medical science supposed these seminal vesicles to be reservoirs, or elongated oval bladders in which the seminal fluid was stored until ejaculation. And probably they were right.

But many today *think* that the seminal vesicles produce a fluid of some sort, which, mixing with fluids secreted

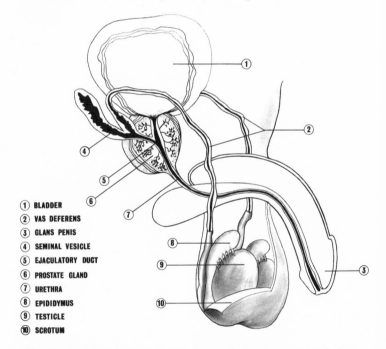

① BLADDER
② VAS DEFERENS
③ GLANS PENIS
④ SEMINAL VESICLE
⑤ EJACULATORY DUCT
⑥ PROSTATE GLAND
⑦ URETHRA
⑧ EPIDIDYMUS
⑨ TESTICLE
⑩ SCROTUM

Sketch showing generative and copulative organs and ducts of male sexual apparatus.

in the epididymus and the prostate gland, form the seminal fluid in which the spermatozoa swim.

However, it seems that all experiments have been made post mortem—on dead bodies. Some doctors say candidly, therefore, that they cannot be sure.

The "authorities," as usual, are postulating—and many assume their theories to be fact. I am not an authority. The one infallible Authority does not tell us. I am inclined to believe, then, that the seminal fluid is produced in the prostate gland, and stored in these vesicles.

Actually the answers to such questions are not pertinent to the object of this book. I merely mention such technical details as a matter of interest, and an example of the very questionable "authority" of the *human* "authorities."

These men, "professing themselves to be wise" (Rom. 1:22), *reject* as foolishness the one reliable AUTHORITY. In so doing, God says they become fools!

But let me remind you again, God does not reveal ALL knowledge through the Bible. It is the FOUNDATION of all knowledge—the foundation on which to build. It reveals only what man *needs* to know and *cannot* otherwise learn. But also it tells us that there are some things which prick human curiosity to great and costly speculation, but which God *hides* from mortal minds because such knowledge is for us unnecessary.

"The secret things belong unto the Eternal our God: but those things which are revealed belong unto us" (Deut. 29:29).

The purpose of this book, after all, is to give the reader that *vital* knowledge which is necessary for right, happy and abundant living; the knowledge of the origin and causes of harmful attitudes of sex; the knowledge of the right and intended attitude toward, and purposes of sex; the knowledge so necessary for fullest adolescent and premarital conduct; the knowledge so essential to marital and family happiness.

The Copulative Organs

And so finally, in describing the genital systems, we come to the organs of copulation.

The copulative organ in the male is a fleshy, muscular organ, or shaft, composed principally of erectile tissue, called the *penis*.

In the normal quiescent condition, it hangs limp and retired. In size, like human noses, ears, hands and other organs, there is variation in different individuals. Average, in the quiescent state, is three to four inches in length, about an inch in diameter. Rigidity, however, is necessary for sexual union.

One "authority" states that "fecundation, if not impossible, is at all events very difficult if the semen is deposited on or in the external genital organs and not in the vagina itself." But numerous case histories—a number of which have been brought to me for serious counselling, advice and spiritual help—prove positively that this "authority" is in serious error. In these case histories, unwed girls, going too far in what they had been led to believe was harmless and socially accepted "necking" or love-making, found they were *physically* in the condition of the prophecy, "Behold, a virgin shall conceive." But *spiritually* they were at the opposite extreme from the position of the virgin Mary. What was conceived in them was not by God's Holy Spirit, but by PLAIN FORNICATION! And though they were still virgins physically, they certainly were not *spiritually!*

I will have more to say about this later, at the proper time, as a serious WARNING to the unmarried.

The truth is, penetration of the vagina IS NOT *necessary* for reproduction, even though it renders the likelihood of pregnancy far greater. But this penetration *is*, in the purpose of the Holy Creator, far more desirable for the expression of God-blessed marital LOVE. And therefore there was, as always in what the Creator does, PURPOSE in designing the male member for arousal to rigidity.

The urethra extends from the bladder, pierces directly through the prostate gland, and continues down the lower or under side the full length inside the penis. Above the urethra, continuing through the shaft, are two spongy cavernous bodies, called *corpora cavernosa*. Along the underside a spongy portion surrounds the urethra. Through the length of the organ run blood vessels, and sensitive nerves. At the anterior end is the head of the penis, called the *glans penis*. The glans has a close network of peripheral nerves, and is the seat of erotic sensation in the male.

The *corpora cavernosa* are so called because they contain a system of *caverns*. In the flaccid, quiescent state, they are almost empty. But under sexual arousal, they become gorged with blood—and also to a much greater than normal extent the spongy area surrounding the urethra. The organ then swells, and becomes stout and hard. In the erect condition, the size will vary from perhaps 5½ to 7 inches in length and 1¼ to 1½ inches in diameter, and in some rare cases slightly larger.

It might be well, here, to correct two baseless fears that occasionally trouble an otherwise happy "cloud nine" bride-to-be.

Some seem to fear that a very large husband will produce abnormally large babies, making the delivery difficult or dangerous at birth. THE SIZE OF PARENTS HAS NEVER PROVED TO HAVE ANY CONNECTION WITH THE SIZE OF BABIES AT BIRTH.

Some young women become a little frightened, fearing that the penis of the future husband may prove to be too large for normal and easy penetration, and that this might cause pain during coitus. But the Creator designed the female vagina with great distensibility. It expands to allow the passage of the head and shoulders of a baby being born— and no male member is anywhere near that large. True, countless wives *have* suffered pain—but only through ignorance. If we had come by evolution, we might have cause for all kinds of worries. But since a benevolent and all-intelligent GOD made us as we are, He simply took care of those things! GOD made no mistakes. Of course, through heredity resulting from transgression of God's laws, there may be, rarely, people born with abnormal conditions in the generative organs. But the average person need have no fears.

Truth About Circumcision

Difficulties in marital love result from ignorance, and from transgression of God's Laws—*never* from inadequacies on the part of the Great Designer. It is the purpose of this book to dispel those ignorances, and to make clear the laws set in motion for human happiness and joy.

Before leaving explanation of the male organs of copulation, a word about *circumcision.*

The glans penis is covered with a foreskin, called the *prepuce.* The size of the prepuce varies. In many if not most cases, it is loose, and barely covers the glans. In rare cases the prepuce is longer, and its orifice so small and tight it imprisons the glans. Under erection the foreskin may not be able to slip back behind the glans—or, if it does, it might, under the swelling of erection, bring about a sort of strangulation of the glans. The solution is, simply, circumcision.

Under the Old Covenant, God made circumcision obligatory under law in Israel. Under the New Covenant, circumcision, ordained FOREVER, is physically, but NOT SPIRITUALLY, abolished. The Apostle Paul instructs that circumcision, as a religious rite, is no longer physical but spiritual—*of the heart*—not of the flesh.

Yet, while it is no longer *commanded* by God as a physical religious rite, it most certainly is ALLOWED, and for pure physical and sanitary reasons, *I do most strongly recommend it* for all boy babies!

Between the prepuce and the glans of the uncircumcised boy—or man—is secreted a tallow-like substance, called *smegma.* Left uncleansed this may cause inflammation and trouble. It is, therefore, necessary, in the case of an uncircumcised male baby, for the mother to regularly push the prepuce back behind the glans penis, and wash it; and as he grows old enough, the boy must be taught to do this regularly. This very need for sanitation causes irritation of the very seat of voluptuous sensation. It is very likely to stimulate sex arousal, and lead to masturbation. This has been the chief *cause* of a serious "sex problem" in the lives of countless young men prior to marriage.

The prepuce forms a protective covering over the easily aroused sensation-producing glans—yet, instead of actually "protecting" it, the cleansing need produces just the opposite. The glans of the uncircumcised boy or man is exceedingly tender and sensitive. After circumcision, the glans gradually loses much of its sensitiveness, until the touch or rubbing of underclothing over it produces no more sensitiveness than clothing does to any other part of the body. Still, the circumcised enjoy all the voluptuous pleasure God made possible in marital coitus.

Some uncircumcised young men, plagued by the masturbation habit formed earlier in life than they can remember, have either had themselves circumcised, or learned to wear the prepuce behind the glans—giving them the same effect as circumcision—so as to lose the tender extrasensitiveness of the glans and thus lessen the tendency of arousal and constant temptation.

I repeat—it is NOT now a physical religious command—but when GOD circumcised Abraham at age 99, and commanded it FOREVER (Gen. 17:9-14), for his descendants—both Israelitish and Arab—it could not have been harmful. And even though the METHOD of the rite as a religious command is transferred from a physical to a spiritual means, I am sure I have the approval of the Lord in making the most urgent recommendation for circumcision, for sanitary, health, and moral protection.

Circumcision, moreover, is coming to be widely practiced today for these very sanitary reasons. Whether or not the obstetrician advises it, I urge all parents to demand it.

Another thing—it is becoming CUSTOM of obstetrical

doctors today to perform the circumcision *at time of birth.*
Do NOT PERMIT THIS! God instructs that it be done ON THE
EIGHTH DAY—the day the baby is eight days old—which is
eight days *after* birth, or actually the ninth day of his life.
The baby is ONE day old on the *second* day of his life, not
the first which is the day he is born (Gen. 17:12).

The only reason doctors are turning to the practice
of performing circumcision at the time of delivery is THEIR
OWN SELFISH CONVENIENCE! And so they simply reason
around the idea—and will so advise patients—that it makes
no difference. They simply do not want to be bothered the
second time, on the eighth day. Perhaps I am a little blunt
in saying this. But I have no patience with such selfish consideration only for *self*-convenience, and inconsideration for
patient and child! Demand it, or go to a different doctor!

One other thing still. Some doctors today are cutting
off too much foreskin—or all of it. Simply tell the doctor
to leave a little of it. If he asks you if you are taking it on
yourself to tell him his business—well, I think I'd simply
decide he didn't *know* his profession and go to one who
does! Perhaps I'm blunt. I do urge you to be courteous and
diplomatic, of course—BUT TO BE POLITELY FIRM! I do know
whereof I speak! If too much, or all of the foreskin is cut
off, the skin is drawn back from the point of joining with
the glans on erection, and *this causes undue arousal and
temptation.*

Female Copulative Organs

The external genital region of the female, or pubic
region, is called the *vulva.* This term includes all the external genitals collectively—all visible from without.

Connecting the womb with the external genitals is the
vagina. The term means a sheath. It is a tube, or canal, the
special copulative organ of the female, serving the specific
act of coitus. The bottom rounded neck of the womb pro-
jects into the posterior end of the vagina. The direction of
the vagina is downward and forward from the uterus, al-

most at a 90-degree angle with the axis of the uterus.

The interior walls of the vagina are corrugated in folds, making these walls elastic and subject to being stretched, especially during delivery of a baby.

Textbooks used by doctors half a century ago indicated that the vagina is six to seven inches in length. More recent texts list it as three to four inches in depth, but with the explanation that, during intercourse, the penis forces the womb upward—the vaginal wall being sufficiently elastic to permit full entrance.

At the anterior opening of the vagina, the mucous membrane forming its lining continues as the membrane of the inner small lips, termed *labia minora*.

The semicavity inside the minor labia is termed the *vestibule*. Just above the vaginal opening is the orifice of the urethra, the passage from the bladder. Above the opening of the urethra, at the top of the labia minora, is the clitoris. This will be principally described later—and its function.

Actually, the clitoris is much like a miniature male penis. It is subject to erection under sensory stimulation. It has a head, or glans, much like the glans of the penis, in miniature, filled with nerve endings. This is the seat of voluptuous sensation and sexual arousal in the female. Only the head of the clitoris is outwardly visible—its body, an inch or so in length, being covered by the membrane over the top of the labia minora.

Ignorance of this very small organ and its intended function is one of the three principal causes of unhappiness, wretchedness and utter frustration in countless millions of marriages through the centuries! This tiny organ, therefore, becomes an important matter for right understanding. And here, again, the modern "authorities" are in disagreement and in grievous error. This will be explained in a later chapter.

Finally, over the labia minora, and covering the female genitals, are the larger lips termed *labia majora*. They require no further description or comment here (see below).

The functions of the principal female organ of copulation, the vagina, are 1) to provide passage for the menstrual flow; 2) to receive the male member during intercourse; 3) to provide a receptacle for deposited semen; and 4) to provide the passage for the birth of babies.

All these organs, and their functions, are GOD-designed for GOD-ordained purposes. It not only is an unmatched privilege to be able to possess human existence, with its awesome breath-taking potentialities—it also is acceptance of a very grave RESPONSIBILITY to possess the marvelous organs and powers of sex. They may be used to bring happiness, pleasures, and joys beyond our wildest anticipations—if controlled and governed by GOD'S LAWS. But foolish or ignorant misuse, abuse, or perversion, can impose severe penalties that far outweigh any temporary illicit pleasures or gratifications.

God's Way is the only *practical* way, that "pays

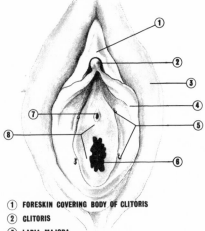

(1) FORESKIN COVERING BODY OF CLITORIS
(2) CLITORIS
(3) LABIA MAJORA
(4) LABIA MINORA
(5) LUBRICATING SECRETIONS
(6) HYMEN AND EXTERNAL OS OF VAGINA
(7) ORIFICE OF URETHRA
(8) VESTIBULE

Drawing showing external female organs, collectively called the vulva.

off" in rich dividends of true happiness and joy. If you use the Maker's INSTRUCTION BOOK as the BASIS of knowledge, and as the directive *approach* to all you *think*, and *do* in relation to sex, properly glorifying God in your body, great shall be your happiness, *now*—and ETERNALLY!

CHAPTER 15

The *God-ordained* Uses
of Sex

WHAT is the real God-ordained USE of sex in marriage? *WHY* have the millions of unhappily married never known either this WHAT, or the HOW? *WHY* is adultery, and other immorality, a SIN? Is it merely because a harsh God gave a command, or was the COMMAND given because its violation robs and harms humans?

WHY is premarital "necking" and "petting" wrong—or *IS IT?*

These are the vital questions that demand plain and clear ANSWERS in this chapter.

Human Male and Female Differences

We have shown the astonishing sex *differences* between humans and animals—especially female differences.

Now we come to decidedly important sex-response differences between men and women. In coming to definite, inexorable ANSWERS to these burning questions, the Maker's INSTRUCTION BOOK is the guide and the AUTHORITY.

And let the answer come right here to the question of WHY God gave commands. Man is not to be punished for sin merely because a God gave an arbitrary command. But God gave the COMMANDS because these violations rob us of joys, and inflict automatic harm.

God's Laws were set in motion TO GIVE us happiness,

peace, security in plenty, and thrilling radiant JOYS. God's Laws are the gift of His LOVE to us. God wants us to ENJOY the blessings they make possible. This is the plain and rational TRUTH! *WHY* has a rebellious mankind insisted on being willingly *ignorant* of that basic FACT of life?

We have covered the sacred MEANING and the divine PURPOSES of sex in humans. We have seen that sex in humans was given for incredibly glorious purposes that do not at all obtain in animals.

The three God-ordained purposes are *marriage; reproduction*, which, in marriage, involves the blessing of God-plane FAMILY life; and *the expression of marital love* to preserve the matrimonial bond and safeguard the home and family.

But now we come to the HOW of the marital love relationship.

The existence and function of the sex hormones have been briefly explained. They produce marked *differences* between men and women. These differences are mental, physical, and sexual. They are responsible for that mysterious, elusive, yet fascinating something we call sex appeal.

Sex appeal causes a man to become romantically *or* lustfully interested in a certain woman. It also prompts a woman to become romantically interested in a certain man.

But *what is* sex appeal?

For one thing, I am convinced it is somewhere between 95% and 99% what one sees from the neck *up!* It is, mostly, what one sees in the face of the other which exerts the appeal. Of course voice and other factors contribute. And a most appealing face might be repelled by a seriously unappealing figure.

We think of it as *mental*—taking place in the mind—and being stimulated primarily by the face. But it would never happen if it did not actually *originate* in the generative glands! But, as explained, these are directly connected with the mind by the nerves. And the sex hormones which make a man masculine, and a woman feminine, pass directly from their "laboratories" into the blood stream, and are carried to the mind as well as other parts of the body.

So, after all, the real origin of sex appeal is in these germinal glands, in cooperation with other vital glands.

Expressing Marital Love

This sexual love-stimulant causes a man to desire to take that one particular girl, not only as his wife—to share his life's problems, troubles and successes—to be his companion, and the mother of his children—but also to desire to take that special little woman into his arms, and express his love in fond embrace.

The same sexual love-stimulant also causes that certain man to be romantically attractive to a girl—not only to want to be his life companion, the mother of his children and the homemaker of his home—but to desire to be taken into his arms and caressed and loved.

In the truly happy marriage, sex is the stimulus for repeated kissing and romantic embrace and love-making. But it also serves to provide that frequent *supreme* expression and consummation of love-embrace in the sexual relation.

THIS IS WHAT AN ALL-WISE, LOVING GOD INTENDED AND DESIGNED IT TO BE! This, in a marriage bound for life by the very Creator, is a most righteous, clean and decent, HOLY relationship.

God made humans of physical matter, and equipped them with five physical senses. These may be expressed in a God-ordained *right* way, or in a sinful *wrong* way.

I repeat—it is God-endowed and *right* that we enjoy the *taste* of delicious, wholesome health-building food; that we *enjoy* the *sight* of a beautiful English landscape or the breath-taking snow-capped Swiss Alps; that we *enjoy* the *sound* of beautiful and inspiring music.

And it is just as *right*—and just as God-CREATED and God-ORDAINED—that a husband and wife, joined in marriage by God Himself, receive perhaps the pinnacle of all enjoyment in the ecstasy of occasional coitus in marriage! This is the SUPREME expression of love between husband and wife. It is entirely *too* intense an experience through the senses to be indulged in to excess. As in all things, God's WAY for our maximum good is the way of intelligent temperance. Temperance is one of the fruits of God's Spirit.

Excess corrodes and makes common this supreme pinnacle of all physical expression. The newly-weds do often have a problem of adjustment to work out. But then, rose bushes have thorns. And the need for adjustment not only builds character and strengthens self-discipline, but renders the experience so much *more* precious, enjoyable and rewarding.

How often, then, is proper for this occasional *supreme* expression of marital love? The human "authorities" generally say two or three times a week for younger married people. The infallible Authority does not reveal any directions for proper frequency. God endowed us with minds and sufficient intelligence to arrive at proper values in this particular. Individual cases vary. Certainly, for maximum happiness and joy, the proper spacing increases the intensity and ecstasy of this ultimate in physical expression of love. It is worth reasonable self-denial.

Differences in Responses

In marriage, a loving embrace, a kiss, an affectionate caress is a loving expression that *should*, within bounds, be repeated often (I do not mean in public).

But when it comes to that more occasional ULTIMATE of love-expression between husband and wife, a second *most important sex difference*—this one between human male and female—must be thoroughly understood.

The first of these two vital *differences*—between human and animal females—was explained in an earlier chapter. But failure to understand the difference in stimuli and time required for arousal in humans has turned untold millions of marriages into tragedy. And here, too, the conditions functioning in HUMAN sex are totally different than in animals.

Before the supreme experience of coitus is engaged in, for mutual love and happiness, *great changes* must take place in both male and female sex organs.

The male penis must become enlarged, stiff, hard and rigid. But changes also must take place in the female genitals, or there will be tragedy.

The vaginal walls are composed of a mucous membrane which is corrugated, in folds. In the quiescent condition, this skin is dry, and the folds drawn so that the inner cavity, or tube, is shrunken to a width of perhaps an eighth of an inch or less. It is, in this condition, *totally unprepared* to receive the enlarged and stiff male member. A *great change* must first take place. Arousal must be induced.

It has been explained, in an earlier chapter, that female animals come "in heat" at a regular rutting season. Between seasons it is impossible to arouse them for sex mating. These rutting periods come at regular intervals, or seasons, *uncaused by the animals*. When the season arrives, arousal for coitus is *automatic*. The animals do not cause or control it.

But in women, as previously explained, arousal must be *produced*. The time or season has nothing to do with it. A woman is virtually as susceptible to arousal at one time of the month as another. In humans, this arousal is self-allowed or self-induced. It is regulated *by the mind*.

But sex hormones cause male minds to function differently than female minds. Male hormones travel through the blood stream to the brain, and evoke erotic desires in a manner different from that operative in female minds. Male minds are affected by stimuli different from female.

Male sex organs may be aroused by a dream, or by a picture, or imagination if the mind is allowed so to drift, by remembrance, thinking of a certain person, picture, or experience, or by direct physical contact. Males are readily aroused by *psychological* stimuli; women by direct *physical* stimuli.

The principal source of feminine arousal is the embrace, the kiss, the caress.

Upon physical contact, in embrace, male arousal occurs in a matter of seconds, and very few seconds, at that. It begins almost instantly.

Many girls, participating in "necking" on dates, do not realize at all that the boy friend is sexually aroused, ready for and desiring coitus, in a matter of five or ten seconds' time. And some girls, devoid of right understanding and character, on learning this, deliberately resort to an embrace on the next date to "try out" their feminine powers. This is very foolish, very stupid, and very WRONG! To any such girl, I say, "You have only the very same power possessed by all the other billion and a half females in the world! Every cheap prostitute also has this power. That is what she sells in her despicable trade. Don't be like *her!* Don't pollute and misuse this wonderful power! God endowed you with these charms to be preserved for the one man to whom He will some day join you—to be used then in a chaste and wholesome manner that will produce blissful happiness. You will be required to answer in the Judgment for the manner in which you use your God-bestowed power."

The Time Lag—and WHY

Sex stimuli are not only *different* in wives, but arousal normally requires *much more time.* Sometimes ten, fifteen minutes, or perhaps half an hour. Of course, as in other human characteristics, individual responses vary. And much depends on mental attitude. There *are* rare cases where the wife is more readily aroused than her husband. But I am speaking, here, of the normal average.

And, mark this well! GOD MADE THIS AS IT IS! There is a vital REASON!

God made man to be the leader—to take the initiative

—to be the aggressor. But there is *YET ANOTHER VITAL REASON!*

For emphasis I repeat—sex in animals serves *only* the purpose of reproduction. But in humans it serves also the purposes of *marriage, love,* and *family!* God made it to express the intimate LOVE-relationship between husband and wife.

So now CONSIDER! If the wife were aroused as instantaneously as the husband, coitus would be concluded immediately. In fact, through *ignorance,* it generally and tragically *is!* This eliminates the LOVE relation.

God intended coitus in marriage to render the REAL HAPPINESS OF TRUE LOVE. And *that* is *WHY* feminine responses are *different*—yes, different from those of animals, and also different from those of their husbands!

However, if the divine PURPOSE of love-expression is to be fulfilled, husbands and wives must possess this KNOWLEDGE. God did not provide them with instinct.

The deliberate repression of this knowledge, under the diabolical sex-is-evil dogma, wreaked havoc on marital happiness for centuries! It reduced women—potential HEIRS OF GOD—to the level of dumb animals!

Of course, by the damnable heresy of evolution, Satan has invaded even the supposed "intellectual" and "educated" classes in his deception of leading humans to think they are nothing but animals! Satan does not want humans to know their true destiny as begotten, and, finally, BORN children of GOD!

But GOD designed sex in *humans* to EXPRESS LOVE in MARRIAGE!

Now UNDERSTAND THIS!

The very *fact* that the response in wives is *slower*—the very *fact* that wives are aroused by stimuli *different* from their husbands—by the LOVE embrace—by the LOVE caress—by the ardent *love talk* of their husbands, each telling his wife she is the most lovely, the most dear, the most darling woman on earth—telling her she is the sweetest, the

most *honored*, the most admired, the most precious of women
—all this sincere ardor and earnest love-making—with the
kissing and fondling of the one so dear and precious to him
—all *this* produces sex arousal in wives!

At a time like this, a husband realizes, IN HIS MIND,
as at no other time, just *how* delightfully lovely and precious
his wife really is to him.

How DIFFERENT is this marital LOVE from premarital
promiscuity or a cheap and degrading *animal* relation with
a prostitute! In either latter case, it is mere self-gratification, not the *giving* of love to THE ONE not only loved, but
respected, admired, and honored above all others—THE ONE
for whom he has the very greatest outgoing concern! Did
you ever notice that the intense love-talk in Solomon's Song
of Songs, expresses this outgoing admiration, not lust? It
was written *before* his polygamous relapse.

To the unmarried, I say, this is such a precious thing
it is a million times over worth waiting for! Any premarital
sex—any perversion—mars this potential marital happiness
—puts irremovable SCARS on the marriage before it happens!

Love-Making NECESSARY

But under the stern sex-is-evil code, none knew the
delights of marital LOVE—unless discovered by accident—
and then under penalty of a "guilty" conscience!

Deliberately, the All-wise, benevolent GOD created in
women the very type of sex stimuli that requires love. And
for man to violate this law, or bypass this love-need, is to
impose the penalty of physical pain and emotional anger
or resentment.

If a husband, immediately aroused, attempts to force
the rigid male member into a quiescent and unprepared
vagina, real disaster may result. As explained above, the
vagina is shrunken, almost closed, and dry. Such a brutal
penetration would tear the unlubricated dry membrane along
with it, causing pain, and producing a mental sense of re-
vulsion in the wife.

But God has provided a wonderful means of bringing about the happy coital love-union between husband and wife. This requires preliminary *love-making.*

The husband's *quick* arousal provides incentive for initiating the love embrace. But also it imposes on the husband the responsibility for the mental control of restraint against a too hasty climax. It was meant for the husband to *take the time* to express his love for the wife God gave him, that she, too, may be aroused and properly *prepared* to share in the supreme and ultimate climax in love-giving!

This love-play *preceding* actual coitus produces feminine arousal. This *love*-giving thus produces the *drastic change* in the wife's generative organs, making them *ready* for the coital union.

And all this love-making—this caressing, embracing, kissing—this "necking" and "petting" as it is called in current slang vernacular—is actually A DEFINITE AND MOST IMPORTANT PART of the act of sexual intercourse!

What Teen-agers Should Know!

Of all the books on sex available today, one especially that I have used as a text in my *Principles of Living* classes in our colleges, is, strangely, 50 years out of date in some biological respects. Nevertheless, for a general approach, I have found it the most satisfactory. The 50-year-old biological errors are easily corrected and brought up to date.

This text describes coitus as ONE WHOLE, but composed of *four parts*, or acts, of the one drama—four successive phases, one blending into the next.

And the first phase of sexual intercourse, this text explains, is the love-making stage. In other words, the very thing adolescents today indulge in freely on dates—"necking" and/or "petting."

These two modern terms, of course have various meanings among various young groups. But I use them here as thus defined: By "necking," I refer to love-making primarily confined to the neck, face, and shoulders. Only it is seldom

LOVE! It is usually sensuous self-gratification on the part of the boy; and on the girl's part it may be the same, or it may be merely what she's willing to give, in order to receive, as payment, future dates and favors. This latter puts it on the cheap and shameful basis of the prostitute, who merely exchanges what she gives for *money*, instead of dates and favors! By "petting" I refer to petting which descends below the shoulders—to places where unmarried hands do not belong! And the term "heavy petting" is sometimes used for a sort of heterosexual type of masturbation, or, as many authors state it, "petting to a climax."

Today "necking" by teen-agers has society's acceptance —and even "petting" is not much frowned on.

But acceptance by society does not define righteousness or SIN!

MAN has no power to determine *WHAT* is sin. GOD has determined WHAT is sin. He allows man to decide only *WHETHER* to sin. And if he does—even with society's approval—he must REAP the PENALTY of sin—ETERNAL PUNISHMENT of *DEATH!* It imposes curses here and now, and robs the sinner of the true happiness and joys a loving Creator made possible!

But, many a young person may exclaim, "Necking a SIN? Oh, come, now! Doesn't everybody 'neck'? How can that be a sin—if we know where to stop?"

The answer is TWO-fold: 1) God ordained this love-making to be the necessary first and most important part of sexual intercourse. It, therefore, deliberately breaks the Seventh Commandment, "Thou shalt not commit adultery," when indulged in outside of marriage. That Commandment *includes* premarital fornication, or any other misuse or perversion of sex. It is a CAPITAL sin. It imposes automatically, without court trial, the CAPITAL PUNISHMENT of the DEATH SENTENCE! And 2) the dating couple all too often *don't know* when to stop—and, if they *know*, they too often fail to DO what they know!

As to WHY this is a sin, the answer will come later. It

is a sin for the same reason that ADULTERY is a sin. It is NOT merely because the Great God said so—He only said it because it is *so seriously harmful to* US HUMANS! God denies us NO PLEASURE—no happiness or joy—that is GOOD for us and for others!

God deliberately *so designed* male and female sex stimuli—and timing—so that humans might ENJOY the LOVE-relationship in marriage! It was definitely and intentionally done to prove the BOND which securely *binds* a marriage in happiness for life! It was purposely so designed in order to constantly *increase* a husband's love for his wife, and a wife's love for her husband.

That very private, very intimate, very personal and very precious LOVE relationship, never shared with any but one's mate to whom GOD bound one, does increasingly endear each to the other—it makes them, truly, ONE! It preserves the HOME and the FAMILY for the welfare and the needs of the children. It protects the most basic and necessary unit of a right society!

And all these are GOD-PLANE relationships!

WHY, then, is UNFAITHFULNESS to this godly relationship a CAPITAL SIN? Because it violates and destroys a sacred CAPITAL blessing!

Adultery, fornication, masturbation, homosexuality are SO COLOSSALLY SINFUL *BECAUSE* they violate, pollute, profane, and destroy something so HOLY and so monumentally RIGHTEOUS in God's sight!

What "Cheating" Does!

People today don't like to use God's plain-language term, adultery. When a husband or wife commits adultery, each uses a more modern less-sinful-sounding term, "cheating."

I have explained in a previous chapter a case history typical of millions. A young man I knew was married to a lovely young wife. They had a fine little son. They were very much in love. Then he decided to "enjoy" the fascination of the "chase" after an "affair." He succeeded. Then another "affair." Soon he discovered that somehow his wife had changed. She was no longer so beautiful and attractive. She seemed no longer desirable. He couldn't figure what had happened to her. Of course nothing had happened to *her*—it had happened to *him!*

As explained before, GOD set in motion a LAW! That law always works—automatically! It worked on him. He was unfaithful to the union to which a loving GOD had joined him. He *broke* not only his marriage, but God's Holy Law. He defiled a GOD-PLANE relationship which even the angels are not given to enjoy! He divorced and married a self-centered, scheming woman. That marriage didn't last. How many others he has entered into since, I never knew. He did try to find solace in a false and deceptive religion, devoid of God's Truth, and ignorant of the WAY to happiness.

Fornication *before* marriage, it has been stated before, also, puts a scar on the future marriage that can never be erased or healed. Many today commit fornication, and then marry the partner in fornication. I do not say such a marriage cannot be happy—it may, and ought to be. But I do say that scar will always remain! It has taken something away from the marriage. Even though happy, it might have been happier!

Fornication never pays its participants!

GOD ordained that "necking" should be used *only* in MARRIAGE. But what does MAN do? He indulges in "necking" promiscuously *before* marriage, and then, too often, omits it *in* marriage!

Actually, believe it or not, *IF* God had made it beneficial and issued a command for all young people to "neck" promiscuously *prior* to marriage, NOBODY WOULD! Whatever GOD says "DO," people *don't!* Whatever GOD SAYS "DON'T!" people *do!*

Deterrents to Marital Happiness

And so the *greatest* deterrent to happiness in marriage —to the very stability and security of the FAMILY and HOME

—is the *misplacing* of "necking"—resorting to it in dating *before* marriage, neglecting it *in* marriage!

This is probably the *main source* of marital troubles. The lack of this knowledge of *differences* in sex stimuli and timing, under a religious regime that forcibly withheld the information, wreaked enormous tragedy. Wives have been cruelly *hurt*—virtually raped—disaster resulted.

And even today, in this era of supposed newer physical enlightenment, the very *mental* attitude of many wives reared in the sex-is-shameful teachings, prolongs tumescence, even when husbands *do* observe this first rule of marital coitus. If a wife has been "seared with the hot iron" of this unrighteous teaching—feeling subconsciously that she is *doing wrong*—or *submitting to wrong*—her mind greatly retards the process of preparation.

Another VERY IMPORTANT deterrent is the widespread *fear of pregnancy.* This *fear* repels many wives. But let intelligence and love drive out fear. WHY should pregnancy be feared?

Is *planned parenthood* wrong?

The Roman Catholic Church has always responded: "YES!"

But if the BIBLE—the Holy WORD OF GOD—the Maker's INSTRUCTION BOOK to mankind—be your true AUTHORITY, *it says no such thing!*

Sometimes the case of Onan is cited, in an effort to sustain the false dogma against intelligent planned parenthood. But that incident upholds no such teaching.

Judah, father of the Jews, had three sons. Er, Judah's eldest son, died, leaving a childless widow. By Israelitish law, it then became the legal duty for Judah's second son, Onan, to marry the widowed Tamar, *for the very purpose* of begetting a son to bear the deceased brother's name. The legal statute involved here is stated in Deuteronomy 25 (RSV trans.): "If brothers dwell together, and one of them dies and has no son, the wife of the dead shall not be married outside the family to a stranger; her husband's [unmarried] brother shall go in to her, and take her as his wife, and perform the duty of a husband's brother to her. And the first son whom she bears shall succeed to the name of his brother who is dead" (Deut. 25:5-6).

Now continue the story of Onan:

"But Onan knew that the offspring would not be his; so when he went in to his brother's wife he spilled the semen on the ground, *lest he should give offspring to his brother*" (Gen. 38:9-10, RSV).

So God destroyed Onan. WHY? *Not* for planned parenthood—*not* for intelligent *spacing* of the arrival of children in a happy family. Onan's purpose in preventing conception was nothing of the kind. He prevented conception because he knew that the son born *would not belong to him*—he did it *"lest he should give offspring to his brother."*

Onan's SIN was *not* planned parenthood. There is no Biblical law forbidding planned parenthood. His sin was his refusal to OBEY THE LAW which required him to beget a son to bear his brother's name. His disobedience of THAT LAW was his sin.

Animals do not practice planned parenthood, because they have no MINDS to do the thinking, reasoning, and planning. With animals conception takes place as a result of instinct. It is automatic. Reproduction is the *sole purpose* of sex in animals.

NOT SO with humans. Sex serves the wonderful purpose of LOVE-giving in marriage. Humans are endowed with MINDS. Humans were placed on earth for the express PURPOSE of developing Godlike CHARACTER—learning to make *right decisions*, with prayerful guidance from God and His Word, and to exercise the self-direction to rightly act on those decisions.

Planned parenthood violates NO LAW OF GOD! Planned parenthood is *a definite contribution* to this supreme purpose of character building. It entails, of course, the responsibility for right and wise planning.

Any teaching or legislating which violates this divine PURPOSE of God—which instills in wives the dread and *fear* of pregnancy—is a religious heresy, and/or a violation of the higher Laws of Almighty GOD!

No wife should ever need to suffer the *fear* of pregnancy. It is natural for every wife to want to become a mother. To *prevent* having children and producing a FAMILY would be a direct violation of God's command: "Be fruitful, and multiply, and replenish the earth." But to PLAN a family in an intelligent manner, as to the *time* of the first arrival, and the time-*spacing* of other children—that is a different matter. Nothing in the Bible forbids this. MUCH in the Bible, in principle, supports it!

Another deterrent to marital happiness has often been a false view of the real MEANING of marriage. Many have been victims of the false notion that marriage bestows on husbands certain *"rights"*—to satisfy a concupiscent selfish gratification—without *waiting* for love-making and preparation for the wife's enjoyable participation. And this false idea assumes also that marriage imposes certain *duties* on the wife—to submit to being virtually raped. Marriage confers no such *"rights"* and imposes no such *"duties."*

Conversely, some scheming women have supposed marriage conferred upon them the *"right"* to a man's money—to take their half, giving nothing. Many women have married wealthy men for their money. Any such marriage is fraudulent in God's sight!

Another deterrent is "letting down" after marriage. During the dating and romance stage, both groom and bride-to-be put a "best foot forward." They are careful about manners, grooming, the courtesies. Then after marriage comes the "let down."

If you want a happy marriage, be far more particular about all such things *after* marriage than before. Be careful about your sleeping garments—be sure they are neat, clean, attractive to the other. Be careful about your hair—especially on rising in the morning. The very first thing I try to do on rising is to get a comb and brush, before my wife sees tousled and mussed-up hair!

Wives, I do not exactly *know* the solution of pricking and stabbing a husband in the face with all those hairpins with which so many females think they must tightly bind their hair overnight. Don't just giggle at this—I hope you wives may find a way to relieve suffering husbands, and still have your hair looking radiantly beautiful next morning.

Ever notice how people answer the telephone? A wife calls her husband at his place of business or work. He answers: "Oh, it's *you*. Well, I wish you wouldn't bother me now. I'm busy." But if some other woman might call on a matter of business, his voice is cheerful, courteous, warm and friendly. And of course it's the same when hubby calls the wife during the day. She's warmly cheerful and polite to all but him. She feels, "Oh, he's only my husband."

Whether I am at St. Albans, England, or Big Sandy, Texas, or my office at World Headquarters in Pasadena, I do have to be shielded to a certain extent from constant telephonic interruption. But there is one voice that *always* gets right through to me—Mrs. Armstrong's. All my secretaries and switchboard operators are instructed that I'm never too busy to be interrupted by *her!* Little things like these are some of the reasons our marriage has been so happy for more than 47 years.

If you *must* be cross, discourteous, or appear tired before someone, let it be *anyone* else—but *never* your husband or your wife! Don't ever utter the alibi: "Oh, but we're married, now." BE LOVERS, as long as you live!

And always REMEMBER: *Love* is an outgoing concern; "*Love* is very patient, very kind . . . is never rude, never irritated, never resentful" (I Cor. 13:4-5). That is God's definition of LOVE. God ordained that husbands and wives should be *that kind* of LOVERS!

The All-wise and All-loving CREATOR designed sex for MARRIAGE, and for the expression of LOVE in marriage as well as the bringing of children into the FAMILY. He designed marriage to be a LOVE-relationship.

The Other Three Phases

This first phase of the sexual act is the most important, because it is the most abused.

Some books dealing with the physical details of marriage may devote many pages to the next three phases. For our purposes here, a brief few words will suffice.

The textbook alluded to, which I have used in classes, lists the other three phases, as: 2) the union of the organs; 3) the motion of the organs, and 4) the orgasm.

I feel that no description is needed here. Yet the following comments are very important in regard to the 2nd.

Never come to this second phase *until* the first is thoroughly accomplished—until the wife is fully prepared. When she is sexually aroused, the shrunken folds of the vaginal walls will loosen up. There are lubricating glands which will provide adequate lubrication for the easy and comfortable penetration of the penis.

Just outside the vaginal entrance, inside the labia minora, are lubricating glands called *Skene's glands* and *Bartholin's glands*. During sex arousal these glands exude a lubricating fluid so necessary for any enjoyment in coitus by the wife. It means the difference between pain and pleasure.

Even after arousal, with blood filling the generative region, the vagina softening up and lubricated, in some cases there may be some pain caused the wife by entrance of the male organ. In such case, the penetration must be gentle, slow, and careful. Let the husband hold more or less still, and the wife do the "pushing."

Also, in the case of the first act of coitus by a newly-wed virgin, absolutely no effort at union of the organs should be made until the wife is sexually aroused and prepared. Then let the husband hold rigidly still, and the wife do what pushing or make what motions are necessary for breaking the hymen. This may be a little painful—but the wife knows how much pain she can stand—and if she does the pushing and breaking, she knows precisely when it is coming. Full instruction regarding hymen-breaking is given in Chapter 18.

How is the husband to *know* when his wife is fully aroused, and ready for the second phase? *She must let him know!* She should not be too shy with her own husband to tell him. But if she is, she may simply cease resisting at this point!

The All-important Clitoris

And now it becomes necessary to say a few words about a small feminine organ which is of great importance.

The *clitoris*, previously described, is simply a miniature of the male penis. This is not generally realized, because only the glans (head) is visible. The small shaft, or body, of this organ is covered with the skin just above the upper end of the labia minora.

The nerve-endings in the clitoral glans are even more acute than in the glans of the penis, so that, even though much smaller, it is the seat of female sexual arousal.

Inside the labia minora is the region termed the *vestibule*. In the case of a wife who is not sexually stimulated to complete preparatory arousal by normal kissing, and caressing in loving embrace, it may be hastened by allowing the organs to come together—but without penetration of the vaginal canal. Instead, let the position be such that the glans penis is placed in the vestibule—but in the upper portion, *in contact with the clitoris*. A continuous gentle movement, in this position, will hasten arousal. But the wife should be *careful* NOT to allow this means of stimulation to proceed to the point of orgasm. As soon as sufficient arousal is attained, she should immediately withdraw from this position, and proceed at once to the second phase—the union of the organs.

Now we come to the third phase, and just one point is of VITAL IMPORTANCE here. Unless this is realized, and care taken, the position of the bodies may be such that no contact is formed with the clitoris.

For this very reason, millions of unhappy wives, through the centuries, have never realized that women are intended to ENJOY the pleasure of love in coitus, the same as their husbands.

In fact, probably millions of women have been married, become mothers and grandmothers, and finally died never knowing they possessed such an organ as a clitoris. Of course, at the other end of the pendulum, many little girls accidentally discover this, and start masturbating. Mothers should be diplomatically watchful for signs of this. Just about every so-called "authority" whose book I have seen, and the medical associations, universally chorus the minor discordant error that masturbation does no harm. I say to you on authority of Jesus Christ and the Word of God that it *does* do harm—not only physically (even though temporary), but psychologically, emotionally, mentally, and, most of all, MORALLY and SPIRITUALLY.

Masturbation is not so prevalent among girls as boys, but nevertheless a too-large percentage indulge in it, either occasionally or habitually.

Most boys and men practice masturbation to a greater or lesser extent. In many it becomes an almost unbreakable HABIT. This would never be if parents realized their RESPONSIBILITY, were *vigilant*, ever watchful imperceptibly, and took proper means to protect their children from this CURSE!

AND DON'T BE TOO EMBARRASSED! It's your responsibility as a parent! You are not fit for parenthood if you feel too embarrassed to protect your children!

BE SURE to read the full instruction about masturbation in Chapter 16.

But back, now, to that all-important little organ, the clitoris. We had come to the third stage of this marital coitus.

It is vitally important that the bodily position of husband and wife be such that contact is established with the clitoris. If the husband's body is placed too low in relation to the wife's, there will be no contact. The male body must, then, be a little higher in relation to hers, so that the base of the penis, near the abdomen, is in contact with the clitoris—the seat of female sensation.

When proper contact is established, the clitoris will be almost directly between the husband's and wife's pelvic bones.

I am well aware that many "authorities" today claim that a clitoral orgasm is immature, and that orgasm should be produced by vaginal contact alone. One doctor, a professor in a very large university, goes so far as to recommend that the bodies of husband and wife ought to be across each other, forming a cross—instead of face to face.

If GOD be our Authority, and the Bible our approach, it refutes and voids all such nonsense immediately. It is

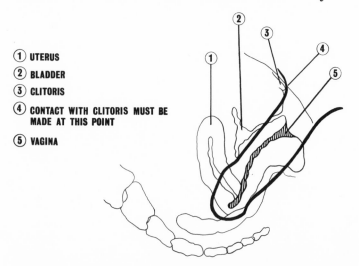

① UTERUS
② BLADDER
③ CLITORIS
④ CONTACT WITH CLITORIS MUST BE MADE AT THIS POINT
⑤ VAGINA

This illustration shows relative size of quiescent, unprepared vagina (shaded area) compared to erect penis (heavy black outline). If a husband attempts to force erect penis into shrunken, dry, unlubricated folds of tender vaginal membrane, the wife may suffer great pain, being virtually raped. Feminine arousal prepares and lubricates vagina to easily receive male member without pain. This illustration shows also the point at which contact must be made with clitoris.

not through ignorance, but on AUTHORITY, that I say dogmatically, marital coitus should be in the general position
of the love embrace, face to face—since God ordained this
act, for humans, to be that occasional *supreme* expression
of *love*.

It could well be concupiscent LUST, in the manner certain authors recommend in this flood of sex books available
today. But God made it for LOVE. Perhaps by now the reader
understands WHY we are unable to recommend any existing
book—*WHY this book had to be written!*

In most of these books much is said about the many
possible bodily positions. I do not deem it necessary to comment on that here. All married people know the two most
natural and commonly used positions. Sex can *become* a
matter of lust, perversion, or plain SELF-gratification and
concupiscence, even in marriage. Any such experimenting
with abnormal positions and unnatural or perverted ways of
performing coitus should be avoided.

The author mentioned here calls this third phase of
sexual intercourse "the motion of the organs." The organs
of *both* husband and wife should engage in this motion. If
the husband is above, he should be careful to avoid resting
his whole weight on his wife, by largely sustaining himself
on elbows and knees. This allows her to lift her hips up and
down slightly, or sway them from side to side, or swing in a
circling motion, as she may choose. This is better made possible by the wife placing her heels, from outside her husband's legs, in the rear knee-hollows of his knees, also clasp-
ing his body with her arms. This gives her leverage to draw
toward him and so gain contact with the clitoris—and with
whatever pressure she may desire.

Nothing more will be said about this third phase of the
act, except that both husband and wife, in full assurance that
this entire drama of love-making is God-designed, and God-
blessed, should strive to make an art of it. Learn to move
gracefully. And each try to please the other. In a God-bound
marriage, rid your mind of all inhibitions. Wives should learn

to "let go"—*giving* themselves in utter and loving and blissful surrender to the husband with whom God has made them ONE.

Now we come to the climactic fourth phase of marital intercourse—the *orgasm*. This possibly is the most intense physical sensation possible, delightful beyond description if not too frequently indulged. It need not be further described. But several things do need to be said about it.

Misconceptions About Pregnancy

Every husband and wife should strive for one objective, here. That is to arrive at this climax simultaneously. I said *strive!* It will take striving—and perhaps time and experience. Perhaps *never* will any couple be able to perfect this technique to a point where orgasm is simultaneous regularly and every time. But it is a goal worth striving for.

This may require mental retarding on the part of the one arriving at this climax faster—concentrating the mind on something *else* temporarily, and complete abandonment of all inhibiting or interfering thoughts on the part of the other.

At the instant of orgasm, the semen is thrown in repeated jets from the penis into the vagina in the region of the cervix.

However, orgasm on the part of the wife brings no corresponding emission of fluid.

Many mistaken ideas abound in regard to pregnancy, at this point. Some have supposed that unless the woman experiences orgasm, there can be no pregnancy. THAT IS FALSE! *Orgasm by the wife has absolutely NOTHING to do with conception*, one way or the other!

Then WHY do (or *should*) wives experience orgasm at all? This voluptuous explosion in women was designed by a Holy GOD for one purpose *only*—for her supreme pleasure, delectation and delight, in the LOVE embrace with her husband! It has nothing to do with conception or reproduction!

It is something animals know nothing of! Animals repro-duce—but they do not marry, or express the delights of LOVE in marriage! WOMEN DO!

Yet for centuries, millions of women were denied even the knowledge of this, by the suppression of information during those dark-age years of prudery and repression!

Millions of women have borne and reared their children, never knowing that WOMEN are supposed to experience the joys of orgasm the same as husbands! Yet, now, today, under the avalanche of "New Morality" "enlightenment" millions of teen-age girls learn all about it in premarital *SIN!* Thank God, Jesus Christ is soon coming to straighten out this crooked, ignorant, mixed-up, God-defying world—and bring it peace and real HAPPINESS!

There are other misconceptions about pregnancy.

Some think there can be no conception, as long as the female hymen is unbroken and no male penis has ever entered the vagina. But again hundreds of thousands of babies have been conceived in this very manner. Young unmarried couples, "necking," going as far as they think they dare, short of "the limit," go far enough to let the organs be in contact—but only in the vestibule—not pene-trating the vagina. Weeks later the girls notice their skirts are becoming too tight. One mentioned this to Mrs. Arm-strong.

"You're pregnant," explained Mrs. Armstrong.

"But I *couldn't* be," exclaimed the girl. "I'm still a virgin!"

"Well, you'd better see the doctor," replied Mrs. Arm-strong. "Perhaps you'll believe him." The girl and the young man married immediately—they were in love and engaged, anyway. They repented bitterly. Of course God forgave, upon real repentance, and their marriage has been happy, with additional children—but that scar will always remain! It just can't be erased! Some mistakes are *SO* PERMANENT!

A single drop of semen deposited anywhere in the outer

vulva may easily lead to an unwanted pregnancy.

But to return to the desirability of simultaneous orgasm. Once complete sexual arousal has taken place, it is some-what—at least temporarily—injurious to break off without proceeding to the climax of orgasm. This orgasm is a nerv-ous release of built-up tension.

Husbands and wives should restrain caressing and love-making in between the times of full intercourse, to a point short of such *complete* arousal. The very fact that the male penis becomes erect in a matter of seconds does *not* mean that this full and sustained arousal has been reached. It is something that *builds up*, more and more, to a state of tension, IF physical contact is continued. Kissing and em-bracing for a moment or two may be enjoyed several times daily, without this built-up, fully charged, nervous condition. Yet, in times of full coitus, if husband and wife enjoy the close bodily contact of full love embrace for as much as 30 minutes or more before the second phase of the act is en-tered, there are some evidences that indicate this sustained bodily contact, up to 30 minutes, actually produces a health-ful relaxing of nervous tensions, and a stimulus to mental and physical well-being, when climaxed by orgasm.

But when this full tension of arousal has been gener-ated, there must be the release of orgasm, or nervous ten-sions continue.

Many a wife suffers all night long, with unsatisfied desire, her generative organs tumescent, her nerves "un-strung"—because on achieving orgasm her husband selfishly turned over and went to sleep!

Whichever party reaches this summit first is DUTY-BOUND to continue until full release of tensions is gained by the mate, through orgasm.

Yet, after this climax, tensions relax, interest is gone, and a desire to turn over and go to sleep seizes one. On the part of the husband, the penis will gradually lose its stout-ness, and after a few moments it will be impossible to keep it in coital contact. If this should happen, a considerate husband will, if necessary, set the alarm clock for about two hours later, and *then* finish *his duty* to his wife.

All rose bushes have thorns. This one of marital sex will present its problems. They require KNOWLEDGE—they require the INTELLIGENCE of human minds—and they require love, consideration, patience, and CHARACTER to work out.

But they pay the richest, most happy and joyous dividends possible in the physical lives of humans made from the dust of the ground! And they are only a TYPE of the sexless but SPIRITUAL joys which we may inherit FOREVER!

CHAPTER 16

Dating—and Teen-Age Morality

*D*ATING PROCEDURES have undergone radical changes in the past seventy-five years. But has it been beneficial progress—or has dating become a lost art?

What about "going steady"? What about "necking," "petting," premarital sexual experience?

It's time to come truly up-to-date—*with the facts and with the* TRUTH!

Let's have reasons, for or against, that are rational and that *make sense!*

First, look at today's teen-age world. Realize how it has *changed!*

NOT ONLY is a moral revolution in cyclonic progress around the world. There also is a teen-age revolution. It is, of course, a large part of "The New Morality" as a whole.

Are Today's Teens Really Worse?

There are those who, in their self-confident uninformed optimism, assure us that today's adolescents are no different —and certainly no worse—than those of past generations. But the *facts* prove otherwise.

Human nature is the same. But we simply live in a *different world* today. The emergence of the phonograph, the automobile, the motion picture, radio and television and other productions of the machine age have brought new in-

fluences and changing customs. Human nature, adapting to
changing times, expresses itself very differently today.

Some would hush up the naked FACTS. But the welfare
of our youth is at stake. The adolescents, drifting with the
immorality tide, are speeding past their elders in the downward plunge. There is a trend. It is an immoral trend. It
is speeding up at accelerated pace. It is only natural for
young people to follow the trend. They want to belong. It's
time to face the facts squarely.

People are like sheep. They all follow the leader to the
slaughter. But they don't *know* they are being led to the
slaughter. They are just a little stupid. Yes, quite a little!
But they still want to belong! It's natural to just go with
the group.

From Chaperones to "Loving Up"

Look how times have changed—and moral standards
with them!

When my mother was of dating age, in the middle
1880's, chaperones were in vogue. She wore long sleeves, high
necks, and skirts that dragged the dust. Young men didn't
know what girls' legs looked like. In her embarrassment,
my mother, I remember as a boy, called them "limbs." When
a young man began dating a young lady, it was called
"courting." There was little or no caressing—only when the
young couple could give the chaperone the slip. It was then
called "spooning" or "sparking." And even on such rare oc-
casions, the very proper young ladies quickly drew the line.

A generation later, when I arrived at adolescence, the
chaperones had disappeared. But in the earlier years of dating—after age 16—this caressing, today called "necking,"
was not yet the general practice. Or if it was, I must have
been highly ignorant.

I distinctly remember one incident—after I had passed
twenty. A girl I frequently dated and I were being driven
to her home by a young man with his girl friend. In those
days all cars were *completely* air-conditioned—they were

open cars. It began to rain. We buttoned on the side-curtains. To hold the curtain down, on my girl friend's side, I was obliged to stretch my arm over the seat behind her. I shall never forget the difficulty I experienced in keeping my arm far enough to the rear to avoid any contact with the back of her neck. I was terribly afraid she would think I was "fresh" if any part of my arm touched her!

Today's bold young people will get a real laugh at that. Yes, indeed—TIMES HAVE CHANGED!

Later I knew of an experience involving a young man about 21 whom I knew very well. He and a 21-year-old chum were double-dating two girl chums. The other couple had begun "loving up" as the younger generation then termed it. So this friend of mine began to fear he would be considered "slow," or behind the times. "Loving up" was then beginning to be considered the thing to do, after the first two or three dates. So this fellow began cautiously putting his arm around this girl's shoulder. She didn't shove it back. A date or two later, he worked up enough courage to kiss her. She made no objection. He remained very proper, otherwise.

The girl's father was dead, and her stepfather was a dealer in Buick automobiles. He and his wife often took the young couple out on Sunday afternoon rides. Very few families owned automobiles in those days. The young people sat in the back seat, and his arm usually was around the girl's shoulders. There was no objection from her mother or stepfather. It seemed to be accepted as normal.

One night, sitting in a front-porch swinging seat, the girl began to tell this young man how much money her father had left her. It was not a fortune, but a few thousand dollars. She began suggesting what they might do with it.

"Wait a minute!" he suddenly exclaimed. "Just what are you getting at?"

"Why," she replied, "I thought we ought to begin to plan what we will do after we are married."

"*Married!*" he exclaimed, in sudden alarm. "Who said

anything about getting married?"

"Why," she came back, equally surprised, "what have you been loving me up for, if we're not going to be married?"

The flabbergasted young man then explained that he had never indulged in "loving up" before, but had begun to feel out of date, supposing it was expected. The girl burst into tears, jumped up and ran into the house, slamming the door behind her. Next day the boy tried to contact her by telephone. Her mother answered the telephone.

"Lucile told me all about it," said the indignant mother, icily. "She never wants to see you again." And she never did!

But in those "loving-up" days, prior to World War I, girls were kept "decent." Actual sexual intercourse was "unthinkable." The girl who did submit to it "lost her honor."

Have times changed?

Let's not be naive!

The Teen Influence

Few people stop to realize to what extent the teen-agers have taken over, today. They pretty well dominate the world picture.

Isaiah foretold this day. Here is a portion of the prophecy: Speaking of our people—TODAY—in these very last days—God says: "And I will make *boys* their princes [Moffatt translates it, "I will make mere lads their leaders"], and babes shall rule over them. . . . the youth will be insolent to the elder, and the base fellow to the honorable. . . . My people—children are their oppressors . . . the daughters of Zion are haughty [Moffatt continues]: holding their heads high as they walk, and ogling with their eyes, walking with their mincing steps. . . ." (Isa. 3:4-16 RSV). And this latter expression, about ogling eyes, when properly translated, actually refers to painted eyes—make-up on the face, and sensuous manner of walking to arouse boys.

Now look at the facts!

WHY do so many radio stations turn to a "rock-and-roll" format today? Because the rating agencies will show that they have the highest "ratings"—that is, the largest listening audience. But WHO is listening? Nearly altogether just "kids" in the lower or middle teens. But the rating agencies do not show the time-buyer *WHO* is listening— only how many! So Big Business, and local "little business" spend millions of dollars for radio time on the stations with the "highest ratings."

But then, they say that these youths pretty well dominate the nation's consumer SPENDING!

WHO determines what is "popular music" today? The "teens." Even the radio stations who do not go to rock-and-roll, in the main, play what is called "popular" music. But *is it* MUSIC? Or is it a moan, a groan, a wail, a dirge, and a screech?

WHY do ten-, twelve-, and up to fifteen-year-old little girls go virtually INSANE, and actually invite demon-possession, over the British "Beatles"? That could never have happened fifty years ago.

Adolescents determine dancing trends, motion-picture themes, radio formats, and even advertisements and most fields of entertainment!

What many do not realize is that this teen-age influence on the whole society *is predominantly sexual influence.* There is much more intense preoccupation with sex during these years than in later maturity.

Therefore SEX became the basic formula for motion pictures—along with crime, including murder.

In the past twenty or thirty years teen-agers have come to recognize that there are advantages in organization and numbers. Actually it started back in the 20's, with the sheiks, the flappers, and the Charlestonites. Then came jitterbugs, bobby-soxers, and then actual sex-clubs and gangs. In Britain, there were the Teddy-boys, succeeded by the "Mods" (Moderns), and the "Rockers" (Rock-and-Rollers).

In many communities, police and citizens alike have

been shocked at the exposure of existing "non-virgin clubs." Many disguised themselves as "teen-agers' social clubs." They played "sexual games." In some clubs, partners were drawn by lot. Club rules required illicit relations not less frequently than once a week. Girl members were initiated by sacrificing their virginity in a "ceremony" witnessed by all members.

There have been teen-age drinking-and-sex parties. Many such girls expressed the attitude that there was nothing wrong with illicit or promiscuous sex.

There are facts and statistics on teen-age immorality and juvenile delinquency to fill this entire book many times over.

But WHY? What is the cause?

Take one typical example. A 19-year-old boy had been in a certain town only six months. He named to police eleven girls with whom he had engaged in illicit sex. Many from "the best" families. "You can 'make' almost any girl in town, on your first date," he said. In this particular scandal, which got into the newspapers, revealed facts were significant.

Of all involved, not one had received any formal sex education—boys or girls. Every boy had engaged in premarital sex before age 15. Not one was close to either father or mother. The police chief exclaimed that it was too bad he was unable to take a horsewhip to the neglectful parents!

One of the mothers whitewashed herself of blame, saying: "You can't blame *me* for Janie's predicament! Why, you can rest assured she never learned a thing about sex in my house. The word was never even so much as mentioned!"

Teen Sex and Violence World Wide

The fast-growing surge of teen-age violence is WORLD-WIDE! Accompanying sexual promiscuity, news dispatches pile up an avalanche of reports of wreckage, destruction of property, pillaging, violence, and often MURDER!

In Britain the *Mods* (Moderns) and the *Rockers* (Rock-

and-Rollers) have succeeded yesterday's "Teddy-boys." While I was in England in the spring of 1964, some 800 boys and 400 girls invaded Clacton, a coast resort, on motorcycles and scooters. There were three days of rioting and disorder.

Hundreds of Rockers and Mods took a one-day excursion across the English Channel to Ostend, Belgium. There they wrecked bars, went completely wild, smashing store windows, attacking waiters in restaurants, fighting for girls. Through the spring and summer the Mods and Rockers terrorized a number of localities, scandalizing Britain.

At Sydney University, in Australia, students shocked the world with "hamboning"—a new fad of throwing off all clothes during informal dances, and dancing naked. Police picked up 300 girls between 13 and 17 years of age. Some 250 of the 300 had indulged in sexual intercourse more than fifty times!

Of course Sweden has led the immorality parade. Sweden has a high standard of living, *economically* (not, regrettably, morally). An organized group of teen-agers in Sweden is the *raggare*. They come from upper, and upper-middle economic classes. They have spending money. Yet drunkenness, venereal disease, illicit sex and prolific premarital pregnancies are their common "fruits." They engage in shoplifting and violence. But they have no sense of *purpose* in life, are utterly aimless, have no idealism, and are completely *bored!* Their only aim in life seems to be a *revolt* against society, authority, decency and morality. *How long can Sweden remain an economically prosperous country*, with its notorious immorality receiving official and public encouragement and acceptance?

Teen-age crime is skyrocketing in France. There an organized gang of teen-age terrorists is known as the *blousons noirs*. Here is the report of a recent escapade. Their current singing "idol" was booked for a performance at the Palais des Sports, in Paris. Six thousand of these *blousons noirs* jammed themselves inside the theatre. But there was no performance. Before "curtain time," they started methodically to tear up the plush seats and wreck the theatre.

The same restless, immoral, violent, teen-age rebellion is sweeping South America. In Argentina drug addiction, drunkenness, robbery, rioting, prostitution, promiscuity and abortion are rampant. Many of these are children of economically prosperous parents.

In Mexico an organized teen group is known as the Little Tarzans. They select certain adults at random as victims to be beaten up. Then they draw lots for the privilege of doing the beating.

The organized teen gang in Venezuela is known as the *Pavoa*. They are a terrorizing gang, operating in the well-to-do suburbs of Caracas.

Canadian teens shock the public with wild orgies, and naked boys chase nude girls through public parks at night.

You never heard of such a GENERAL state of affairs fifty years ago! Most definitely *times have changed!*

And WHY?

WHY Teen Immorality and Violence?

Yes, WHY?

The world doesn't want to hear the true answer!

The world refuses to *face* the tragic TRUTH!

The TRUE answer is this: Something has been *taken away* from this earth that sorely needs to be restored! That "something" is knowledge of, respect for, and obedience to THE GOVERNMENT AND THE LAW OF GOD!

But will *any like* that answer? Most want to go on rebelling against their Maker, trying to find some *other* solution to their problems. *There is no other!*

Once there *was* peace, happiness, orderliness, joy, on this earth. You don't have to believe it, but its TRUE. Angels populated the earth. The Almighty GOD has placed a top-ranking archangel, Lucifer, to administer the Government of God on the earth. Lucifer was a brilliant cherub. He sealed the sum-total of wisdom and beauty. It went to his head. He became vain. Vanity gripped him. His mind swelled with resentment because he ruled only this earth—a mere speck in the universe—while GOD ruled all the universe.

A third of the angels followed him in warlike aggression to knock God off His throne, and take over the UNIVERSE rule. But they were driven back to the earth. Physical chaos struck the earth as a result of this stupendous mutiny. In six days God restored the earth, and created MANKIND upon it. God made man mortal, of material substance. But He gave man MIND power. He placed in man HUMAN NATURE. Human nature is the natural *attitude* that had become Satan's (Lucifer's name now changed to Satan). Human nature is a PULL, like the power of gravity, in the direction of vanity, greed, self-love, and spirit of competition, hostility, indifference, resentment, or hatred, toward others. That is man's natural attitude and tendency. It is a constant PULL on man in that direction. It is the WAY THAT COMES NATURALLY.

Human Nature—Minus Purpose!

Let's *understand* the real *basic* reason for these present problems. Basically, it is simply human nature.

Yet God endowed man with MIND power, capable of recognizing the error of this WAY, *if willing.* Adam could have obeyed God, resisted Satan, and qualified to replace Satan as earth RULER, administering the GOVERNMENT OF GOD. But Adam disobeyed God, succumbed to Satan. His children have done so ever since.

Jesus Christ obeyed God, kept God's Commandments, resisted Satan, conquered the devil, and qualified to administer the world-ruling GOVERNMENT OF GOD. Then He ascended to heaven to officially receive this world-RULE. The heavens have received Him *UNTIL*—notice it, Acts 3:19-21, only *"UNTIL* the times of RESTITUTION of all things"—that is, the RESTORING of what had been taken away—THE GOVERNMENT OF GOD!

That time is almost upon us, NOW! This very outburst of universal VIOLENCE is one of the signs! "As it was in the days of Noah," said Jesus, "so shall it be," just before the days of Christ's return to RESTORE THE KINGDOM OF GOD, and bring us PEACE! Just before the Flood, there was illicit sex and VIOLENCE! It was not thus fifty years ago. IT *IS* A TIME OF ILLICIT SEX AND VIOLENCE TODAY!

Can't we see the handwriting on the wall?

WHY all this violence—this immorality?

HERE is the cause! Human nature—which is VANITY— without any PURPOSE, and absence of parental training and discipline!

There is no sense of PURPOSE today. We are told we must adjust to living in a world of problems *with no solutions!* Nuclear war—the erasure of human life from the earth—appears to be just around the corner—liable to strike us any second.

Young people today are given NOTHING TO LIVE FOR! No HOPE! No FUTURE! They are more prosperous than ever before. THEY ARE *BORED!* They are *rebellious*. The spirit of REVOLT is in the air! They resent all AUTHORITY!

Yet VANITY within them seeks to exalt itself!

WHY did Lee Oswald shoot and kill President Kennedy? Frustrated VANITY! He sought status. He sought it the wrong way. America turned him down. Russia turned him back. He was a *little* man, incapable of greatness, yet he desperately craved to do something that would make him stand out in history—make the world *take notice* of him!

Even the Warren Commission could find no other motive!

WHY do aimless, purposeless, bored, yet prosperous teen-agers resort to violence? Says an article in *Reader's Digest*: "Boys explode into violence to prove that they are grown up. Some, unable to succeed in school . . . seek status through hooliganism."

There it is—"TO SEEK STATUS"—plain VANITY, but minus any constructive or healthy PURPOSE!

Their parents have FAILED!

One father said of his boy in police trouble: "It isn't *my* fault! Why, I've always given him everything he wanted.

I can't understand WHY he did this terrible thing!"

Yes, this father gave him MONEY. But he failed to give him right teaching, training, a PURPOSE in life, proper discipline, instilling in his boy a sense of responsibility and respect for authority! And he probably denied him love and true father-and-son companionship! Also he failed to teach him the TRUTH about SEX!

Teen-Agers Need Factual Instruction

It is not exactly a paradox that millions of teen-agers have had considerable sex *experience*, and yet possess little sexual *knowledge*. It is largely *because* of ignorance—or right instruction in the right manner at the right time—that adolescents seek to satisfy curiosity by *experience*. And, of course, they are "sheep," and when it becomes a trend—when "it's being done"—human nature wants "to belong." So they go with the crowd—and parents know nothing of it.

Even when growing children and adolescents do receive some formal sex education, it is always presented from the physical, the material, and therefore the sensual approach.

If teen-agers had been *properly* taught what they *needed* to know about sex, from the very first and second years of their lives, by informed and loving parents, the frightful tragedies of teen-age and premarital sex would have been reduced to the barest minimum.

Today, if you tell a teen-ager that "necking" is WRONG —that it ought *never* to be indulged in—that it is a definite SIN—that it robs their future marriage of much of its possible joys, delights, and blissful happiness—the young man or woman will probably look at you rather pityingly, wondering how you could be so naive!

He would probably *reverse* the truth and exclaim, "Oh you poor, poor ignorant soul! Why, *where have you been*, that you don't know the *facts of life* yet? WHY DON'T YOU GROW UP? This is the twentieth century!"

Actually, it is the adolescent who is naive, ignorant,

and untaught in the TRUTH about the *facts of life!*

"Going Steady"

The *basic* cause of today's immorality, of course, is HUMAN NATURE. Human nature is the basic cause of all violence, war, crime—all our troubles in this present evil world!

But, as stated in the beginning of this chapter, human nature expresses itself in different ways, and adapts itself to changing times.

Human nature is, simply, the subconscious *pull* of a *definite attitude* of mind. It is the attitude that became Satan's. It is the *natural* attitude of vanity—of *self*-concern —of lust and greed. It is the attitude of hostility to others, and resentment of authority over it. Of course, the *self*, as explained before, *expands* into the "empirical self"—which includes those with whom individual self is associated, or connected. This may include one's family, his club, his gang, his church, his country.

Patriotism is an example of the empirical self expanded to include one's country. But patriotism is expressed in the form of loyalty to country, *as opposed to* OTHER countries. It includes an automatic hostility toward *other* countries— either passive or active. The Bible (Moffatt translation) classifies this as "party spirit," (Gal. 5:20) and one of the "deeds of the flesh"—as opposed to the "fruit of the Spirit."

The natural tendency to want to *belong* is merely the expression of this phase of human nature. This leads to the desire to want to *go along*—with those one accepts as his group, team, gang, or whatever. This nature expresses itself in young people by the natural *pull* to want to *go along* with the *teens*, as opposed to their elders. If the teens have a new custom, frowned on by their elders, then *self* associates itself with the teens, and feels automatic and *natural* (from human nature) hostility and resentment toward the opposing elders.

Now what about "going steady"? This started several years ago as an American custom. The custom has spread.

It is a new *way* started by those in the middle and late teens. But when 18- and 19-year-olds began "going steady," 16- and 17-year-olds desired to emulate (Gal. 5:20) and to *go along*. Then 14-and 15-year-olds responded to the *pull* to *go along*, and today even the 12-and 13-year-olds are beginning to "go steady."

This subject has been discussed before in this book. Going steady brings familiarity, and familiarity breeds a certain contempt—in this instance, contempt for chastity, virtue, and honor.

This going steady is simply the natural response to the *pull* of human nature. Human nature is essentially lazy. When a boy or girl goes steady he feels assured of dates. The boy is spared the embarrassment of asking new girls for dates, and the possible humiliation of being turned down. The girl feels a sense of security, knowing she will have dates.

The very familiarity of steady dating makes it easier for the boy to make bolder advances in "necking," and then going on further into sexual intercourse. It makes it more difficult for the girl to say "NO." It tends to lower bars of resistance, and increase the temptation to carry intimacies to the limit.

The FRUITS of going steady are definitely *not good!*

It is one of the most difficult things in the world to convince an adolescent of the wisdom of doing what he *ought* to do, instead of what he *wants* to do. But yielding to what one *wants* to do is surrendering to human nature. It is travelling the road to sin. And sin is man's greatest enemy, inflicting on him every pain, heartache, suffering and anguish he ever experiences. It inflicts *unwanted* penalties. But, again, it is hard for people to understand *why* they can't put their hands on a red-hot stove and not get burned!

If a parent has not taught his child basic rules of character from infancy, it is a little late, by age 14, 15, or 16, to convince him that he ought not to "go steady." He is now too big and set in his ways to listen readily, and his mind is still too young and immature to recognize TRUTH. But "going steady" is not good—*for those who do it!*

Now what about "necking"?

Is "NECKING" Wrong?

To even ask the question, "Is 'necking' wrong?" would sound rather silly to the average adolescent today.

WHY?

Because of *ignorance!* Because of wrong teaching, and a lack of *right teaching!* Because there are some of the *facts of life* they have not yet learned!

Is the Bible an out-of-date Book? If it is, how does it happen that it so accurately foretells *today's* WORLD NEWS— so understandingly pinpoints human nature? It says: "The carnal mind is *hostile* toward God." And that is certainly true. Where God says, "Remember," everyone immediately *forgets!* When Jesus said, *"Think not* I am come to destroy the law," everyone proceeded to think He DID destroy it! If God, in the Bible, said, "OBSERVE Christmas, New Year's and Easter," *then nobody would!*

GOD created humankind *male and female.* GOD blessed humans with the wonderful God-plane marriage and family relationship. GOD designed sex, to bring indescribable delights and joys with His blessing, IN MARRIAGE! In His great wisdom, GOD created men so that sex arousal and desire takes place more rapidly than in their wives—and He designed women so that they are not physically or mentally *prepared* for actual coitus *until* arousal is brought about *by the love embrace—by caressing—by the love-talk and endearing words of the husband!* In other words, by "necking" and by "petting."

There was vital PURPOSE in this!

Had God made women to be aroused by the same means, and the same quickness, as their husbands, sexual intercourse in marriage *would seldom*—if ever—*be that supreme expression of* LOVE that God intended—in order to

BIND and HOLD TOGETHER the marriage and the home and family! Marriage would be robbed of its blessings—of its supreme joys!

But when boys and girls engage in premarital love-making, called "necking," "petting," and even "heavy petting" (these terms are defined in an earlier chapter), it is NOT the love that binds more firmly that which GOD has bound for life. It is mere sensual gratification. It is LUST, no matter what you wish to call it! It CHEAPENS, TARNISHES, CORRODES the entire, wonderful experience God intended as a repeated lifelong experience IN MARRIAGE! And it detracts from, and robs the participants of the *full* happiness they might have had in a future marriage!

This love-making—this "necking" or "petting"—this caressing—is all a PART OF, *and actually the most important part of*, SEXUAL INTERCOURSE IN MARRIAGE!

A Capital Sin!

Therefore, when indulged in *prior to* marriage—or outside of marriage—*IT IS A CAPITAL SIN!*

Teen-age CUSTOM does not determine what is SIN!

College-campus practices do not define right and wrong!

Acceptance by Society does not decide what is SIN!

GOD ALMIGHTY has already determined WHAT is sin!

God does not allow humans to decide WHAT is sin—but He forces us to decide *WHETHER* to sin! He has called me to lift up my voice and show people WHAT is sin. That is what I am doing here. I did not devise that LAW, or set it in dynamic, *living*, if invisible MOTION—*GOD DID!*

How can you *prevent* the tragedy of a premarital pregnancy? How can you *prevent* the disgrace and terrible predicament of venereal disease? By knowing *when to stop? NO!* By simply not starting the "necking" in the first place!

If it were GOOD FOR young people, God would have instructed them to engage in it! But SIN is not good for people —SIN *HARMS* PEOPLE!

In an earlier chapter we described how people are drawn into sin. It is explained in James 1:14-15, "Every man is tempted, when he is drawn away of his own lust, and enticed. Then when lust hath conceived, it bringeth forth SIN: and sin, when it is finished, bringeth forth DEATH."

The temptation is not a SIN. It is when the MIND harbors the temptation—retains it—keeps *thinking* of it—keeps desiring it, UNTIL the desire conceives into the ACTION of SIN. How does one avoid SIN? By NOT RETAINING THE DESIRE! By pushing it out of mind *immediately!*

But to *start* in the action of sin, and think you can "draw the line"—that you know "when to stop" is to COMMIT SIN!

The time to PREVENT SIN is before it starts!

This world's Society and its customs are based on human nature—which is to say, on SATAN'S ways—and are diametrically CONTRARY to God's ways!

Go along with the crowd, and you are stumbling along with the other dumb sheep TO THE SLAUGHTER! Why be one of the CROWD? Why not stand out from the crowd of ignoramuses and weaklings, as one who has knowledge, wisdom, and CHARACTER! Any old dead fish can float downstream but it takes a *live* one to swim up *against* the current!

This is not prudish talk. It is not "old-fashioned" talk. It is intelligent, rational UNDERSTANDING, based on the instruction of the Creator!

What a shame that the adolescents of today were not taught properly by their parents from babyhood!

It is THE GOD-REQUIRED *DUTY* of every parent—a responsibility for which parents will be held accountable IN THE JUDGMENT—to *properly* teach and inform their children of the FACTS of sex.

This teaching ought to begin while children are still small.

Dating a Lost Art?

Has dating become a lost art? It would certainly seem so. Certainly there is no "art" to the manner of dating today.

It seems young people no longer know what to do with themselves on dates. Perhaps most dates today are spent either in a car, parked by the roadside in a dark and secluded spot, where the time is spent in "necking," or in sexual intercourse, or else in a darkened motion picture theatre letting their minds drift with a ready-made daydream.

Dating is no longer stimulating mentally, upbuilding, socially and intellectually beneficial. It tends not to build but to destroy character.

Some dating, of course, is spent at various kinds of dances. Some of these may be invigorating physically and at least somewhat mentally. Some are downgrading and morally and mentally harmful—depending on environment and character and quality of participants.

In my dating days, I had a "system." I was unconverted, and the motive undoubtedly, in part at least, was vanity. But I did try to date only top-level girls. Of course we sometimes went to the theatre, occasionally to the motion pictures (it was during the "silent" days), occasionally to a dance—but never to a public dance. Public dances, then, were not in good repute.

But usually our date involved a walk, a scintillating and enlightening conversation, and possibly a soda or sundae at an ice cream parlor. I devoted considerable time in public libraries, in the philosophical, or travel, or biography departments, acquiring knowledge for interesting conversation.

On a first date I analyzed and sized up the girl. I didn't know how a fellow "fell in love," but I supposed it might happen unexpectedly in some mysterious way. And I didn't want it to happen to me in the case of an unqualified girl. If my first-date appraisal of the girl indicated definitely that, should I "fall" for her, she would be unsuitable as a wife and the mother of my children, there was never a second date.

I was taking no chances on "falling" overboard with

the wrong girl to the point I might be so blinded by love I would be unable to see it!

I remember one girl, pretty, attractive, good conversationalist. She got a second date. But then I discovered she was lazy, would not help her mother with dishes, making beds, and housework. I never dated her again.

I dated two or three girls, frequently but not regularly or like "going steady" in any sense, who had absolutely *no* "sex appeal" for me whatsoever. There would have been no temptation to "neck" as teens call it today. Of one I said I would as soon have my arms around a cold iron lamppost. Yet I dated her on occasion because she was an unusually fine girl whom I respected highly.

Dating can, and *ought to be* made a real art. Some thinking and planning ought to go into the preparation for a date. A date should be an event which adds to the mental, social, moral and spiritual character development of both boy and girl. Such a date is *so* much more rewarding, and leaves a far more palatable feeling afterward. In today's warped and perverted thinking I suppose that suggestion seems very old-fashioned and naive. But for those who have a little sense and understanding, it would be wise to heed it.

Dating should be made *interesting*. But a date can be both interesting and at the same time stimulating, uplifting, and a contribution to the very PURPOSE of life—character-building.

If my "system" did nothing better, it protected me until the Eternal God brought the finest little woman in the world and me together. Our dates were stimulating, challenging, dynamically interesting. *They still are*, more than 47 years later!

Instructing Small Children

This instruction should begin as early as little minds begin to show curiosity about little bodies—and that might be as early as age two or three.

The "birds and the bees" method has been ridiculed— but it is a sensible way, nevertheless. To little children, explain first about GOD. Explain about creation. If you have a copy of Volume I of Basil Wolverton's *"The Bible Story"* (which we sent out free—a second printing to be ordered), use that to explain how God created the plants, the flowers, the birds, the bees, and the animals.

Then explain how God is a SPIRIT Being, who *looks like a man*—who has a face, eyes, ears, nose, mouth—who has a body, and hands and feet—only GOD is composed of SPIRIT, and His eyes are like flames of FIRE; and His face shines as brightly as the SUN—so bright no human could look at Him without having his eyes blinded by the great light. God has ALL POWER, and so He caused all these things to come into being.

Then explain how God decided to make MAN in His very own likeness—not like animals, or birds, or plants—and to give us MINDS like His—only He made us out of matter, and so we do not know as much as He, or have as much power. But, just as all plants and animals were created to be male and female, and to reproduce their own kind, so God made humans male and female so we could have little babies who become children and grow up to be just like Daddy and Mommie.

Then explain how wonderful it is that even a little baby starts from a tiny "seed" or "egg" which is kept, as it grows, where the mother can best protect and watch over and nourish, as it develops. *You'll* be able to fill in the details—I won't attempt it here. And show how HUMANS can be a loving FAMILY, like God—and how a baby has a HOME, and a Mother and Father to love it—and not have to be out all by itself, like baby animals. Connect it all with God, and with LOVE, and with FAMILY RELATIONSHIP.

And above all, explain to your child that *YOU* will answer all his questions, and instruct him to come to YOU with all questions, but *never* to talk about this very wonderful but *private* subject with other children.

Of course you cannot tell a two- or three-year-old more than a small part of sex knowledge. But as the child grows older, explain more from time to time. Keep ahead of the "gutter."

Child Discipline—A Parental Responsibility

One of the greatest SINS, CRIMES, TRAGEDIES of this world's society, is that great sin of OMISSION—the neglect of parents to teach their children.

Not *only* about sex. Most parents neglect to teach their children—*period!*

But first, *before* you attempt to teach your children—especially about sex—EDUCATE YOURSELF! To enable parents to do that is a major purpose of this book. After you have finished it, go back and read it all again!

Always give your children an abundance of LOVE. *Show* your affection. Then, from tiniest infancy, by *loving* but unquestionable *insistence*, bring your child to absolute recognition of your AUTHORITY—and before he reaches the end of his first year! If spanking is necessary, use it—always being careful not to injure the child, yet making it smart enough to get results. Most mothers spank too lightly—that may do harm rather than good—especially psychologically.

Some fathers spank, beat, or paddle too hard. Make it *hurt*,—enough to accomplish the purpose—but without injury. The main point in spanking is to apply the principle of the adage that "the stitch in time saves nine." *Do not* spank your child *into obeying* you.

One mother couldn't understand why her spanking never got results—she spanked only in final desperation—to *force* the child to do what he was told. She told her four-year-old boy it was time to go to bed. He didn't want to. She threatened to spank. That was her first mistake. She should *immediately* have spanked him FOR DISOBEDIENCE. Instead, she threatened. He was accustomed to her threats, and knew by experience she probably would neglect to carry it out. Ten minutes later, she threatened again, a little impatient—a little angry. Then, another ten minutes and it was repeated. Finally, half an hour after her first command, she forcibly *spanked him into bed*. And wondered why this spanking had to be repeated so often!

Never spank in anger. Always *be sure* your child UNDER-STANDS your command or instruction. If this is made sure, then *spank*—crisply enough that the child doesn't want it repeated!—for DISOBEDIENCE TO AUTHORITY. The parent who hesitates is LOST! Do it *immediately!* First *be sure* the child UNDERSTOOD! Second, *be sure* you TEACH—get in the *lesson*—make plain, and in love, WHY you are spanking! Third, *spank without delay!*

Don't say: "This is going to hurt *me* more than it will you." Make it hurt *him* enough (without injury) that he won't want to disobey again—but make him understand *he* made you do it—not because you wanted to, but because he *made you*. Don't be afraid, as the crackpot child psychologists warn against, to make him feel "guilty." When a child disobeys, he *is* guilty, and must be made to realize it!

When *we* disobey GOD, He tells us plainly, in the Bible, that we are GUILTY! Yet God *loved* us enough to give Christ to die for us, that the sin may be forgiven, upon repentance.

So let the child *know* he is guilty—but he can be forgiven upon repentance—which means to *change* from the spirit of rebellion to an attitude of willing obedience.

But, don't *humiliate* your child—especially before others! The most cruel thing one person can do to another is to make him feel whipped, or to cause him to lose all confidence, or induce an inferiority complex. True HUMILITY is required for right Godly character—but one can be HUMBLE and still properly confident. True confidence is not *self*-confidence, but FAITH in GOD.

Space does not allow more along this line in this work. Every parent needs Garner Ted Armstrong's booklet on *Child Rearing*. Write for your copy. It's FREE.

Instructing About Puberty

NEVER lie to your child. NEVER refuse to answer questions about sex. NEVER say, "You're not old enough to know that yet." Always find a way to give a *right* explanation in a *right* manner, and within the understanding and capacity of your child.

NEVER reproach your child for asking questions about sex, by accusing him of interest in "indecent" things. Be sure you represent sex, as God ordained its *right* uses, as decent, good, and actually something sacred and pure—and to be *kept* that way! Make your child understand, early enough, that GOOD THINGS may be put to sinful USES.

When the little child asks his mother, "Where did I come from?" tell him the TRUTH. Let the mother say, "You grew into a baby inside of me, here under my heart," and she can point.

In teaching little children to keep pubic regions covered, never talk about it being "indecent," in a way to give the impression sex is indecent. But explain it is *not proper* to be exposed to others—sex is something God wants *kept private*. If a little boy and his little sister ask about sex differences, it's certainly time to begin instruction about sex, and why God made it so.

Answer! Don't tell your child the "stork" lie.

One little fellow said to another little boy: "I found out that all that stuff about the stork bringing my little sister, and about Santa Claus, isn't true—and so now I'm going to look into this Jesus Christ story, too!"

"Oh, BUT," some may protest, "am I to rob my children of their Christmas?" If you want the true answer, write for our free booklet on THE TRUTH *About Christmas*. NEVER LIE TO YOUR CHILDREN!

Doctors report cases of twelve- and thirteen-year-old girls being brought to them by distraught parents, on the occasion of their first menstruation. The parents didn't know how to explain. And it was "too embarrassing!"

This should never be! If children have been properly instructed about sex, gradually, as they grow up, all girls should have been fully instructed about menstruation before they reach the age of puberty.

Any mother can and should completely explain what is found in the early and last portions of Chapter 13 in this book, in a manner to cause her daughter to consider with reverence and awe how wonderfully God has designed her body and its functions—especially of the marvelous "laboratories," the ovaries. If the mother is dead, the father should have no difficulty in explaining this with the help of Chapter 13, and other portions of this book.

Every boy should be completely instructed before he reaches the age of puberty. And the *proper* explanation is found in Chapter 13—especially the middle portion.

A boy reaches puberty when he discharges semen in his sleep. Every boy should be fully and properly instructed about this before he reaches this stage of physical maturity. He should be made to understand that night emissions—termed nocturnal emissions—are natural and normal—the natural "safety valve" which God designed to eliminate the excess semen as it develops, so that neither masturbation nor premarital sex experience are necessary—and neither should ever be resorted to.

Truth About Masturbation

Nearly all books on sex—produced by the medical doctors, psychiatrists, and others from the purely physical approach—assert that masturbation is not harmful. THEY *ARE WRONG!*

WHY must humans—even the "professionals"—always go to one or the other *extreme*, as *far from truth* as possible?

On the one hand, many boys have been told, falsely, that masturbation causes insanity, loss of virility, sterility, pimples, etc., etc. This is not true. Scaring boys with lies is not the thing to do!

On the other hand, masturbation is a form of PERVERSION. It is a SIN! It *does* harm the boy—*or the man*—physically, over a period of twelve to twenty-four hours by dulling the mind, even causing often a partial blurring of sight, and acting as a partial anesthetic to the memory. Often a boy will experience absent-minded proclivities following masturbation.

It is harmful *psychologically!* Invariably it produces a guilty conscience, and destroys normal confidence. Sex experience *belongs in marriage!* The *mental attitude* is the *all-important* factor. God intended it to be that sacred and WONDERFUL relationship of expressing LOVE in that most intimate and personal of all human physical and psychological experiences, which binds husband and wife together truly as ONE FLESH! When sex is expressed in any other way, it ROBS one of a portion of that blissful, delightful, and truly WONDERFUL God-ordained experience! Remember LOVE is *giving*—an *outgoing* concern—as well as *sharing*. Masturbation is neither.

Masturbation is either plain LUST, or else a desire for relief. But God provided for relief, through the means of nocturnal emissions during sleep. If such *natural* relief is needed, the boy or man may induce it by sleeping on his back.

Most boys and some girls get into the *habit* of masturbation at an age so young they simply cannot remember its beginning after growing up. It is a nasty habit, often almost impossible to break. There is no greater plague!

Even a baby may discover a pleasurable sex sensation. It could and often does happen accidentally. Even before one year old, some babies may discover this and start masturbating. The parent should be constantly on guard. Treat it, in infancy, in the same category as thumb-sucking, or putting his finger in his nose. *Teach* the child that he should not play with parts of the body. Do not frighten him. Do not lie to him. Just tell him his thumb, or his penis, or his nose, was given him for a *different purpose*—and he must not misuse it. And back up your teaching with discipline—and punishment if necessary!

And don't assume that only boys and men masturbate.

It is a perversion practiced by girls—and grown women—also. The difference in sex is only relative. A higher percentage of males practice it, but more females are guilty of it than commonly realized.

This will require *constant vigilance!* DON'T NEGLECT IT! It is a serious parental responsibility!

Circumcision

The matter of circumcision was treated in an earlier chapter. At cost of repetition, it should be mentioned in this connection.

As a religious rite, as the Apostle Paul explained, circumcision under the New Testament is spiritual—of the heart, and not the flesh. Although it is NOT TODAY A RELIGIOUS RITE, nevertheless, *it is urgently recommended* for all male babies, for purely *physical* reasons. Check the index, turn back and reread what was written before on the subject. Circumcision will greatly lessen the danger of masturbation.

CHAPTER 17

The Best Age for Marriage

*I*GNORANCE ABOUT SEX is not, of course, the only cause of unhappy marriage and divorce. Even though some nine out of ten such cases result from ignorance and misuse of sex, many causes contribute to the other ten percent.

Religious differences is one. The Roman Catholic Church is very emphatic in restraining its members from marrying non-Catholics. And in this, they most certainly are right.

Neither should a truly converted Christian ever marry a non-Christian. God *commands* Christians: "Be ye *not* unequally yoked together with unbelievers: for what fellowship hath righteousness with unrighteousness? and what communion hath light with darkness?" (II Cor. 6:14.)

That fellowship with unbelievers should be avoided, *even in dating*. For dating too often *leads* to marriage!

What About Dating?

In different ways, according to varying customs, dating has been practiced as far back as history records. But, as in all things, dating has a right and a wrong *use*. The *right* kind of dating has become virtually a lost art today—especially in America.

Enough has been said, in Chapters 15 and 16, in regard

to the almost universal modern custom of "necking," "petting," "heavy petting," and premarital intercourse. These immoral practices dominate modern-day dating. Most dates consist of either this sort of thing, or a ready-made daydream watching a motion picture.

Enough, also, has been said about "going steady." This should not be done by teen-agers. After one is mentally, emotionally, and spiritually mature, and qualified to assume the *responsibilities* of marriage, steady dating with the most likely choice for an engagement to be married becomes a different matter.

But until then, avoid "going steady." Date different ones. Let the dates be on a higher mental, intellectual and ethical plane. Let the dates be up-building, contributing to mutual self-improvement.

When I was a young man, a date was a challenge. My effort was to make the date stimulating, and enjoyably beneficial. Of course, some of them included dances, the theater, an occasional "movie." But often they included ice skating or other such interests, and often simply going walking— with a scintillating conversation.

In Ambassador College we encourage dating. But we very definitely discourage "going steady"—until the middle of the senior year.

And remember this: It is GOD who *joins together* in marriage a husband and a wife. Therefore it *ought to be*— in your own interest—GOD who selects *for you* the husband or wife you are going to marry! And GOD WILL do this, if you ask Him, and then refrain from getting in a hurry and taking it into your own hands! This may require self-restraint and patience; yes, and also FAITH. But if you rely on God, He will not fail you. And if HE selects your lifelong mate, you'll have the RIGHT ONE!

I didn't realize this before I was married. Yet I have always known that, in His mercy, God did select for me the young woman I married. And now, more than forty-seven years later, we are both more sure of it than ever before!

If you are a parent of one or more teen-age children, should you try to *force* your children to date only converted young people—or those of your choice? YOU'LL DRIVE THEM DIRECTLY THE OTHER WAY, IF YOU DO! Your responsibility is to TEACH your children the TRUTH—and teach them, as they grow up, gradually to assume more and more responsibility themselves. Of course, this teaching ought to begin during their first year of infancy. For many of our readers it will be too late for that, now. Then USE TACT. Your children may now be past the age where you can guide their lives. They have minds of their own. But, in sympathetic understanding and tact, try to induce them to be willing to counsel with you in regard to general principles and truths. But NEVER try to pick for them the one they are to marry. If you have a choice, above all, NEVER let them know it—unless they voluntarily ask your counsel and advice. Otherwise, you'll drive them the opposite direction!

But, in more than thirty years of counselling in the problems of unhappy marriages and divorces, the overwhelming majority of those, involved couples who married too young.

Thousands have asked us, "What is the best age for marriage?" An article on this subject has appeared twice in *The* PLAIN TRUTH. The answer to that question is so vitally *important*, it simply cannot be omitted from this book. Therefore, it is here reprinted to complete the remainder of this chapter.

Too Young to Marry!

Some time ago I officiated at a wedding in stately Memorial Hall at Ambassador College in England. My next-to-youngest grandson, Richard David Armstrong II, then age two and a half, thought the ceremony so very nice, he said,

"Mommie, *I* want to get married!"

"Well!" answered his mother, a little shocked—a little amused, "and whom do you want to marry?"

"Karen," replied little Dicky promptly.

"But Karen has just been married. She can't marry anybody else, now."

"Well then," decided Dicky, "I'll marry Sheila." Sheila is a very nice Irish colleen, and was then a student in the college.

"But Sheila is grown up now, and in college," protested "Mommie." "What if she won't have you?"

"Then I'll marry you, Mommie," came the quick decision.

Marriage Is Not for Children

We may smile at the idea of a two- or three-year-old's getting married. It *would* be a bit irregular! Marriage is not for children! Marriage is for ADULTS. Marriage is pretty serious business!

Marriage entails the assuming of very serious responsibilities. Children do not realize this, of course. Marriage is a lot more than romance. It is more than daydreams about a "Prince Charming," or floating around on Cloud Nineteen, or being in a lover's arms.

But when do we become adults?

Are not boys and girls adults at around age 14? No. Far from it! Let's understand WHY!

Age for Acquiring Knowledge

Human beings know *nothing* at birth. We have to learn, or be taught—EVERYTHING! Without any knowledge, or with erroneous knowledge, we are helpless—as newborn babes. But there are some things many fail to learn. One of these is the right age for marriage.

Whatever an adult knows, true or false, has come into his mind since birth.

It may sound surprising or incredible, but a person actually learns more during his first year of life than in any succeeding year. If a one-year-old baby could talk plainly with complete and adequate vocabulary, you'd be completely amazed at how much he has learned that first year!

The second year he learns a trifle less than the first, and

the third year a little less than the second. Gradually, his capacity for learning decreases year by year, if only slightly. This is hard to believe for the simple reason that a two-year-old *adds* his second-year acquisition to what he learned the first year, the third to that, and so through the years his *total* store of knowledge increases continually.

But a person past 60 cannot learn something new in a field new and strange to him as readily as a young person of 22 or 23. Does this mean that a well-educated man of 60 knows less than a young man of 22? Of course not. Other things being equal, he knows infinitely more—because he has the accumulated knowledge of all those years since age 22 *added* to what he knew then—and he has learned much by *experience*. That is one reason wisdom comes with age!

But a two-and-a-half-year-old cannot delve very deeply into the study of advanced mathematics, philosophy, nuclear fission, business administration, economics, or child rearing. He would have very different ideas on the latter than he probably will have when he becomes a parent!

The first five or six years of life are, so we believe from experience, most profitably spent in learning the basic things of infant and child learning—how to walk, talk, eat, run, and play—knowledge about lots and lots of things. The little child learns what an automobile is—an airplane—he learns about animals—many things.

He may even be taught to count, and part or all of the alphabet. However, the kind of knowledge taught in school (kindergarten excepted) seems most effectively taught beginning age 6. At that age the child can learn to write, to read, and to spell simple words. In some countries he begins to learn a second language at that age. For the next ten years he acquires gradually all the foundational elementary knowledge, and during the last two of the ten perhaps a bit of preparatory knowledge for higher education.

All these years the normal individual has been learning rapidly. There is a great deal to know before maturity, and he is not mature *yet!* Of course, by age 16, the juvenile may think he *knows it all.* Many, in their own minds, know more than Dad or Mom. You see, what they do not yet know, they don't *know* that they don't know! But there is still much to learn.

But by age 16 the average normal young person of good mind is ready to *begin* a little more advanced study into more solid fields.

When Bodies Mature

But along in these early and mid-teen-age years, usually 12 to 14, the physical body suddenly speeds up its growth and development. The teen-ager at this point sprouts up much taller within a single year, with *bodily* changes from child to man or woman.

Suddenly the young person feels "grown up"—adult. He usually does not realize that at this stage the body makes a rather sudden leap toward maturity, *while the mind makes no corresponding advance!* The mind continues on at only the same year-to-year *gradual* development. *The mind is still more child than adult.* Its interests are still mostly "having fun," games, entertainments. Sexual maturity is suddenly reached, long in advance of mental, emotional, and spiritual maturity.

A human being is not a mere body. The married state needs maturity of mind, emotions, and spiritual qualities as much as physical adulthood.

A boy or girl is physically able to become a father or mother years before he or she is qualified to assume the *responsibilities* of parenthood.

But, suddenly becoming taller and physically developed, the boy or girl *feels* mature. A new awareness of the opposite sex is present. What the child of this age does not yet know, I repeat, he usually fails utterly to realize.

The attraction of the other sex acts as a magnet. The girl dreams of her Prince Charming; desire is awakened in the boy to hold an attractive girl in his arms.

The girl often falls in love with love, a certain boy being the focal point of her fantasy. Of course she only sees this particular boy as she imagines him to be, not as he really is. She is dead sure she is in love. And no one can awaken her from this entrancing dream. There are many facts of reality about this puppy-love affair of which she is totally unaware.

But, again, what she doesn't know that her parents see so plainly, she simply doesn't know that she doesn't know! She simply has to outgrow it! The very *fact* that she is not mature enough to recognize her immaturity is proof that she is still too immature for marriage.

At this stage, the parents have a problem on their hands, and need great wisdom to deal properly with it.

I repeat, marriage is not for children.

The Preparatory Years

But when does a child become an adult? When is one ready for marriage?

Marriage is in itself a career. One is not ready to enter upon any profession or career until after full preparation. This *preparation* may be divided, roughly, into three stages. First, that of infancy, preparing the child for school. Second, elementary and preparatory schooling prior to, thirdly, more advanced education and specialized training for the adult life's work.

There are really three stages, roughly, of mental development that parallel these stages of preparation. First, the change from babyhood to boyhood or girlhood around age six. Then the mind, as a rule, has absorbed enough elementary and semi-mature knowledge, by age 16, to *begin* more mature thinking and learning. Age 16 is a crucial year in mental development.

Prior to age 16 the average youth has little awareness of the seriousness of life, of world conditions, of human problems or the purposes of life. In our American public school system, he enters senior high school, or the last two years of preparatory school at about this age.

But the mind does not really become mature, on the

average, until age 25. At age 25 a more definite adulthood of mind, attitude, interests, is reached. The mind becomes more "set" in its ways.

The years between ages 16 and 25 are the *vitally important* years of adult preparation for life's work. These are the *crucial* years of *PREPARATION*. During these years the mind is capable of *acquiring* faster than at any other stage of life the advanced knowledge needed *before beginning* one's adult career—whether it be business, profession, occupation or marriage. Before age 16, the mind has not acquired the basic elementary knowledge needed as a foundation for entering more advanced study—and the mind has not developed in serious comprehension to the level of advanced knowledge. After age 25, the mind which has stagnated since age 16, finds it difficult to enter upon more mature study.

Before age 16, the mind simply is not mature. At age 16, it is merely prepared to *begin* acquiring the more mature *preparation* for either career, business, or marriage.

It should be borne in mind, I am speaking of average ages. There are, of course, exceptions to all rules—but in my experience about 99 in 100 follow this pattern.

Another stage of maturity seems to be reached at about age 30. I have noticed that, although most young people reach a certain mental maturity at age 25, a far more complete maturity of mind, personality, performance, and influence on others is reached at age 30.

By age 30 the man or woman has added five years of practical *experience*, in addition to further study, to the preparatory knowledge and final reaching of mental maturity attained at 25. Prior to 25, the young man is often called just that—"young man"—by older men. I can remember how, in my carnal preconversion vanity, I smarted under being spoken to as "young man" by business executives I dealt with. This expression simply meant they did not accept me, yet, as a fully mature man, and I knew it.

Somehow, the vanity in a young man of 18 and older makes him want to be considered *mature*—as a completely adult, fully experienced MAN. He wants to be considered older than he is. But as soon as young women are past 20 to 25, female vanity usually causes them to want to be considered *younger* than they are!

The Right Age for Marriage

The fact that a man attains a more complete maturity of personality, leadership and influence by age 30 seems fully recognized by the Eternal God. In ancient Israel the Levites were ordained to full priesthood at age 30—although they were put into physical *service* at age 20.

Jesus Christ, our Example, did not begin His active ministry until age 30. All years prior to that were years of learning and preparation.

Yet in ancient Israel men *began* actual service, adult work, and even military service, at age 20. This, however, does not mean that they were fully and completely educated at that age. Actually, their first years of service were those of apprenticeship—training, preparation. They probably were not accounted fully prepared for adult responsibilities until 25, though the exact facts are not given.

Apparently God has not given specific and direct instruction or command as to the proper age for marriage. God did not even count people in the census, as adults, until age 20. While there appears to be no punishable prohibition against marriage prior to age 20, there is every indication that on God's instruction juveniles were considered children until 20. At 20 they were considered "of age." *This by no means implies they were expected to marry by age 20!* Rather that they were expected not to marry *until* at least 20—OR MORE!

Based on actual experience, my judgment is—and I think it is sound judgment guided and approved by God—that until out of the "teens" a boy or girl is too young to marry! And it is also my judgment—and I think it is sound and approved by God—based on lifelong experience counseling on marriage problems of hundreds of people—that even

20 is too young to be *the best age for marriage.*

Two factors are the major causes of broken marriages, or of unhappy problem marriages, in the hundreds of cases that have come to me for advice and counsel: sex ignorance and marriage prior to age 20. Quite often these two are merged in the same case. A great majority of all unhappy or broken marriages that have been brought to my attention were those of people *who married too young!*

Only too well I know that teen-agers who *think* they are in love will not listen or heed. That very *FACT proves* they are too young for the responsibilities of marriage. Marriage is so much *more* than romance, necking, love-making and immature emotional bliss. Thousands of young people have gone ahead heedless, and been sadly disillusioned to learn that lesson—TOO LATE!

But in my judgment, except in rare cases or circumstances, even twenty is too early an age for marriage. I can only give my judgment. But it is based on experience. It is based on facts and knowledge. It is based on what Biblical revelation God has given us. It is based on hundreds of case histories.

But here it is, and young people will do well to heed it —and later be glad they did! The *best* age for a man to marry is around 24 to 26, after he has devoted those *top aptitude years* between 16 and 25 for mature education, experience, and preparation—*after* he has acquired the knowledge, preparation and preliminary experience to assume adult responsibilities—*after he is able to assume the responsibility of supporting a wife—and family!* And the *best* age for a girl to marry is between 23 and 25, when she has utilized those top aptitude years for preparation, and is prepared to assume the *duties* of wifehood and motherhood—the responsibilities of planning, decorating, arranging a home, keeping it, and being a help and inspiration to her husband.

I sincerely believe, in view of what God has developed, that He brought about circumstances and influences to shape my early life, and also my wife's, as a preparation for a very great world-wide work He willed to accomplish. I believe I was steered and guided by His unseen Hand in ways I did not realize then. And Mrs. Armstrong and I were married when we were both 25. We were mature enough to assume the responsibilities.

Our marriage has been *happy*, and blessed beyond words to describe. And, after all these years during which God has blessed us with four fine children, equally fine sons- and daughters-in-law, and eleven fine grandchildren, our marriage is still happy beyond words to describe. In fact it is happier now than ever before, because it has grown constantly more and more happy. WHAT A BLESSING!

Wouldn't you like yours to be equally so? Then heed! Use wisdom!

CHAPTER 18

Engagement—and Wedding Night

O NCE A COUPLE are engaged to be married—*then what?* What should be their standard of conduct?

Virtually everybody, today, would assume that "necking" is completely within the bounds of propriety after a definite engagement. But *is it?* Let's look rationally at *facts* unconsidered in the almost universal *assumption*.

What about premarital sexual intercourse between engaged couples? Does it help prepare for adjustment *in marriage*—or does it prevent or make more difficult that adjustment? What are the true *facts?*

The "New Morality" trend has changed the thinking—and the behaviour—of a very large portion of young people. Perhaps the overwhelming majority. These "emancipated" moderns view premarital sex as entirely acceptable between engaged couples. Such experience is fast coming to have public acceptance even where there is no engagement.

WHY Premarital Sex is SIN!

It seems *so hard* for humans to realize that whatever is becoming customary is not necessarily good. But there is a LAW! Put your hand on a red-hot stove, and your hand will be painfully burned! But people can't seem to understand WHY they can't put their hands on red-hot stoves, and *not* be burned!

These inexorable LAWS are GOOD, not bad! They are THE WAY to well-being, happiness, enjoyable living! People can't seem to believe that.

Let's see what are the inevitable results of actual experience!

Look at a couple of case histories.

Here is an actual experience brought to the editors of this book for counselling and help in finding a way out.

A couple in high school, age fifteen, began "going steady." Dates usually ended in a parked car. The boy made the usual advances. Boys usually go as far as they are allowed. Boys pride themselves on having a "clever line." They can twist truth, and make wrong seem *so right!*

Occasionally this girl submitted. Of course the boy was sexually aroused as soon as his arm slipped around the girl. She was not. Actually she didn't really *want* sex intercourse. In spite of the modern immoral drift, she knew it "wasn't nice." But boys with a line are hard to resist. Though she often protested, "I'M not interested," she did frequently give in. The boy was ignorant about sex. He merely followed the *pull* of his nature. He didn't wait for girl-arousal. He didn't know about the *preparation* phase of sexual intercourse. He plunged right in where angels most certainly would fear to tread.

Now, some years later, this fellow admits he got "a temporary thrill" out of each conquest. He then supposed the thrill was physical—sexual. In reality, he now admits, it was more psychological, mental, and emotional. It was primarily the thrill of conquest—of "putting it over" and breaking down the girl's resistance.

Before completing high school they decided to marry. Parents consented, without giving it the forethought parents should. He married the girl, he now says, "for sex." But "sex" is not the right MOTIVE for getting married—and can only lead, generally, to tragedy. One of the reasons God created sex was to make *marriage* possible—but He did not institute marriage merely to be an outlet for sex. There's a vast difference!

The girl, she now confesses, married him because she wanted to "get away from parental discipline," and have a home of her own. If she had been given the right kind of parental discipline she would not have fled it!

In marriage, the girl "submitted," as a wife, to his sex passion. But the young husband *suddenly found the "thrill" missing!* There was no longer the chase—the spirit of conquest. No longer was there the *self*-gratification of winning the psychological battle! There was only *physical* gratification. There *never had been* any real LOVE for the girl. Always it had been *self*-seeking—*self*-desire—never outgoing concern.

The sex relationship in marriage, under these conditions, *became cheap!* He knew he could go out and satisfy his physical desires with any other loose woman. He did not respect the girl who had been so *easy* for him to "make" prior to marriage.

In this marriage, there was NO LOVE expressed for, or toward the other, by either mate. There was only the attitude of *getting*—not giving or sharing.

All this occurred during the Korean war. Soon he was in the army. There he committed adultery repeatedly. She gave in to other men at home. The result was divorce!

Fornication, for this young man, had been a wholly selfish act of physical gratification. *It warped his thinking! It perverted his outlook! It robbed him* of the precious God-endowed capacity for LOVE, with honor, respect, and outgoing concern. And *she* had robbed herself of the priceless, God-intended, joyous privilege of being respected, loved and cherished.

Does Premarital Experience Help Marital Adjustment?

Another case history. These were college students, both of respected families of good social standing. They thought they were well-informed about sex, including contraceptive knowledge. Their frequent sex relations were secretly and carefully planned. They were sure "nobody would know." But after a few months the girl discovered she was pregnant.

"We reasoned," the young man said later, "that it was nobody's business but ours. It involved only ourselves—so we thought! But we had to learn—*the hard way*—that what we were doing involved both our families, their social connections, our respective churches, the college where we were students, and quite a host of people. And it involved, most of all, the child that was illegitimately conceived. These brief moments of occasional fleeting pleasure have now caused real pain, suffering, and disappointment to many other people. I guess it's true—nothing is ever done in a vacuum."

Of course the "educated" and "scientific" world rejects all knowledge of the invisible but living LAWS of God. It seeks answers by purely physical, experimental, and research expedients. Research studies have attempted to arrive at the final answer to the question: "Does premarital experience affect later marital happiness—and if so, how?"

They have found that those who had indulged in sex relations prior to marriage were less well-adjusted in marriage than those who married without previous experience. But they found so many complicating factors they could arrive at no "scientific" conclusion. Premarital experience nearly always must be carried on under very unsatisfactory conditions, as to environment, need for secrecy, psychological disturbances, fear of pregnancy and/or possibility of venereal disease, and many other impeding and unsatisfactory factors.

A couple in a large university began "going steady." Since premarital sex was the accepted custom, they indulged in "the usual." The girl, a brilliant all-A student, became pregnant. They decided immediately they had to marry. But they didn't tell their parents about the pregnancy.

Both parents objected violently. The young man's parents were socially prominent, the girl's were not—though the girl's parents were actually of superior intellectual level. The girl had career ambitions, expecting to continue on in graduate school to work for a Ph.D. Of course her career dreams were now shattered. It was only after the students confessed the pregnancy that the parents consented to the marriage.

The marriage was never happy. The young wife was bitterly resentful of being unable to continue her career. She resented her baby. She allowed this resentment to be transferred to her husband. Although she had consented to sexual intercourse before marriage—because it seemed to be "the thing to do," she became frigid *in* marriage. The young husband began going elsewhere for sex. The marriage ended in divorce.

"We're going to be married, anyway," argue many engaged people. "So what's the difference?"

Engagement Period Conduct

What's the *difference!* It's the difference between *SIN* and righteousness—between RUINING the marriage, and SAVING it for a true *God-plane* relationship—between corroding and seriously detracting from this lifelong companionship, and keeping it clean, pure, and full of joy.

An engagement, as considered today, *is not a marriage.* It is merely the understanding or agreement between a man and woman that they intend to *become* married. But the engagement does not involve the marriage vow.

Sexual intercourse prior to the actual marriage vow is FORNICATION, and the Law of God is inexorable—it will exact the penalty—CAPITAL PUNISHMENT! It is, in the sight of God, as great a crime as MURDER!

Read again Chapters 8 and 9. Catch anew a vision of the sacredness—the supreme *God-plane* blessing of the marriage and family relationship, bestowed on *no other* creatures or kind of life *except* human!

It ought to be looked forward to by the bride as the very PINNACLE of human experience! A bride should—and many do—have dreams of the coming marriage so idealistic and lofty they touch heaven!

To commit *fornication* prior to that wedding is to profane that sacred state of marriage—to drag it through a filthy cesspool into the depths of degradation. Any man who would suggest, or make advances toward, such a defiling of his marriage is not fit to enter that sacred relationship. And any woman who would submit to it is not fit to be the mother of her husband's children!

But what about plain "necking"?

This, it has been made plain in the 15th chapter, is a PART—and *the most important and necessary part*—of sexual intercourse! Therefore IT IS FORNICATION!

What, then, are the true facts? They are far different from modern immoral customs! The engaged couple *should be doubly careful* to avoid any form of love-making by physical contact in any way! Doubly careful because of the temptation to say: "Oh well—we're going to be married anyway," and so be unable to resist the temptation to continue on into fornication.

This is *not* to say that a fond embrace and a kiss—if not prolonged—are wrong. But remember, the male is sexually aroused in five to ten seconds—or less. Any such embrace or kiss ought never be prolonged sufficiently to produce arousal and desire. This is the time to practice self-restraint. This is the time to demonstrate honor with power of WILL.

These facts in themselves argue strongly against prolonged engagements. It is far better for young people resolutely to put thoughts of marriage out of mind *until* they are qualified to assume the *responsibilities* of marriage and parenthood. Until you reach this status, date different ones. But avoid "getting serious."

Fallacious Ideas

There are certain fallacious ideas held more or less generally by those not properly informed.

Some young men, and many girls, become engaged believing that the relative sizes of sexual organs may become a serious problem in sexual adjustment after marriage. They wonder if they are properly mated sexually. They may be tempted to experiment to be sure. This is an UTTER FALLACY!

God Almighty placed the female hymen at the orifice of the vagina to protect young ladies until marriage. God has set a LAW in living motion that makes fornication a CAPITAL SIN. Would an All-wise, All-loving GOD have made people so that they cannot be sure whether they are mated, unless they commit a CAPITAL SIN to find out?

You may be SURE that God, in His wisdom, made no such mistake. True, sex organs, like hands, ears, feet, or other parts of the body, do vary slightly in size and shape. But *size has nothing to do with being properly mated!* No adjustment will be necessary because of any size variations! The smallest vagina is made so that it will stretch sufficiently to allow the passage of a baby's head and shoulders when it is born! And no penis is ever *that* large! Also the smallest penis will fit perfectly into the vagina of a man's wife— regardless of whom he marries!

You *do* need to be sure you are properly mated—mentally, socially, religiously, emotionally, and that you are IN LOVE! But *forget* the sex until you are married. The GREAT GOD has seen to it that you'll be mated in that one category in which HE forbids premarital experimenting!

Many a bride has become nervous as the wedding approaches, in real fear that she may discover that the husband's penis is so large it might cause severe pain. THAT IS AN UNFOUNDED FALLACY!

The only reason some wives—and they have been MANY —have experienced severe pain upon penetration of a husband's penis, is because both have been IGNORANT of the need of the preparation that comes with preliminary LOVE-MAKING. If they will be careful to follow the instruction in Chapter 15, and the husband will be careful, considerate, and gentle, there will be no cause for concern. Even then there may, occasionally, be a case where entrance must be slow, careful, and gentle. But any considerate and informed husband can co-operate to avoid any difficulty.

Some boys believe that continence will reduce sex vitality. THAT IS ABSOLUTELY UNTRUE. Total refraining from sex intercourse, masturbation, or other sex outlet DOES NO HARM WHATSOEVER. But the self-discipline of continence *develops character!*

Many boys and young men think they can detect a homosexual by his appearance, or manner. That is FALSE. Some homosexuals are effeminate. Others are not. Even the Bible recognizes the two kinds. In the 6th chapter of I Corinthians, quoted in an earlier chapter, speaking of those who *shall not* inherit the Kingdom of God, we find: "Be not deceived: neither fornicators, nor idolaters, nor adulterers, *nor effeminate, nor abusers of themselves with mankind* . . . shall inherit the kingdom of God" (verses 9-10). The "effeminate" are one type of homosexual. The "abusers of themselves with mankind" are another type—*not* effeminate in manner. GOD, in the vernacular, "has their number." Homosexuals reveal themselves *only by their behaviour!*

Some girls, and some wives, believe that if females do not reach orgasm there can be no pregnancy. THAT IS A DANGEROUS bit of ignorance! Orgasm, as previously explained, has absolutely *nothing* to do with pregnancy. All that is necessary for pregnancy is the presence of male semen in the vagina, uterus, or Fallopian tube. Thousands of women have become pregnant through artificial insemination when no man was near, and no sexual arousal occurred. Others have become pregnant when a bit of semen was left *outside* the vagina, but within the labia majora.

A very general false conception is the idea that premarital intercourse is a good and necessary test of marital sex compatibility. JUST THE OPPOSITE IS TRUE. It not only is a CAPITAL SIN—it will give a WRONG ANSWER! Illicit sex *must be* carried out, in nearly all cases, under strain, sense of guilt, doubt, nervousness—and in poor or improper surroundings. This is about as far as it is possible to get, psychologically, from the circumstances of a happily married couple, knowing GOD has joined them, and that GOD now blesses their union. Girls by thousands today are losing emotional stability, moral security, the happy and joyful anticipation of GIVING THEMSELVES to their husbands as virgins on their wedding night—and also risking premarital pregnancy and venereal disease—by following this FALSE idea.

The Wedding Night

Although statistics supplied by the National Research Council indicate as high as 80% of brides, since 1950, enter marriage as nonvirgins, it is believed that a considerably higher portion than 20% of those who shall read this book will be virgins at the time of marriage.

The study conducted by this Research Council, however, is shocking, and shows how times have changed. Their statistics show that prior to 1912, 82% of brides entered marriage as virgins—only 18% of all women had "lost their honor," as it was termed in those days. By 1922, 26% had lost their virginity. By 1931 it was 49%. The immorality curve soared upward until by 1937, 68% of brides entered marriage having lost their virginity! And by 1950 an incredible 80% of brides were no longer virgins on their wedding day! And yet *some* say conditions are not getting worse!

Nevertheless, a *few*, even though a minority, still become brides in full retention of their moral HONOR! And for them, and their well-blessed bridegrooms, some important instruction must be given.

What a WONDERFUL, blessed and thrilling event it *ought* to be for a young woman who has kept herself a virgin to *give* herself, at last, to the man of her dreams—the man whom she dearly LOVES—the man to whom GOD has just joined her in holy wedlock FOR LIFE! Most assuredly this is the pinnacle of human emotional experience for a right-minded young woman of high ideals!

The wedding night will be a spiritual, as well as a physical experience. But the crux of the *physical* experience is that of *defloration*—the removal of the hymen. By now it shall have served its purpose.

There are two ways of accomplishing the defloration. One is by stretching, the other must be by rupture.

In a very small percentage of women the hymen is sufficiently flexible that it may be *stretched* during the first experience of intercourse, without the necessity of being broken. In such cases—and they are somewhat rare—if the penis is very slowly and carefully introduced, it may be wedged in gradually. There will be a certain drawing pain, but if preceded by preparatory caressing and love-making until arousal is experienced, and a sexual *desire* has been stimulated, this pain will be mixed with sensations of pleasure.

It may take several minutes, under careful pressure, but it may thus be possible to produce complete penetration of the penis without tearing the hymen—merely stretching it. This may need to be repeated several times in the same manner, and finally the hymen will completely relax. The defloration will have been completed in a bloodless and comparatively painless manner.

But in most women, the opening through the hymen will be too small to allow this stretching process. In such cases, the penis must be thrust with sufficient power—but not necessarily rapidly—to break open the hymen. Yet *the husband ought not to do the thrusting*—but the wife as we shall explain.

Fallacious Ideas Again

Both men and women often have ridiculous and unfounded ideas about this act of defloration. Many a bridegroom has worried for fear he may be unable to accomplish it. But every normal man will have a penis of sufficient stoutness to break the hymen. Besides, *he* should not do it—but the bride.

Some women, on the other hand, are seized with fear

of being "torn apart." This is due to ignorance! It seems too bad that the 80% of unmarried nonvirgins didn't worry more about it—or the approximately 95% of males who have had premarital experience!

There need be only slight pain to the bride—and that, in such manner that *she* may control it, as well as when and how it occurs, herself!

Let the Bride Do It

On this particular night, of all times, there should be no direct contact of the sex organs until after there has been love-making in abundance. The preparation must be fully carried out, first. The bride must be brought to arousal and desire. The vaginal area must be thoroughly lubricated.

Then, when the wife is ready, let the penis be placed at the entrance to the vagina. A clumsy bridegroom may not know where to find it. The wife should not be too timid to guide the penis to the right spot. Then, the husband should remain rigidly STILL! He should not attempt to plunge on through the hymen—for that might *really* cause pain. Instead, while he holds rigidly still, the wife should do the pushing. She will soon learn whether the penis can be slowly wedged in. Probably not! And if not, it must be powerfully thrust on through—but *while the husband remains rigidly and firmly still*. She knows what pain she can stand—and when she does the shoving, she knows *when* the pain is coming! In most cases, it will not be great. And it will be accompanied with great joy, and also with pleasurable and voluptuous sensations and delights!

In very rare cases, the hymen will prove too thick and stubborn to be broken in this manner. If success is not attained the first night it is attempted, try again the next night. And, if necessary, a third. If it appears that it is going to be impossible, then go to a physician, and he can open the hymen with a very simple, harmless, and probably painless surgery. But by all means avoid the surgeon if possible.

Some "authorities" recommend going to the surgeon

for this defloration prior to marriage. But we answer, *NEVER!*

The Wedding, and the Attitude

Forty-five or fifty years ago many young men would discuss the idea of whether they should not wait a night or two after the wedding before approaching their brides sexually. The theory was that a bride would be so nervous after her wedding that she ought to be given a day or two of quiet and relaxation. But times have changed. The average bride, today, *wants* her husband to approach her sexually on the wedding night.

Still, there is certainly no harm in any considerate bridegroom taking the precaution to *ask* his bride if she wants to wait. But, unless the bride is completely done in, and upset with nervousness, the husband surely ought to take her into his arms in bed, and quiet her nerves with LOVE! It is certainly to be recommended that he do this *first*, and delay any questions about deferring the sexual contact until LOVE has been expressed—unless she herself asks otherwise.

Every bridegroom ought to realize the bride's psychological situation on her wedding day. It is her greatest hour! In most cases she will be leaving her parents and her home. She is embarking on a new and different life.

If there is a reception following the wedding ceremony, the bridegroom (and, of course, also the bride) should be careful, if any alcoholic beverages are served, either to abstain, or to partake with extreme temperance. He must retain complete mental and physical alertness. He may be driving a car immediately afterward. He must be completely sober as he takes his bride into his arms on the wedding night. To ruin this night might be to ruin the marriage for life.

Above all, he must now show consideration, tenderness, kindness, and love as never before to the girl he has married —and this must continue into the wedding night. He should realize solemnly that the purpose of *this* night is not to give *him* pleasure. Only a selfish ignoramus would consider it so. This should be *her* night.

Many a wedding is wrecked for life on the wedding night. Many a bride has been cruelly *raped* by a self-centered, ignorant lout who was seeking only his own gratification.

This, above all, is the night to be gentle, tender, considerate, and loving. This is perhaps the most critical night of his life—*and hers!* The fate of the lifelong, or divorce-short marriage is at stake! First impressions are lasting. Make your bride's first impression of sex one of respect, admiration of her husband, and of God-ordained LOVE and TENDERNESS and consideration!

And, finally, a few very necessary cautions.

The bride-to-be should, of course, be careful to set the wedding shortly *after* a menstrual period—being very careful in her calculation—and leaving a safe margin for error, or irregularity due to the nervous tension of the time.

The bridegroom should REALIZE, and NOT FORGET, that on this wedding night above all, he must not embarrass his bride. If she wishes to undress in privacy, give her the opportunity. When ready for bed, REMEMBER, nearly all women want either darkness or very subdued light. That's *one* of the *differences* between human male and female.

Remember, too, that although the Maker of us all made the female body to be attractive, beautiful, and even sex-arousing to the male, the female mind is altogether different. No man should display his body, or especially the pubic region before the new bride—above all on this wedding night.

The fact that God talked to the first man and his wife in their complete nudity—that they were not ashamed (Gen. 2:25) and God made no effort at that time to cover them —does indicate that God imposes no command that husband and wife always be covered before each other. It is after the public—other people—"ALL LIVING"—are mentioned, in Genesis 3:20, that God (verse 21) clothed them. This would indicate that there is no prohibition against nudity between husband and wife in the privacy of their own bedroom. But, REGARDLESS, no bridegroom ought to embarrass or shock his new bride by displaying his body, or demanding that she display hers, on this wedding night.

Take plenty of time to get used to one another! As you value your future marriage together, BE CAREFUL—avoid embarrassment—take time!

Read again the instruction given in Chapter 15 about how a husband and wife ought to appear before each other in bedroom privacy—the bedclothes, undergarments, careful grooming.

The new husband should not think of this wedding night as a night of sensual pleasure—but a night of LOVE! This is the most critical night of his life! The fate of a lifelong marriage could be at stake. The experience of this night may determine the bride's attitude toward the sexual relationship *for life!* And *her attitude* is the ALL-IMPORTANT thing! She has, in all probability from girlhood, had an idealistic picture in her mind of marriage and husband. Don't destroy it!

All-Important Bride's Attitude

The CURSE of so many millions of marriages through the centuries has been the *attitude* of wives toward it— and toward the sexual relation. This attitude, of course, has been formed by false repressive teachings, and by ignorance.

The reader of this volume is blessed with the right and proper teaching, and with true and wholesome knowledge.

Still, much of the entire lifelong marriage relationship depends on a *right attitude* on the part of the wife.

The properly instructed bride, with a correct view of love and marriage, looks forward to this moment—the wedding night—as the fulfillment of the purpose of her youth. She has accepted the right man. He is her ideal. She is in love. She doesn't fear him as a stranger. As he now takes her into his arms, she happily and impulsively embraces him.

She must now realize that he is the complement of her

mind and body. Alone, she has been incomplete, imperfect. He is the stronger of the two. Now they are to be joined as ONE. His strength is to be added to—combined with—her weaker nature.

This is the moment for her to simply *give herself to him* —to *surrender* herself to him—in loving embrace, and in the pleasure and ecstasy of the moment.

As one writer has stated it, this surrender to her husband is a modest tribute to be paid for the present and future happiness of marriage and motherhood!

Conclusion

In final conclusion, remember that sex, in humans, was designed and created by the Ever-*Living*, All-wise GOD as the symbol of LIFE (for through it human life is begotten) and the expression of LOVE.

The Eternal God is working out His greatest and grandest PURPOSE here below. That purpose is the reproduction of *His own Kind*—holy, righteous and perfect CHARACTER in the divine FAMILY of the Ever-*Living* God! Humans, physically begotten and born through sex, may be spiritually begotten and divinely BORN of GOD—entering the ETERNALLY LIVING GOD FAMILY!

As physical reproduction is the type and forerunner of spiritual begettal and glorification, so marital LOVE is the type of Christ's LOVE for His Church, and our love for Christ.

The wife's *giving* of herself, in the ecstasy of love and in obedience, to her husband, is the type and physical counterpart of those in God's Church *giving* themselves, in love and obedience, to the Christ who bought and paid for us with His life's blood!

God Almighty is the source of LIFE, and of LOVE. Human sex is the symbol and physical counterpart of both—the source of physical LIFE, and marital LOVE.

These are holy, righteous, and sacred things!

The marriage and family relationships are GOD-PLANE

relationships, which God shares with humans, and *humans only!*

A perverted, hostile devil has deceived *his* world into two extremes *away from* this beautiful and central TRUTH. First, he represented sex—physical sources of LIFE and marital LOVE—as something degrading, shameful and evil. Today he leads people to the opposite extreme *away from* TRUTH, into accepting the *perverted* and profaned and lustful *uses* of sex as being acceptable and good.

In this volume those lying, foul, deceptively false attitudes have been exposed, and the blessed TRUTH made plain.

But remember, the all-important thing is MENTAL ATTITUDE!

Most marriages are rendered unhappy by wrong attitudes. Most people marry for *selfish* purposes. They think only of what they can GET *from* the other. They want to extract gratification, pleasure, money, security, or something for SELF *from* the mate. True outgoing concern and LOVE is usually lacking.

It is hoped that this volume shall have brought to many thousands a right knowledge of the TRUTH—helped thousands to a changed and right attitude toward sex, toward wife or husband, toward life, and toward God.

God's Law is THE WAY to every happiness—whether in marriage, in business—in LIFE.

If you are one whose marriage has not been happy—perhaps "on the rocks"—*change your attitude.* Follow God's LAWS. Avoid the penalties of unhappiness, troubles, and curses. Reap the joys of divinely intended blessings!

If you are unmarried, follow these living inexorable LAWS—seek God's wisdom and guidance in the selection of a mate when the right time comes—trust the *Living* God. He has a deep and tremendous outgoing concern for you. Get your attitude toward sex cleaned up and in harmony with the Maker's purposes. Avoid every misuse or perversion. Reap the glorious rewards a loving God has intended and made available!

The editors and producers of this volume wish God's richest blessings on every reader—and they *will* be yours *if* your attitude and your actions are in harmonious obedience to God's Laws and His TRUTH!

Index

virtue, 156-157
implants sense of shame, 45-47
sense of guilt about expressing
love in sexual intercourse
inspired by, 176

SCHOOLS, PAGAN
dotted Roman Empire, 31, 52
attended by Christians, 32, 40
used only pagan textbooks, 32, 40
collapse with fall of Empire in
476 A.D., 53
monastic schools take place, 53

SCIENTISTS
revise moral standards without
authority, 1
lack authority for ideas on sex,
15-17
do not speak dogmatically, 16, 211
cannot disprove either the
existence of God or the
inspiration and authority of
Bible, 19

SCOPES TRIAL
sounded death knell of Bible in
secular education, 24

SCRIPTURE (see also Bible)
interprets itself, 172

SCROTUM (see also Testes)
description of, 202
is marvelous temperature gauge,
208-210

SEMEN (see Prostatic fluid)

SEMINAL DUCT (see Vas
Deferens)

SEMINAL VESICLES
location and function of, 205, 222

SEMINIFEROUS TUBES (see also
Testes)
definition and description of, 203

SEMIRAMIS (see also Nimrod)
original paragon of licentiousness,
53
spread pagan doctrines throughout
world, 53

SENECA (see also Augustine)
Latin Philosopher, 55

SENSES
right use of, 163-165
to impart enjoyment and pleasure,
162-164

SEX (see also Attitudes, Augustine,
Catholic Church, Knowledge,
Materialism, Morals)
God, the Architect who designed,
xi, 7-9
the Supreme Authority on, xii-xiii,
30
Bible is God's instruction book
on, 17, 18
falls within spiritual category,
13, 172, 176
perverted by Satan, 44-47, 50, 176
Satan implanted sense of shame
and guilt concerning, 44-47,
50, 176-179
not sinful, but wholesome, 8, 176
misuse of, brings penalty, 9, 85,
86, 175
Bible commands proper use of,
181-182
pagan religions pervert, 34
Simon Magus introduces as
"Christian" the pagan
interpretation of, 37-38
Catholic concept of, 4, 74-76, 140,
153-154
Protestants inherit from Catholics
repressive attitude toward,
158
three modern movements affect,
23
modern approach to, based on
evolution, 18
a great national problem, 88
people have only partial
knowledge of, 12
Bible speaks out frankly
concerning, 180-184
illustrates the God-plane
relationship, 171
purposes of, 133-134, 171-172, 232
not for reproduction only, 139-
140
marriage is second purpose of,
141-142, 173
binds husband and wife together,
49, 172-173, 176
an expression of love in marriage,
160, 167-170
its commanded functions, 171-173
differences between males and
females, 231-241
how to instruct children
concerning, 274-278

SEX APPEAL, 232

influences on, 259-261
vice among, 261-264
fail to control their human
nature, 264-266
need instruction about dating and
"necking," 266-267, 269-273
should not "go steady," 267-269

TEN COMMANDMENTS
are a spiritual law, 9, 13
their violation is sin, 8
regulate physical actions, 13
safeguard the marriage institution,
xii
define proper use of sex, 8-9
condemn sexual lust, 9
not basis of traditional Christian
morality, 111

TERTULLIAN
condemns Nicolaitanes, 37

TESTES (see also Castration,
Scrotum)
are miniature "colossal"
laboratories, 203
produce germinal cells in males,
199
produce male hormones, 205-206
why one is suspended lower than
other, 202

TESTICLES (see Testes)

THEOLOGIANS (see also Clergy,
Protestant Churches)
admit churches have failed in
moral leadership, 90
blamed by churchmen for moral
decline, 100-101
employ deceit, 88-90
condone sex vices in the name of
"compassion," 88
employ permissive attitude toward
premarital sex relations, 6-7

THEOLOGY, PROTESTANT (see
also German Rationalism,
Materialism)
victim of anti-God rationalism,
24

"TREE OF KNOWLEDGE"
represented Satan's philosophy,
31
typified way of rebellion against
God's Law, 31

"TREE OF LIFE"
represented God's philosophy of

life—the way of love, 30
summed up in obedience to Ten
Commandments, 30-31
symbolized the gift of the Holy
Spirit, 130

TRENT, COUNCIL OF (see
Council of Trent)

TRIAL MARRIAGES
advocated by Judge Lindsey after
World War I, 3

UNITED STATES (see also Morals)
morals in, 78, 80, 82-90
homosexuality in, 105

URETHRA
definition and position of, 221,
225

UTERUS
function and description of, 219-
220

VAGINA
female organ of copulation, 199
function and description of, 228-
230
diagram of, 250

VAS DEFERENS
definition and function of, 199,
205, 221-223

VASA EFFERENTIA
description of, 199, 205

"VENIAL SIN"
a Catholic, not a Biblical term,
72

VERGIL (see also Augustine)
Latin philosopher, 56

VESTIBULE
description of, 229
location of, 248

VIRGIL (see Vergil)

VULVA
definition of, 228
diagram showing, 230